DEBATING SEX WORK

DEBATING ETHICS

General Editor

Christopher Heath Wellman

Washington University of St. Louis

Debating Ethics is a series of volumes in which leading scholars defend opposing views on timely ethical questions and core theoretical issues in contemporary moral, political, and legal philosophy.

Debating Sex Work

LORI WATSON

JESSICA FLANIGAN

OXFORD
UNIVERSITY PRESS

OXFORD
UNIVERSITY PRESS

Oxford University Press is a department of the University of Oxford. It furthers the University's objective of excellence in research, scholarship, and education by publishing worldwide. Oxford is a registered trade mark of Oxford University Press in the UK and certain other countries.

Published in the United States of America by Oxford University Press
198 Madison Avenue, New York, NY 10016, United States of America.

Library of Congress Control Number: 2019012357
ISBN 978–0–19–065989–9 (pbk.)
ISBN 978–0–19–065988–2 (hbk.)

1 3 5 7 9 8 6 4 2

Paperback printed by Marquis, Canada
Hardback printed by Bridgeport National Bindery, Inc., United States of America

CONTENTS

PART 1: A SEX EQUALITY APPROACH TO PROSTITUTION

Lori Watson

PART 2: IN DEFENSE OF DECRIMINALIZATION

Jessica Flanigan

ACKNOWLEDGMENTS

WATSON'S ACKNOWLEDGMENTS

This book has been several years in the making, and I would like to acknowledge the support and contributions of the many persons who helped this project come to fruition. First, I would like to thank Kit Wellman and Lucy Randall for their guidance and support as editors. Jessica Flanigan is also owed a huge thank you for being a pleasure to work with, as well as a gracious and generous interlocutor. The anonymous referee for the original manuscript made important and substantive suggestions for improvement, and I am deeply grateful for the referee's comments.

Christie Hartley and Susan Brison each read the entire manuscript; their comments and contributions improved the final manuscript immeasurably. Melissa Farley provided generous feedback on chapter 3, which improved it greatly. The support and encouragement from Catharine MacKinnon in this project and all my work is a gift that I am so fortunate to receive. I am incredibly lucky to have a philosophical community full of friendship and inspiration. The following persons have offered their care and support to me over the years, including through the writing of this book, and their work inspires me to be a better philosopher: Elizabeth Barnes, Remy Debes, Robin Dembroff, Clare Chambers, John Christman, John Corvino, Liz Goodnick, Lori Gruen, Sarah Clark Miller, Cindy Stark, and Helga Varden.

While working on this book, I was fortunate enough to present versions of various arguments to generous audiences and hone the arguments in light of their feedback. I would like to thank the hosts and the audience members at the American Society for Bioethics and Humanities, Georgia State University, Georgetown University, University of Kentucky, University of Wisconsin-Milwaukee, Dartmouth College, New York Society for Women in Philosophy, Society for Analytical Feminism, San Diego State University, the Eastern and Central Divisions of the American Philosophical Association, California State, Los Angeles, and Trinity College.

The support of the University of San Diego, through research grants, helped create the time to finish this project. My colleagues offer continuous and generous support and make my daily life richer through their friendship. And, finally, the constant companionship of Grace, my sweet, sweet dog, made long days of researching and writing this book more bearable through her gentle nudging to stop working in order to play.

Flanigan's Acknowledgments

Debates about sex work and public policy raise challenging questions about identity, economic justice, political authority, and consent. It is often easy for people who disagree about these questions to talk past each other or to fail to engage with the other side. It is for this reason that I am especially grateful to Lori Watson, who has consistently been a charitable and open-minded interlocutor. I learned a great deal from reading her contribution and from our conversations about the ethics of sex work. I am also grateful to Kit Wellman and Lucy Randall for their guidance and support as editors. In addition, an anonymous referee for the original manuscript provided extensive comments that truly went above and beyond what any author can reasonably expect, for which I am very thankful.

My thinking about this topic benefited from many conversations with Javier Hidalgo, who encouraged me to think more about this topic and provided helpful written comments on a draft of the manuscript. I would also like to thank my colleagues in the Ethics Working Group at the University of Richmond, Ryan Davis, and Matt Zwolinski, who suggested that Lori and I work together on this project. In addition, opportunities to discuss this work in two public debates with Lori improved the manuscript substantially. I would like to thank Andrew I. Cohen for organizing our first debate at Georgia State University and John Alcorn for hosting our second debate at Trinity College and for providing extremely helpful comments on a draft. Audience members at both debates provided helpful comments as well.

While writing this book, I read many sex workers' accounts of their experiences in the industry and I learned a lot from sex workers who write online. In particular, I would like to thank and acknowledge the writers at titsandsass.com, whose writing has been especially informative and insightful. One thing I learned from reading sex workers' accounts is that people in the sex industry often feel that academic discussions of sex work abstract away from the complexity of workers' own lived experiences in ways that obscure the true normative questions involved in everyday sex work. Though some degree of generalization is required to develop an effective normative critique of public policy, I tried to acknowledge the diversity of sex workers' experiences and include their voices throughout the manuscript. The arguments I develop here build on arguments that sex workers and advocates have been making for years. In recognition of this, I dedicate my contribution to them.

DEBATING SEX WORK

Introduction

LORI WATSON AND JESSICA FLANIGAN

"PROSTITUTION" IS OFTEN SAID TO be "the oldest profession." Some feminists have argued that this saying is
better rendered as "prostitution is the oldest oppression."[1]
These feminists analyze prostitution as a form of sexual
exploitation, as a form of sex-based inequality in which
women are subordinated and used for sex on men's terms.
That prostitution was harmful to women was a foundational aspect of feminist organizing for much of the 20th
century.

More recently, in the later part of the 20th century and
into the 21st century, some feminists, and others, have
come to reject this view of prostitution. In fact, they reject the term "prostitution" itself. Rather than analyzing
women selling sex as a form of oppression, or a practice of
sex-based inequality, these feminists see selling sex as an
exercise of agency, a pathway to liberation from sex-based
oppression, and reject analyses that place "sex work," in
their terms, as inherently degrading or unequal. Sex work

---

1. Catharine A. MacKinnon, *Sex Equality*, 3rd ed. (St. Paul,
MN: Foundation Press, 2016), 1535.

Debating Sex Work. Lori Watson, Jessica Flanigan, Oxford University
Press (2020). © Oxford University Press.
DOI: 10.1093/oso/9780190659882.001.0001

is work, like many other forms of work, they claim. In their view, denying this claim rests on unjust stigmatization of sex workers, and such stigmatization is a primary harm that sex workers face, according to these feminists and their allies.

This book aims to put these two contrasting views in conversation with one another. Each author aims to defend a particular analysis of prostitution/sex work, and from this analysis argues for a particular form of regulation. Lori Watson argues that prostitution is not like other forms of work and defends criminalizing the buying of sex while decriminalizing the selling of sex. Jessica Flanigan argues that sex work should be treated like other forms of work and argues for full decriminalization.

I.1 PRELIMINARIES AND DEFINITIONS

A few preliminary caveats are needed prior to providing the overview of the book's structure. First, the book is primarily concerned with the practice of selling and buying sex, rather than all the activities that may fall under the umbrella of sex work. Pornography, stripping, phone, and Internet sex fall under the wider net of "sexual services" that many call sex work. The core arguments presented here certainly will give guidance and insight about how to think about these other forms of sex work. However, each requires its own full analysis for thinking about public policy and law: for example, pornography potentially raises free speech concerns, and thus any serious analysis of pornography, from a legal standpoint, must engage with such concerns.[2] Likewise, stripping and phone or Internet sex require their own analyses that account for the facts of their specificity, neither of which strictly speaking involves actual sex. Each author will refer to these other forms of sexual services when they are relevant to the arguments; however, this book is about debates concerning legal approaches to the buying and selling of sex.

Second, as noted, this book is primarily about the dominant and most prevalent form of prostitution, where women are the sellers and men are the buyers. Male prostitution exists, of course. However, it is a significantly smaller portion of the market, estimates range between 10% and 20% of all persons in prostitution. And importantly, there are no brothels, in any legal or decriminalized context, where men are for sale. Male prostitution occurs through the Internet, apps, and other contexts, but it is unlike the prostitution of women with respect to brothel prostitution. Nonetheless, many of the same issues that arise in thinking through the best public policy for prostitution apply equally to men and women. For example, men may become sex workers for similar reasons as women, and concerns about bodily integrity, sexual freedom, and equality, as well as occupational health and safety and security from violence, are relevant for women and men. Watson's and Flanigan's respective arguments about these matters can apply straightforwardly to all forms of prostitution. Nonetheless, men in prostitution are far less researched than women. As many of Watson's and Flanigan's arguments draw on the available

2. See Andrew Altman and Lori Watson, *Debating Pornography* (New York: Oxford University Press, 2019).

empirical data concerning the costs and benefits of specific public policy and law, and the overwhelming majority of the data concerns women because they constitute the primary persons in prostitution, our arguments are largely focused there.

It is also helpful at this point to define a few terms. There are four forms of regulation of prostitution: criminalization, decriminalization, legalization, and the Nordic Model. *Criminalization* refers to a system of regulation in which statutes criminalize both the selling and the buying of sex. Additionally, under criminalization regimes, pimping, pandering, solicitation, and so on are criminalized. The severity of the crime and punishments vary across nation-states and jurisdictions. In the United States, the dominant approach to prostitution is criminalization; the only exception in the United States is some rural counties in Nevada in which prostitution is legalized. Most other countries also fully criminalize prostitution, though of course there are a substantial number of countries that either decriminalize or legalize prostitution. Both Watson and Flanigan reject criminalization, on the grounds that it makes women in prostitution worse off in nearly every respect.

The Nordic Model, first developed in Sweden in 1999, decriminalizes the selling of sex but criminalizes the buying. The model is premised on the view that prostitution is a practice of sex inequality that differentially harms and disadvantages women. Additionally, the Nordic Model, based on empirical evidence, rests on the view that demand for sexual services is the driving force of the prostitution market, and so it targets demand reduction as a primary strategy. Further, advocates of the

Nordic Model do not draw any sharp distinction between sex trafficking (typically defined as relying on force, fraud, or coercion) and prostitution (defined by critics as a separate phenomenon and as fully voluntary). In analyzing sex trafficking and prostitution as both part of a system of gender inequality, the advocates of the Nordic Model emphasize that inequality itself functions as a form of coercion and that prostitution is both a site and a cause of gender inequality. In her contribution, Watson defends the Nordic Model.

In contrast, legalization removes criminal laws and penalties for both the sellers and the buyers, but it also consists of a system of prostitution-specific laws. In contrast to what is referred to as decriminalization, legalization typically involves more robust regulation that is prostitution specific. Prostitution is legalized in Germany, the Netherlands, and some counties in Nevada, United States. Under legalization regimes, brothels are permitted and state regulated.

Decriminalization entails removing criminal laws and penalties for both the buyers and the sellers of sex. In some places it also involves removal of criminal laws and penalties for pimping or living off the prostitution of another. Many sex workers and sex worker advocates or unions prefer this approach. In the summer of 2015, Amnesty International formally endorsed decriminalization. Although decriminalization is often contrasted with legalization with respect to whether prostitution-specific regulations are legally instituted, in practice decriminalization often does involve some industry-specific legal regulations. For example, even in New South Wales (Australia) and New Zealand, both of which have decriminalized sex work, there are sex work–specific regulations such as mandatory health screening and zoning laws. Thus, in practice the line between legalization and decriminalization can be unclear. Still, the decriminalization approach generally favors treating sex work like other kinds of work, acknowledging that some industry-specific regulations may be warranted but rejecting policies that aim to reduce the scope of the industry. In her contribution, Flanigan defends decriminalization.

I.2 THE CASE FOR THE NORDIC MODEL

Watson's contribution argues in favor of the Nordic Model. She begins her contribution by rejecting the title of the book, "Debating Sex Work," arguing that the phrase "sex work" is a pernicious cover-up and attempts to legitimize prostitution as "just another form of work." In the first chapter of her contribution, Watson aims to present the initial positive case for the Nordic Model as a sex equality approach to prostitution. She argues that social conditions of inequality (based on sex, age, class, race) structure the conditions of entry into prostitution and structure it internally. Moreover, prostitution is harmful and constitutes the denial of basic human rights. Legal approaches that tolerate, support, or normalize prostitution violate equality principles. Yet given the asymmetrical inequalities between buyers and sellers, laws concerning prostitution should not treat them the same. Decriminalizing persons in prostitution (those that sell sex) raises their social status, and thus no law against selling sex is justified (for it entrenches inequality). Moreover, persons in prostitution should be provided state support for their basic needs as well as means for exit, should they choose to exit.

Further, Watson contrasts two methodological approaches to arguments concerning public policy with respect to prostitution. Some theorists approach the questions concerning prostitution from the perspective of ideal theory. Crudely put, ideal theory involves making idealizing assumptions that abstract away from the actual practice under consideration. In contrast, non-ideal theory draws on the wealth of information concerning the ways in which prostitution functions here and now and frames the policy questions at stake in terms of what is achievable (or best) in light of those facts. Thus, Watson argues in favor of a materially grounded approach to thinking about what should be done about prostitution that requires an understanding of the actual facts that structure it as it occurs now, and that includes knowing who is there, why they are there, who benefits from prostitution, and who is harmed.

After providing some initial facts and analysis of sex inequality to further ground the argument for the Nordic model, Watson addresses a series of objections to arguments in favor of restricting markets in sex. Those objections include that any position aiming to curtail prostitution must rest on some form of unjustifiable moralism or paternalism; that prostitution should be understood as a fully voluntary choice and protected as such; that even if prostitution is exploitative, allowing such exploitation makes persons in prostitution better off than they would be otherwise; and, finally, that persons have rights to markets in sex such that any prohibitive policies violate rights.

In chapter 2 of her contribution, Watson critically engages with the often-repeated argument that "sex work is work, like any other form of work." Advocates of this argument rely upon it as a basis for either decriminalization or legalization. Watson dismantles this claim by showing that where sex is the "service," occupational health and safety standards applicable to every other form of work cannot be met. Further, she explores the various ways in which persons in prostitution may be thought of as "workers" and argues that relevant legal standards in the context of discrimination laws and employment law cannot be met in the context of "sex work." Thus, she shows that the burden of argument falls on advocates of decriminalization to legalization to argue for a series of exemptions from generally applicable laws. However, she argues such exemptions are unwarranted, do not achieve their aims, and would require institutionalizing inequality for persons in prostitution. In the final section of that chapter, Watson explores the possibilities for recognizing "sex contracts." There she argues that contractualizing sex is incompatible with equality.

After presenting the initial case for the Nordic Model and exposing the flaws of the alternatives, chapter 3 of Watson's contribution returns to provide the full defense of the Nordic Model. There she presents the evidence that policies of toleration (whether decriminalization or legalization) are proven to increase the trafficking of persons for sexual exploitation. She also presents the evidence that demand reduction is the most effective legal approach to prostitution. Further, recent research on the behaviors and attitudes of buyers is presented to further make the case that targeting demand is central to eliminating the harms of prostitution. Finally, she considers a series of objections to the Nordic Model and replies to them.

I.3 THE CASE
FOR DECRIMINALIZATION

Flanigan's contribution argues in favor of decriminalization. She begins her contribution by arguing that sex work is, largely, just another form of work. In the first chapter of her contribution (chapter 4), Flanigan argues that the Nordic Model violates the rights of sex workers and their clients. Furthermore, decriminalization has better consequences for sex workers, their clients, and the general public than either criminalization or the Nordic Model. In addition, criminalization is profoundly inegalitarian, and in practice the Nordic Model may be as well. In sum, many of the same reasons in favor of rejecting criminalization are also reasons to reject the Nordic Model.

Flanigan then considers objections to decriminalization, focusing on arguments in favor of the Nordic Model in chapter 5. She first considers the possibility that selling sex is not an especially important right, so public officials can restrict people's ability to sell sexual services on the grounds that selling sex is often insufficiently voluntary, exploitative, or degrading. In response, Flanigan agrees that the sale of non-consensual sex or sex with children ought to be legally prohibited (of course) but that these conditions are not intrinsic to sex work. The fact that a person has poor economic prospects or exists in a state of social marginalization due to her sex, sexuality, race, gender, or citizenship status does not entail that she is incapable of consenting to work or that it is wrong to pay her for her labor. Rather, by enacting policies that limit socio-economically marginalized people's economic prospects, such as criminalization or the Nordic Model, public officials make members of these groups worse-off by perpetuating stigmatizing judgments and reducing their bargaining power in the labor market.

Another objection to decriminalization stems from the idea that officials are sometimes justified in treating people paternalistically. On this view, if paternalism were sometimes justified and if the enforcement of the Nordic Model or criminal penalties would promote the well-being of sex workers, then officials could be justified in enforcing these policies. In response, Flanigan argues that officials should generally avoid paternalism but that even if paternalism were justified, paternalistic arguments cannot justify limiting the sex industry because even if sex work is difficult and distressing labor, sex workers are better judges of their own well-being than uninformed public officials who know nothing of their values and experiences that led them to choose sex work.

Watson and others reject decriminalization on egalitarian grounds. They argue that a decriminalized sex industry would entrench or exacerbate existing economic or social inequalities. As an empirical matter, Flanigan rejects the claim that the decriminalization of sex work would make inequality worse. And as a conceptual matter, Flanigan argues that recognizing the legitimacy of sex work needn't conflict with embracing egalitarian values.

I.4 CLARIFYING THE DEBATE

Though Watson and Flanigan disagree about whether public officials should prohibit citizens from paying for sex and whether sex work should be treated like other forms of work, they agree that any defensible approach to sex work should not target, stigmatize, or punish sex workers. In this way, Watson and Flanigan broadly agree that the moralistic and punitive approach that characterizes many nations' approach to prostitution/sex work, including that of the United States is unjust.

The criminalization of prostitution/sex work is unjust for several reasons. First, police officers often enforce the laws against buying and selling unequally. It is women, the sellers, who are targeted and arrested. For example, data from the Bureau of Justice Statistics from 2012, the most recent year in which data are available, report a total of 56,575 arrests for "prostitution and commercialized vice."[3] Of the total number, 18,610 of those arrested were male, 37,965 female. Data from 2010 reports 62,670: 19,480 male and 43,190 female, respectively.[4] Given that there are more buyers than sellers, these data especially suggest selective enforcement targeting women.

Even when buyers are arrested or ticketed, depending on jurisdiction, the consequences of arrest are far less severe and burdensome than for prostituted persons. Given the relative social and economic position of buyers as compared with sellers (mainly men compared with women), buyers can much more easily make bail, hire effective lawyers, plead to lesser charges, attend diversion programs, and the like. Women, the sellers, are less likely to make bail, or they may depend on an abusive pimp to bail them out, putting them further in the pimp's debt. The women are more likely to lack the resources to hire effective lawyers;

3. https://www.bjs.gov/index.cfm?ty=datool&surl=/arrests/index.cfm#
4. https://www.bjs.gov/content/pub/pdf/aus9010.pdf

have prior criminal convictions for prostitution, which increase the severity of punishment for repeat offenses; suffer greater economic consequences as a result of longer jail time, which may lead to homelessness; be the primary care-givers of children (than buyers) and face state intervention with respect to custody arrangements; and face additional obstacles to "leaving the life" as a result of a criminal record.

Additionally, under criminalization regimes, persons in prostitution have an adversarial relationship with police. Police are known to coerce and extort sex acts from sex workers, using the threat of arrest to force compliance. Moreover, persons in prostitution are reluctant and unlikely to call police for assistance when they are victims of crimes both inside and outside of prostitution. And even when they do, their complaints are often dismissed based on stereotypical thinking that prostitutes cannot be raped or be victims of sexual assault.

Criminalization also makes persons in prostitution/ sex workers more vulnerable relative to buyers (johns) insofar as buyers know that police intervention is unlikely and persons in prostitution are unlikely to rely on police for support, safety, and enforcement. Moreover, there is no evidence that criminalization of both the buying and selling of sex is effective as a deterrent for either buyers or sellers. Its primary purpose does indeed suggest a moral condemnation of prostitution, with no real purpose of improving the lives of persons in prostitution.

Sometimes, in light of profound disagreement, one might conclude that political and philosophical arguments are doomed to fail, that progress is impossible, and that we will never know the truth about which policy is best. But historically, the criminalization and policing of women's bodies has been the norm. It is only in the last century that people have begun to see that incarcerating persons in prostitution is unjust. Rather than relying on antiquated moralisms that blame and shame women, in particular, for engaging in prostitution, the debate here, and globally, concerns what is best for women made vulnerable by systems of prostitution. This is, indeed, a radical shift in orientation. Though Flanigan and Watson strongly disagree about which policy is the best approach, both offer arguments framed in terms of the interests of women and drawing on principles of sex equality. A key disagreement between them concerns precisely what taking women's equality seriously entails, but this debate is a long way from the stigmatizing and shaming of women in prostitution so prevalent in the recent past and sometimes still a part of dominant discourses.

PART 1

A SEX EQUALITY APPROACH

TO PROSTITUTION

LORI WATSON

1

Prostitution and Sex Equality

1.1 INTRODUCTION

"Sex work" as a description of prostitution is a misnomer at best, at worst a pernicious lie. To address the reasons the book is so titled: some people engaged in such "work" and those who have a vested interest in its continuation have waged a public campaign against the words "prostitution" or "prostituted persons" in favor of the terms "sex work" or "sex worker."[1] This campaign to redefine prostitution as work is part of a strategy to normalize "sex work" and strengthen public support for either decriminalization or legalization.[2] Generally speaking, it is a good idea to refer to people with the terms they prefer, and certainly one

---

1. Carol Leigh claims to have invented the term "sex work." See her chapter "Inventing Sex Work," in Jill Nagle, ed., *Whores and Other Feminists* (New York: Routledge, 1997), 225 (She says, "I invented sex work.").

2. I use quotes around "sex work" to indicate I reject the term. However, continuing to use quotes throughout the whole text clutters the sentences and, I think, challenges readability. Thus, I will often drop the use of quotes throughout the rest of the text, but this is for aesthetics and readability.

Debating Sex Work. Lori Watson, Jessica Flanigan, Oxford University Press (2020). © Oxford University Press.
DOI: 10.1093/oso/9780190659882.001.0001

must have very good reasons for not doing so. However, and this is important, not all persons impacted by systems of prostitution embrace or prefer the terms "sex work" or "sex worker." These people, largely women, document their experience in systems of prostitution as exploitative, degrading, abusive, and violent.[3] Calling such practices "work" serves to cover up and erase the harms constitutive of the actual practices and inequalities upon which they are based. Treating prostitution, in particular, as "just another form of work" is a position that is ultimately indefensible, my contribution will argue.

A second reason that "sex work" is a commonly used term is because many think it captures the broad array of activities in which sexual acts are provided for money beyond prostitution, such as in pornography, stripping, and phone or Internet sex. These forms of transactional sex require their own distinct analyses, in many respects. However, insofar as they share some of the core features of the practices of prostitution, including resting upon and perpetuating sex inequality and treating sexuality as an economic transaction, many of the arguments I make here can be extended to them as well. Most relevant is that it attempts to "normalize" practices in which women are required to service men's sexual needs by assimilating them into "just another form of work" functions to cover-up the sex inequalities at stake.

Those who defend the term "sex work" view of prostitution typically argue for across-the-board decriminalization or legalization. Often they rest their case on arguments that

---

3. Women who have exited prostitution are important voices for exposing the abuse and exploitation that structure prostitution. See for example, Rachel Moran, *Paid For: My Journey Through Prostitution* (Dublin: Gill & Macmillian, 2013).

claim one or more of the following: those who engage in prostitution typically do so freely and voluntarily; prostitution has always existed, will always exist, and so we should aim to reduce harms associated with it (and decriminalization or legalization are said to be the best "harm reduction" strategies); the buying and selling of sex is no different from the buying and selling of other goods or services, so there is no legitimate reason to object to markets in sex; those who object to decriminalization or legalization must rest their arguments on some form of unjustifiable moralism or paternalism (forcing someone to do something for their own good). Each of these claims will be evaluated in this chapter.

In contrast to the sex-work approach to prostitution is the Nordic model, a sex-equality approach to prostitution. The Nordic model is increasingly being adopted by nation-states and international political bodies as the best way to address the inequalities that give rise to and structure prostitution while simultaneously attacking the demand that fuels both prostitution and sex-trafficking.[4] As noted in the Introduction, the Nordic model, first adopted in Sweden in 1999, decriminalizes the selling of sex, but criminalizes the buying of sex; it also provides social supports and services for persons in prostitution and those wishing to exit. It is often referred to as an "abolitionist model."[5] This term

4. Catharine A. MacKinnon developed this legal approach to prostitution. For her analysis and defense, see MacKinnon, "Trafficking, Prostitution, and Inequality," *Harvard Civil Rights–Civil Liberties Law Review* 46 (2011): 271–309. See also her "Prostitution and Civil Rights," in *Women's Lives, Men's Laws* (Cambridge, MA: Harvard University Press, 2005), 151–61.

5. MacKinnon, "Trafficking, Prostitution, and Inequality," p. 275. She writes: "The sexual exploitation approach seeks to abolish prostitution."

invokes an association with the abolitionist movement to end slavery in the United States and elsewhere in the 19th century. The association is apt insofar as those that advocated for the abolition of slavery held the position that slavery could not be reformed into a more "humane" institution, as some pro-slavery advocates or others who wanted to avoid civil war in the United States claimed. Some who argue for an abolitionist approach to prostitution argue that prostitution itself is a form of slavery,[6] a form of paid rape,[7] or an unequal practice of sexual subordination and sex inequality,[8] or all of these at once. On this analysis, reforming the institution and practices of prostitution simply isn't possible in ways compatible with equality and other human rights.

The key claims in the argument for the Nordic Model as a sex-equality approach to prostitution, developed by Catharine A. MacKinnon, can be briefly summarized as follows:[9]

1. The overwhelming majority of persons who buy and sell persons in prostitution are men. The majority of those bought and sold in prostitution are women and girl-children.

6. A powerful statement of this view is expressed in Kathleen Barry's *Female Sexual Slavery* (New York: New York University Press, 1979).

7. See, for example, Rachel Moran, *Paid For*.

8. MacKinnon, "Trafficking, Prostitution, and Inequality."

9. This is my reconstruction of her argument, developed from reading the following sources (and in conversation with MacKinnon): See her "Trafficking, Prostitution, and Inequality"; "Prostitution and Civil Rights."; and *Sex Equality*, 3rd ed. (St. Paul, MN: Foundation Press, 2016), chapter 10 "Sex Trafficking," pp. 1533–1687.

2. Prostitution exists due to social conditions of inequality, specifically the social conditions of sex, race, age, and economic inequality (class) through which women and girls are disempowered, disadvantaged, and discriminated against.

3. Social conditions of sex inequality include systematic discrimination against women including the control and use of women's sexuality through norms of masculinity that support practices (rape, sexual abuse, prostitution, pornography) in which women are made to be sexually available to men on men's terms.

4. Thus, the social conditions of inequality that channel and keep women and girl-children in prostitution are part of a practice of systematic gender-based inequality, which includes racial, economic, and age-based inequality.

5. The position of powerlessness women in prostitution are in with respect to pimps, johns, and brothel owners makes prostitution dangerous, violent, abusive, manipulative and difficult to leave; its coercive constitutive practices, thus, deny basic human rights protections to the persons in it (the right to bodily integrity and security of the person, for example, and especially the right to equality).

6. Laws that permit, support, legalize, or normalize prostitution secure the conditions for such sex inequality to continue, promoting the violent, abusive, and degrading treatment that is endemic to prostitution.

7. Therefore, laws that permit, support, legalize, or normalize prostitution violate equality principles.

8. Given the asymmetrical inequalities between buyers and pimps and women in prostitution, laws concerning prostitution should not treat seller and buyers identically (e.g., by criminalizing both).

9. Criminalizing buyers and third-party profiteers (pimps and brothel owners) attacks demand, which fuels the industry.

10. Decriminalizing persons in prostitution (those that sell sex) raises their social status, and thus no law against selling sex is justified (for it entrenches inequality). Moreover, persons in prostitution should be provided state support for their basic needs, as well as means for exit, should they choose to exit.

The aim of my contribution to this volume is to provide a defense of the Nordic Model as a sex equality approach to prostitution. In this first chapter, I will explain the methodological approach that grounds the arguments for the Nordic Model. I will also provide a "snap-shot" of the facts of sex inequality which constitute the conditions in which women's pervasive and substantive inequality vis-à-vis men continues to exist and forms the background conditions against which women are channeled into prostitution. After presenting the initial case for the Nordic Model as a sex equality approach to prostitution, I will turn and examine some common arguments against restricting "free" markets in sex (prostitution). Each argument will be rejected in turn.

1.2 METHODOLOGICAL CONSIDERATIONS

When evaluating arguments for or against some particular legal or policy approach to prostitution, it is critically important to consider the methodological commitments and assumptions underlying those arguments. Philosophers often use the language of ideal theory and non-ideal theory to mark two different methodological approaches to normative questions. Precisely what each of these methodological approaches entails is a matter of debate. However, it is possible to simplify to understand the contrast.

Ideal theorizing involves making assumptions (idealizations) that are contrary to how things actually are. So, economic theory, for example, relies upon certain idealizations about people and then considers what it might be rational for such ideal people to do in an economic market. Such idealizations include that persons as economic actors are rational, have full information, and are situated equally with respect to those with whom they will bargain or exchange. These assumptions do not accurately describe people in the "real" world. We often have incomplete or bad information; we often have irrational preferences or don't reason well about how to fulfill the preferences we do have; and we are certainly not equal with all others with whom we might wish to bargain or exchange.

One of reasons that economists or other theorists nonetheless make such assumptions is because they believe through such idealizations we can imagine "an ideal case" to help us make diagnoses for reform in our non-ideal circumstances. For example, in the case of economic theory, if we are thinking about how to regulate markets (or not), we may want to think about that from the perspective of how markets (ideally) should function. Doing so is thought to prevent the introduction of variables that don't have to do with markets themselves (like the fact that sometimes people act irrationally).

In the context of thinking about prostitution, some theorists approach the question from the perspective of ideal theory. According to these theorists, approaching the questions about how to regulate (or not) prostitution from the perspective of ideal theory is useful for thinking about whether there is anything *in principle* wrong with prostitution. That is, they want to know whether anything is wrong with persons buying and selling sex in *itself*, apart from the contingent and variable ways that the practice actually works. They reason that if we introduce facts like most people are driven into prostitution because of economic desperation into our considerations as a basis for criticizing prostitution, then what we are really concerned about is the economic inequalities, not prostitution per se. Thus, they argue, to think carefully about prostitution *itself*, we should assume that persons engaged in it are equal, and then think about whether it would be wrong in some way. According to these thinkers, idealizations will help us discover *the principled* answer to whether prostitution is bad or wrong or harmful. Once we have that answer, we can think carefully about how to reform (or not) the actual contexts in which prostitution occurs.

Apart from whether any such argument is a good argument, there is a danger in relying on this method for drawing conclusions about what we should do here and now in our very non-ideal circumstances. Relying on conclusions from arguments grounded in assumptions of ideal theory under

non-ideal circumstances can further entrench and perpetuate injustices. Consider this example: many people think
that "ideally" racial distinctions are not morally significant in anyway. This claim leads some to think that in ideal
circumstances we would live in a "color-blind" society in
which racial categorizations are either non-existent or have
radically different meanings than they have at present. Even
if this argument is persuasive, adopting practical policies
on the basis of it now, or relying on it as a principle to guide
one's behavior in a world in which social hierarchies structure and define racial distinctions is very likely to worsen
or further racial injustices. At a minimum, recognizing that
racial distinctions are socially salient, and so continuing to
recognize them, is important for tracking social and political inequalities. If we adopt fully "color-blind" principles
under unequal conditions, and that includes failing to ask
about racial group membership on government forms and
surveys, then we will lack the information needed to understand how racial inequality functions and to develop
concrete plans to ameliorate it. Even more, taking into
account racial group membership may be necessary to directly address racial injustices; this thought underlies some
arguments for affirmative action policies.

These reflections bear on the debate about prostitution insofar as how one approaches the issue matters for
evaluating their arguments and policy suggestions. The
sex-equality approach to prostitution, defended here,
adopts a non-ideal approach. Central to this approach is
the claim that understanding the actual material (real and
lived) conditions that give rise to and structure prostitution, as social practice, is necessary for any effective policy
proposal. In other words, a materially grounded approach

for thinking about what should be done about prostitution requires an understanding of the actual facts that structure it as it occurs now, and that includes knowing who is there, why they are there, who benefits from prostitution, and who is harmed. As the full defense of the Nordic Model is developed over the course of my contribution, these facts will be presented. Prior to examination of the details that structure and lead persons into prostitution, it is useful to have an understanding of the broad and pervasive facts of sex inequality.

1.3 SEX INEQUALITY

As previously stated, the Nordic Model is a sex-equality approach to prostitution. Some discussion of both sex inequality and sex equality is warranted in order to contextualize and illuminate what it means to say that this approach to prostitution is a "sex-equality" approach.

The sex/gender distinction functions as a binary division through which persons are determined to be "male" or "female" and assigned socialization to masculinity or femininity on that basis. (Of course, there are increasing numbers of persons who reject the sex/gender distinction as binary and live and argue for a broader conceptualization of the ways of being human that do not reduce persons to "male" or "female." Nonetheless, the dominant discourse and institutionalization of sex/gender through social norms and penalties rests on an assumption of binary sex/gender categories.) The dominant division of sex/gender isn't merely a division of persons into "different" categories. Sex/gender is a distinction that is organized hierarchically. Even if one accepts a biological basis for gender/sex distinctions, the way in which they function as social categories of persons is not given by biology. Masculinity and femininity are the social categories through which "maleness" and "femaleness" are lived identities and statuses. Masculinity and femininity are mark-out social positions within hierarchically ordered gender. They are not mere "differences."

Masculinity underwrites the social superiority of men as a class. Masculinity is culturally defined, for example, as displaying power, dominance, or aggression. Men who act in ways that carry approval as "appropriately masculine" are rewarded and, often, revered. Men who are judged to "fail" in conforming to social norms of masculinity are often viciously punished. Consider that gay men have all too frequently been murdered for their alleged "transgression" of norms of masculinity, including heterosexuality.

Femininity is defined in relation to masculinity, and serves, by contrast, as a social marker and designation of inferiority. Consider the various ways in which "appropriate" femininity involves passivity, being demur, and adopting a position of being other-oriented ("selfless"). Women who step outside the socially permissive ways of expressing femininity, by for example showing aggression or dominance, are often judged to be "bitches," or called out as possibly being "really men." (Think here of the way in which female athletes who are in fact dominant in their sport are ridiculed as being "men" if they don't also have extremely feminine body and style presentations.)

Nowhere are women the social equals of men. This is true even in western, liberal democracies that have, over time, extended formal legal equality to women and other marginalized groups. Even with anti-discrimination and civil rights laws aiming to promote social equality among persons denied such equality on the basis of group membership (including women and racial, sexual, and religious minorities, for example), substantive equality has not been achieved. Not only is the inequality between men and women—sex inequality—reflected in patterns of distribution of resources, it is also manifest in inequality of social standing. Women, as women, are often denied the requisite respect and authority to stand in a relation of equality with men.

Examples of inequality of standing include the ways in which women are denied equal social authority with men because they are women. One primary manifestation of such inequality is the asymmetry between men and women concerning sexuality. So, for example, men, as men, can engage in casual sex with many partners and if this fact is known it generally enhances their reputation rather than damages them. When women behave similarly, they are sometimes "slut shamed" or regarded as acting outside the bounds of "appropriate" femininity. The obstacles women face in having their experience of sexual violence (including rape) believed by others, whether by family members, friends, police, prosecutors, or jurors, serves as a powerful instance of the denial of equal standing of women. The recent #metoo movement in the United States, and globally, provides some hope that the pervasiveness of sexual violence against women as a fact, as true, is starting to undermine the patterns of disbelief and denial that women have faced for centuries. Whether this will translate into women's ability to secure justice in those instances where they have been sexually harassed, sexually battered, or raped remains to be seen.

A further element of the analysis of sex inequality that is especially relevant to prostitution is the way in which gender-based norms function with regard to whose interests structure heterosexuality. Consider the ways in which men's desires and interests, often, define whether "sex" happened and when "it" is over. In heterosexual sex, male penetration is generally thought constitutive of what "sex" is. Other forms of sexual contact, oral sex, for example, are thought of as "hooking up" but not as "having sex." A man's ejaculation is, often, thought to be the terminus of a sexual encounter. This is reflected in pornography where the so-called cum shot is the climax of the scene. The dominant understanding of heterosexual sex situates men and women asymmetrically: women are often thought as instruments for serving men's needs, and their needs are secondary if they register at all.

Women's inequality relative to men is also manifest across patterns of distribution of resources, welfare, and opportunities. Women and their children are dramatically overrepresented in poverty, both globally and within nation-states like the United States. The National Women's Law Center, drawing on US Census Bureau data, "found that women's poverty rates were once again higher than the poverty rates for men last year [2017]. It also showed that women working full time, year-round continue to be paid just 80 cents for every dollar paid to their male counterparts."[10] Racial inequalities further women's income inequality: "Black women working full time, year-round

10. "NWLC Resources on Poverty, Income, and Health Insurance in 2016," National Women's Law Center, available at https://nwlc.org/resources/nwlc-resources-on-poverty-income-and-health-insurance-in-2016/

were typically paid just 63 cents for every dollar paid to their white, non-Hispanic male counterparts. Latinas working full time, year-round were typically paid just 54 cents for every dollar paid to their white, non-Hispanic male counterparts."[11] Emphasizing the gender-based reality of poverty in the United States, Anna Chu, Vice President for Income Security and Education at the National Women's Law Center (NWLC), states: "For women, the news is grim: being a woman in America increases the odds of being poor." And further, "Women are nearly 1.4 times more likely to be poor than men. More than one in twelve women is poor. Nearly two-thirds of the elderly poor are women. And nearly one in five children live in poverty—with more than half living in families headed by women."[12]

Globally, the poverty rates for women relative to men are significant. The United Nations and the World Bank, together, issued a recent report on global poverty rates, noting gender disparities. They summarize some of the key findings: "[W]omen fare worse than men and boys on a range of factors that may predispose them to poverty, including having their own source of income, ownership and control of assets and decision making within their households."[13] Further, their research notes: women in the

11. Ibid.
12. "Poverty Rate Falls but Being a Woman Increases the Odds of Being Poor in America, the Wage Gap Remains Stalled, and Uninsurance Among Women Dropped by 37% under ACA," Press Release from National Women's Law Center, available at https://nwlc.org/press-releases/poverty-rate-falls-but-being-a-woman-increases-the-odds-of-being-poor-in-america-the-wage-gap-remains-stalled-and-uninsurance-among-women-dropped-by-37-percent-under-the-aca/
13. "UN Women and the World Bank Unveil New Data Analysis on Women and Poverty," UN Women, available at

age group of 20–34 "are more likely to be poor than men"; women's disproportionate and gendered responsibilities for child care contribute to their poverty; women lack equal opportunities and participation in the labor market; much of "women's work" is undervalued and may not be remunerated; and elderly women are at extreme risk for greater poverty.[14]

In addition to substantial inequality and vulnerability to economic deprivation and poverty women face because they are women, gender inequality is also pervasive and enduring with respect to positions of leadership, including, importantly, political office. The United Nations documents some important data on women's political participation: "Only 22.8% of all national parliamentarians were women as of June 2016"; "As of October 2017, 11 women are serving as Head of State and 12 are serving as Head of Government"; "As of January 2017, only 18.3% of government ministers were women"; and "Globally, there are 38 states in which women account for less than 10% of parliamentarians in single or lower houses, as of June 2016, including 4 chambers with no women at all."[15] The underrepresentation of women in political leadership is both an indicator of the lack of social and political power women, as a class, have relative to men as well as a means of depriving them of an equal voice in political decision making.

http://www.unwomen.org/en/news/stories/2017/11/news-un-women-and-the-world-bank-unveil-new-data-analysis-on-women-and-poverty

14. Ibid.

15. "Facts and Figures: Leadership and Political Participation," UN Women, available at http://www.unwomen.org/en/what-we-do/leadership-and-political-participation/facts-and-figures

Gender norms continue to define women's relation to men in marriage and other forms of domestic partnership such that women do the lion's share of care-giving and domestic work. The unequal division of care labor between men and women contributes to women's inequality in other spheres of life, including, importantly, their relative economic standing as noted previously. Beyond the economic impacts of unequal gender division of care work, women's status is devalued relative to men's in connection with gendered assumptions about the value of such work. Such work does not factor into the measurement of gross-domestic product calculations, and thus remains invisible as productive labor. And as the majority of such work is unpaid, its social value relative to paid work is often degraded or unseen. The unequal burden of caregiving work impacts women's quality of life in other ways as well. For example, women, generally, have less leisure time and time for self-development when they are primary caregivers to children, the elderly, or others who require care (family members with disabilities, for example). If they work outside the home as well, their opportunities for self-directed interests are further diminished.

The fact that women and girl-children are vastly overrepresented as targets of sexual harassment, sexual violence, and rape is a central manifestation and mechanism of sex inequality. A full reporting and analysis of the data concerning sexual violence is beyond what can be presented here. However, some important data reveals the scope of the problem. The Center for Disease Control issued a report on sexual violence, including the following facts:

Nearly 1 in 5 women (18.3%) and 1 in 71 men (1.4%) in the United States have been raped at some time in their lives, including completed forced penetration, attempted forced penetration, or alcohol/drug facilitated completed penetration.

More than half (51.1%) of female victims of rape reported being raped by an intimate partner and 40.8% by an acquaintance; for male victims, more than half (52.4%) reported being raped by an acquaintance and 15.1% by a stranger.

Most female victims of completed rape (79.6%) experienced their first rape before the age of 25; 42.2% experienced their first completed rape before the age of 18 years.

Approximately 1 in 5 Black (22.0%) and White (18.8%) non-Hispanic women, and 1 in 7 Hispanic women (14.6%) in the United States have experienced rape at some point in their lives.

More than one-quarter of women (26.9%) who identified as American Indian or as Alaska Native and 1 in 3 women (33.5%) who identified as multiracial non-Hispanic reported rape victimization in their lifetime.

Approximately 4 out of every 10 women of non-Hispanic Black or American Indian or Alaska Native race/ethnicity (43.7% and 46.0%, respectively), and 1 in 2 multiracial non-Hispanic women (53.8%) have experienced rape, physical violence, and/or stalking by an intimate partner in their lifetime.

One percent, or approximately 1.3 million women, reported being raped by any perpetrator in the 12 months prior to taking the survey.[16]

Additional studies and data support these findings and, in some cases, demonstrate the scope of the problem of sexual

---

16. "National Intimate Partner and Sexual Violence Survey," 2010 Summary Report, Executive Summary, Center for Disease Control, available at https://www.cdc.gov/violenceprevention/pdf/NISVS_Executive_Summary-a.pdf

violence to be even greater than these facts show.[17] What is clear is that simply being a woman/girl is a risk factor for sexual violence. Additional layers of inequality, including racial and age inequality, increase the risk of sexual violence for women and girls.

When women are also members of other marginalized and oppressed groups, they face additional forms of inequality as women of color, as women with disabilities, as indigenous women, or as so-called "third-world" women. The intersection and interlocking nature of layered forms of inequality result in social, economic, and political subordination that disproportionately harms and disadvantages women as such. This is especially clear in prostitution, where women of color, women with disabilities, and trans women are disproportionately represented.

The facts presented here aim to provide a broad snapshot of some of the substantive forms of inequality women face. Yet the picture is clear: nowhere do women enjoy full, substantive equality with men. These facts of sex inequality are not inevitable, not based on biological "differences" between men and women, but a product of social norms

17. The methodology relied upon to study sexual violence is critically important to the results yielded by a particular study. Victim-centered methodology yields more accurate data concerning the incidence of sexual violence. How sexual violence is conceptualized and how the questions are written or asked of interviewees matters a great deal for the answers interviewees provide. For example, if the question is framed so that rape-victims must identify themselves as rape victims in order to count as having been raped (in the study), there is significant underreporting. Shifting a question from "have you been raped?" to "have you been forced to have sex" makes a difference for how persons answer the question even though forced sex is rape. For further discussion and analysis of this methodological point, see: Diana E. H. Russell and Rebecca M. Bolen, *The Epidemic of Rape and Childhood Sexual Abuse in the United States* (Thousand Oaks, CA: SAGE, 2000).

and organization, including, importantly, laws that structure human lives. In evaluating particular legal approaches to prostitution, a key and critical question is whether the specific proposal or practice leaves inequality in place or whether it challenges such inequality.

As a sex-equality approach to prostitution, the Nordic Model is grounded in an analysis of the way in which sex-based inequality is a push factor into prostitution and its solution—decriminalization of the sellers while criminalizing the buyers—aims at securing substantive sex equality for persons in prostitution. The asymmetrical approach to persons in prostitution and buyers is a response to the inequalities between them. Decriminalizing the selling of sex in conjunction with providing social supports for persons in prostitution aims to raise their status. Criminalizing the buyers attacks demand, without which prostitution would not exist. Moreover, it holds men who buy sex responsible for their role in perpetuating harms to women and sex-based inequality.

Several initial objections to any argument to restrict prostitution are worth careful consideration prior to a full defense of the Nordic Model. These objections are popular, and unreflective acceptance of them can lead to a misunderstanding of the uniqueness of the Nordic Model. They are (1) Arguments for restricting prostitution must rest on either a form of moralism or paternalistic justifications, and these are unacceptable bases for laws. (2). Persons (women) in prostitution are there by their own free and voluntary choices, and any restrictive law unjustly restricts their freedom (and buyers' freedoms as well). (3) Even if persons/women in prostitution engage in prostitution from a position of vulnerability and inequality that makes prostitution exploitative, such exploitation may be "mutually beneficial exploitation." Mutually beneficial exploitation should not be legally prohibited. (4). There is nothing inherently wrong with selling sex, compared with other goods and services, and in order to justify any restriction on markets in sex, one would have to argue that selling or buying sex is in some way inherently wrong. These arguments will be reviewed and evaluated in the following sections.

1.4 MORALISM AND PATERNALISM

Charges of moralism and paternalism are often a first line of response to any position that opposes open markets in prostitution. Charges of moralism and paternalism are closely related, though not identical. Roughly speaking, moralism is the view that the state can and should use laws to enforce morality.[18] The scope of political authority and its relation to the scope of political morality is a highly contested matter. Liberal political philosophers generally hold that the scope of proper state authority (political morality) is much smaller than all of morality. Thus, liberal political philosophers hold that there are some areas of life in which the state should refrain from interfering in individuals' lives and choices, even when matters of morality (full stop) are at stake. Moralism, per se, then is considered anathema to liberal political philosophy. There are some areas of life, some actions, which the state has no business "telling" people (coercing through law) what to do. Thus, generally speaking, to claim that a law is moralistic is often

18. John Stanton-Ife, "The Limits of Law," *The Stanford Encyclopedia of Philosophy* (Winter 2016 Edition), Edward N. Zalta (ed.), https://plato.stanford.edu/entries/law-limits/#lega

a criticism, charging that the law in question is interfering in an area of persons' lives in which the state should leave them free to act (provided they don't infringe on other's rights). Put simply, to say that a law rests on a kind of moralism is to charge that the law in question rests on a particular view of morality that is beyond the scope of proper state authority.

When charges of illicit moralism are levied against arguments in favor of restricting prostitution, they often take the following form: matters of sexuality, between consenting adults, is not something the state should interfere with. The argument continues: attempts to regulate or restrict sex between consenting adults inevitably rests on a view of the morality of sex, for example, what counts as virtuous sexual relationships, and such enforcement of morality (in this area of life) is not an appropriate subject for state action. Note this argument, in the context of prostitution, rests on the claim that prostitution, generally or almost always, involves free, voluntary, and consensual sex between the sellers and the buyers. Thus, the argument is restricted in scope and depends on the veracity of that claim. The plausibility of that claim will be interrogated in the next section.

Charges of paternalism are closely related to charges of moralism, but are not identical, even if they overlap in practice. Paternalism is the view that it is sometimes acceptable to prevent people from doing things because those things are harmful to themselves, even when those things are freely chosen. Common examples of laws that are thought to be paternalistic are requiring motorcyclists to wear helmets or laws that make the use of certain drugs illegal because the drugs are deemed "too harmful" to users.

Paternalism can also involve actions by the state (or others) to aim to prevent you from doing something, even if it is not expressly forbidden. So, for example, heavy taxation on cigarettes (sometimes called a "sin-tax") can be understood as a form of paternalism, if the goal is to make it more likely that you will quit smoking because that is what is good for you. Those who object to the full-scale criminalization of prostitution—both the buying and the selling of sex—often claim such state actions are paternalistic.[19] In addition, this claim is often paired with the claim that any argument for restriction must rest on unacceptable forms of moralism. In other words, they charge that those who argue for restriction are either explicitly or implicitly relying on some conception of what is good for persons (moralism) that is controversial or rejected by many such that restrictions take the form of "forcing persons to act (or not act) in ways" that are claimed to be "for their own good." Thus, charges of moralism and paternalism are intimately related, even if the concepts are not identical.

Most liberals reject paternalistic justifications for the use of state power. Though some liberals do think that some forms of mitigated paternalism are consistent with liberal principles of justice and respect for persons; Peter de Marneffe makes this argument with respect to prostitution. His argument will be considered shortly. However, for most liberals, anti-paternalism is central to liberal justice. Forcing persons to act in ways deemed to be "for their own good" is an unjustifiable basis for public law and policy in the view of most liberals.

19. Flanigan's contribution discusses paternalism in detail, see, pp. 271–278.

There are various liberal grounds for objecting to paternalistic policies: (1). It can be argued that they deny persons their basic right to freedom to live according to their own conception of the good. (2). It can be argued that they fundamentally disrespect persons as autonomous agents capable of directing their own lives. (3) It can be argued that they unjustly subject persons to the rule of another, in effect subjugating persons to the will of persons (say the majority) with more power. However the objection is precisely formulated, the basic idea is that paternalistic laws are incompatible with the very kind of individual freedom the liberal state is constructed to protect.

Historically, many of the arguments offered for full criminalization of prostitution have rested on paternalistic grounds. Such arguments were often grounded in, or connected to, dominant social beliefs about "proper" uses of one's own sexuality that also served to criminalize nonmarital sex, gay and lesbian sex, or other forms of sexuality deemed "deviant." Such arguments also specifically targeted women in prostitution as "immoral" or "fallen women," while characterizing the men as simply doing what men do, seeking sex.

As noted in the Introduction, both Flanigan and I reject full criminalization as a justifiable approach to prostitution. The reasons we each reject that approach may vary, but we do share the view that paternalistic reasons are an unacceptable basis for social and legal policy. A further shared premise that underwrites our rejection of paternalism is that the use of coercive state power requires special justification, and that coercive laws that rest on moral values that are reasonably rejected by some citizens are anathema to liberal, political values. Yet despite this agreement between

Flanigan and I, we do not share a vision of what liberal political philosophy entails or requires.

Flanigan can be aptly described as a libertarian, that is,
someone who argues for a very restrictive scope of governmental authority on the grounds that such is necessary to
properly protect individual freedom. Flanigan holds a relatively strong (libertarian) view from which it follows that
inequalities per se are not a threat to freedom. In contrast,
I can be described as an egalitarian-liberal, someone who
argues that some level of substantive equality is a necessary
condition for meaningfully protecting individual freedom.
This difference is apparent in our respective contributions,
particularly concerning whether inequalities can function
as coercive conditions that threaten freedom. Nonetheless,
we both reject paternalistic justification for restricting
prostitution.

In my view, a critical starting point for rejecting paternalism is the fact that people reasonably disagree about
morality. Our moral views and orientations are usually
grounded in some larger belief system, whether religious
or secular, about what gives meaning and value to life. In
societies that protect rights to freedom of thought and
conscience, freedom of association and speech, and other
central liberties, persons enjoying such protections inevitably come to hold a range of different moral views, none
of which can be definitively established as true, right, or
justified to all.[20] Another way of putting this point is that
under conditions of freedom, as just described, reasonable
pluralism about the good (full morality) is inevitable.[21] It

20. John Rawls makes this argument in his *Political Liberalism*, expanded edition (New York: Columbia University Press, 2005).
21. Ibid., pp. xix and xxvi.

is important to note that the use of the word "reasonable" here is precise and somewhat technical.

In order to count as reasonable, persons must both be committed to finding shared terms of social cooperation (shared principles of political morality) and willingly accept that persons so committed may come to very different conclusions regarding the values or principles of full morality.[22] To put the point simply, reasonable persons as citizens of liberal democracies are committed to a principle of restraint concerning the kinds of arguments and reasons that can be offered as justification for the use of state power. Such restraint requires that when advancing arguments for some public law or policy, reasonable citizens draw on shared political values, like ideals of free and equal citizenship, rather than full-blown moral theories.[23] Reasonable citizens do not regard the state as the appropriate instrument for enforcing the whole of morality; they respect other person's reasonable disagreement about morality and, thus, view the role of the state as limited to securing the necessary political morality required for securing fair and equal social cooperation.

22. This way of putting it is purposefully simplified, so that that the ideas are accessible. The more technical definition of reasonable persons, offered by Rawls, is the view I endorse. Rawls defines reasonable persons in two respects, first such persons are "when, among equals say, they are ready to propose principles and standards as fair terms of cooperation and to abide by them willingly, given the assurance that others will likewise do so." And, second, reasonable persons are "willing to recognize the burdens of judgment and to accept their consequences for the use of public reason in directing the legitimate exercise of political power in a constitutional regime." *Political Liberalism*, pp. 49 and 54, respectively.

23. Christie Hartley and I advance this argument, and an account of shared political reasons, in *Equal Citizenship and Public Reason: A Feminist Political Liberalism* (New York: Oxford University Press, 2018).

On the basis of such arguments, or very similar ones, many liberals conclude that the state ought not to rely on controversial moral claims or values as the bases for state policies. Doing so would be inconsistent with the liberal principle of legitimacy—the claim that state actions are justified only insofar as those subject to them can in some way consent to them. Relying on a specific and particular account of full morality to justify state actions will invariably require reliance upon reasons that some citizens may reasonably reject.[24] Thus, some liberals argue that the state should forgo comprehensive moral claims in grounding particular laws or policies and rather rely solely on political values.[25] Political values are moral values, of course, but they are narrower and aim to be compatible with a range of comprehensive values, such that all reasonable people can endorse them. Examples of such political values are the values of free and equal citizenship, human rights, equal opportunity, and the like. They are drawn from the public, political culture of liberal democracies and are compatible with a range of differing but reasonable views about what full morality demands.

Thus, one desideratum that will constrain my arguments concerning how to regulate prostitution is that those arguments do not rely on particular comprehensive conceptions of the good life or particular comprehensive accounts of the value of sex or sexuality. In other words, such

24. Rawls, *Political Liberalism*, Lecture II.
25. A political liberalism can be distinguished from a comprehensive liberalism in one respect in terms of the scope of its principles. A political liberalism does not aim to specify values across the whole of life; rather it aims to articulate just principles for regulating the basic structure. See *Political Liberalism*, pp. 11–15.

arguments should not rest upon claims about the right or best way to express one's sexuality from a moral perspective. Political liberals will reject any argument that rests upon claims like: we should only have virtuous sex, where that is defined in turn as sex congruent with other moral values like monogamy or a rejection of promiscuity, or the purpose of sex is to show love for one's sexual partner. Political liberals accept that reasonable people have a range of views about sex and sexuality, and so long as the sexual practices that follow from any particular view don't harm others or deny others' their rights as equal citizens, then the liberal state accepts pluralism about sex and sexuality.

Does the Nordic Model rest on either moralistic or paternalistic grounds? No.

The Nordic Model does not rest on any particular comprehensive moral doctrine, nor does it rest on a view of "moral" sex or sexuality; rather, it rests on the value of equal citizenship, understood substantively. A substantive conception of equality measures equality not in terms of sameness or difference, but rather status or hierarchy. The opposite of equality is not simple difference, but hierarchy.[26] A substantive analysis of inequality reveals that being denied equal power, privilege, access, and standing relative to those with such power and privilege is a denial of equality. As such, dismantling power structures that serve to subordinate some relative to others is essential to securing conditions of equality. This understanding of equality is especially perceptive for identifying patterns of inequality that mask themselves as mere difference, sex inequality being a prime example.

---

26. See MacKinnon, *Sex Equality* 3rd ed., Chapter 1.

Canada has embraced this approach to equality.[27] It has also been the framework from which sexual harassment law in the United States and elsewhere was recognized as a violation of equality and provides a basis for a new approach to pornography that reframes it as a practice of subordination of women, a practice of inequality, rather than merely a form of free expression of sexuality.[28]

Equality is a normative value, and it is foundational in nearly all political moralities. Yet exactly what equality is and how it should be realized is a matter of debate. The substantive theory of equality, upon which the Nordic Model rests, entails that social hierarchies that serve to subordinate persons, based on group identities, relative to other social groups is incompatible with equality. The empirical and grounded analysis of prostitution as a social practice, in which women are both subordinated and exploited in service of men's sexual demands, is an example of such a hierarchy.

The commitment to equality rests neither on paternalism nor any kind of moralism. The scope of the commitment to equality concerns equal civil standing; this point will be elaborated later in this section. Though some defenders of the Nordic Model might also envision broader forms of egalitarianism as a moral ideal for all of life, the justification for the law itself rests on a commitment to equality as a civil right. Nor does the Nordic Model rest on

27. Ibid.
28. Readers will no doubt identify this list with Catharine MacKinnon's body of work. For an illuminating account of the development and success of these legal arguments, see *Butterfly Politics* (Cambridge, MA: Harvard University Press, 2017).

the claim that women should be prevented from prostitution "for their own good" as a matter of morality.

Thus, it is a mistake to classify the Nordic Model as paternalistic law. The Nordic Model is a sex-equality law. It fully decriminalizes the sale of sex. Thus, it does not aim to prevent women from engaging in prostitution "for their own good." In other words, a paternalistic justification necessarily draws on some conception of what is "good" (understood as morally good or as constitutive of some fairly robust ideal of "the good" for persons). Clear cases of paternalistic justifications for specific laws are cases in which appeals to some ideal of what is good for a human life, or persons' interests or welfare, as a basis for restricting *their* liberty or autonomy.[29] To put it simply: paternalistic justifications have the structure of forbidding or threatening consequences for persons for acting in ways that are deemed contrary to their good, interests, or welfare as informed by morally robust specifications of those concepts.

The Nordic Model does not forbid or threaten legal consequences for persons in prostitution. They are not the subjects of the law. Buyers and third parties are the persons whose actions are criminalized. It criminalizes the buying of sex because targeting demand, and abolishing demand, is the best way to secure sex equality. Social and political equality is the ground of the law.

The Nordic Model can be understood, then, as civil rights law. As such, it aims to shift cultural understanding of prostitution away from an immoral occupation of "fallen

29. Dworkin, Gerald, "Paternalism," *The Stanford Encyclopedia of Philosophy* (Winter 2017 Edition), Edward N. Zalta (ed.), https://plato.stanford.edu/entries/paternalism/

women" to seeing it as a form of inequality. It then develops a strategy for rectifying that inequality. Inequality is a form of harm, but it is not a harm that one inflicts upon one's self. Rather, inequality is a product of hierarchical social conditions and relations.

To see this more clearly, consider the US Civil Rights Act of 1964. The act prohibits discrimination on the basis of race, color, sex, religion, and national origin in specific areas of public life, including public accommodations, education, and employment. It also prohibits such discrimination in voting. One might ask, how and why were these specific areas of public and social life included in this Act? In other words, what explains the focus on discrimination in public accommodations, education, and employment as specific sites of inequality? There are some complicated legal reasons, but we can set those aside because they are not critical to the point. These areas of life were the focus of the legislation for two reasons: first, they were significant areas of life in which discrimination was pervasive and through which the second-class status of those subject to such discrimination, primarily Blacks in the United States, was manifest and maintained. Denial of access to equal education, equal employment, and housing was (and in some ways still is) a part of a system of inequality in which Blacks, and other racially subordinated groups, are denied full citizenship and a material existence as equals. Second, activists, over a long period of time, were able to convince judges and legislators that these acts of discrimination were forms of inequality. Thus, the civil rights movement, culminating in the 1964 Act, transformed our cultural understanding of discrimination away from a view that supported such discrimination as a right of those with power to exclude Blacks (and others) to a view of such discrimination as a practice of inequality.

Similarly, sexual harassment laws, which define sexual harassment as a form of sex discrimination, evolved as a response to social conditions of sex-based inequality. Prior to the development of sexual harassment laws, women who were routinely subject to sexualization in their work environments, including unwanted sexual touching and sexual acts (rape, in some cases), did not have legal recourse or a legal concept in which to frame their injuries. The development of sexual harassment law including its analysis that unwanted sexual offers or threats (quid pro quo) and hostile environments (contexts in which "conditions of work are damagingly sexualized or gendered on the basis of sex"[30]) framed such harassment as a form of sex subordination—as a practice of inequality.

Civil rights laws, like those just described, clearly conceptualize inequality as an injury, a harm that sets back the interests of the persons subject to such unequal treatment. However, legislation that aims to secure equality, and prohibit practices of inequality, is not paternalistic either in substance or in form. The justification for such laws rests on preventing other persons (or institutions) from subordinating members of socially disadvantaged groups. Those constrained by the law are others or third parties or institutional structures, not the subordinated persons themselves. Substantively, such laws do not rest on illicit moralisms. They rest on the value of equal social and political standing, and as such, seek to secure the material conditions of such

30. MacKinnon, *Sex Equality*, p. 1050.

equality for persons as members of socially subordinated groups.

Nonetheless, some liberals think that any argument that entails restricting prostitution (including legal restrictions targeting buyers) must rest on a form of paternalism but think that such restrictions are compatible with liberal values. For example, Peter de Marneffe argues that laws regulating and limiting prostitution can be justified on paternalistic grounds consistent with liberalism's respect for liberty.[31] His argument primarily addresses the following harms: "feelings of worthlessness, shame, and self-hatred, damages their capacities for healthy intimate relationships and limits their social and employment opportunities."[32] In brief, his argument is that prostitution is harmful to those who are in it and that forms of regulation should be formulated with the goals of reducing the number of women in prostitution, as well as reducing the harms experienced by individuals in prostitution.[33]

De Marneffe thinks that some of the empirical evidence concerning the impacts and structure of prostitution is difficult to assess or mixed such that knowing which particular policy is best is difficult to determine. He argues that we should choose a model for regulating prostitution (whether decriminalizing some aspects of prostitution or imposing stricter limits on prostitution while permitting it) based on the goal of reducing harms, as he identifies them. His argument does not identify inequality as a primary harm. Nor does he consider that inequality is a distinctive

31. Peter de Marneffe, *Liberalism and Prostitution* (New York: Oxford University Press, 2010), 44
32. Ibid., p. 22.
33. Ibid., pp. 3–44.

harm for which no paternalistic justification is required to address. That a law may restrict the behavior of some per-sons (buyers of sex in the case of the Nordic Model) so as to prevent harms, including the harm of inequality, for those impacted by their behavior, is not paternalism. Again, the Nordic Model does not target or penalize persons in prosti-tution and its justificatory structure does not rely on claims about persons' "own good." It is an equality law.

The underlying assumption that leads De Marneffe to structure his analysis in terms of paternalism is his claim that most prostitution is fully free and voluntary. Thus, he frames any restrictions (even those that only target buyers) as restricting freedom of persons in prostitution for the sake of reducing harm. This assumption warrants investigation.

1.5 MEANINGFUL CHOICES

A common defense for those who argue for either legaliza-tion or across-the-board decriminalization of prostitution is to exclaim, "But it is a choice!" They continue, "If it's a free choice, then laws that aim to criminalize some or all aspects of the buying and selling of sex require a special justifica-tion for restrictions of freedom in this case."[34] And further, they argue there is no warranted justification for restricting markets in sex.

Whether any individual person's entry into prostitu-tion can be accurately described as a "free choice" depends on the particular facts of their situation. To know this,

---

34. Flanigan's contribution makes a version of this argument.

we'd have to know a lot about that particular person such as their age, race, economic resources, and opportunities; country of origin and its political and economic climate; whether they have a history of abuse, sexual or otherwise, and whether someone else was involved and in what way with this "choice"; and the like. When advocates of legalization or decriminalization appeal to "the free choice argument," though, they are not saying each and every person in prostitution has made a free choice; after all, how could they begin to know that? They are, rather, making a general claim that most people in prostitution have freely chosen to be there. This claim must be evaluated in light of the evidence.

No matter one's position on whether prostitution should be legalized, decriminalized, or abolished, everyone acknowledges that the primary reason women (or men) enter into prostitution is desperate economic need.[35] The terms used to describe that need vary, but most recognize it as a "choice" of last resort made in the context of economic desperation.[36] In other words, it is a "choice" made under conditions of severe economic deprivation, often to provide for basic needs for survival. For example, Melissa Farley's

---

35. For example, governmental reports in the Netherlands, New Zealand, and Germany all emphasize this point. These are places in which prostitution is either legal or decriminalized, and each of these reports is commissioned by governments that support continued legalization or decriminalization.

36. EU Parliament Report: "Sexual Exploitation and Prostitution and Its Impact on Gender Equality," [Hereinafter "EU Parliament Report"] The Policy Department on Citizen's Rights and Constitutional Affairs for the European Parliament, completed in January 2014, pp. 7–8, available on line at http://www.europarl.europa.eu/RegData/etudes/etudes/join/2014/493040/IPOL-FEMM_ET(2014)493040_EN.pdf

study into prostitution in 9 countries, with roughly 900 participants, documents that 75% of women in prostitution were homeless at the time of entry.[37] Severe economic inequality is a primary push factor into prostitution, especially when combined with other inequalities, importantly, sex inequality. Many men are also poor, though not as pervasively as women, and yet few men resort to prostitution out of economic desperation. Some men do, but in drastically fewer numbers than women.[38] And even when men are in prostitution, other men, overwhelmingly, are those buying them.

Other documented pathways into prostitution include prior history of abuse (including sexual and domestic abuse), homelessness, addiction, and enticement, coercion or force by a romantic partner or friend.[39] Moreover, women of color, indigenous, aboriginal, and First-Nations women, women from countries negatively impacted by globalization, and trans women are over-represented in prostitution.[40] Such women are also more frequently at the

37. Melissa Farley and Emily Butler, "Prostitution and Trafficking—Quick Facts," Prostitution Research & Education 2012, available at http://www.prostitutionresearch.com/Prostitution%20Quick%20 Facts%2012-21-12.pdf

38. SeeMichel Dorais, *Rent Boys: The World of Male Sex Workers* (Ithaca, NY: McGill-Queen's University Press, 2005) and Donald J. West, *Male Prostitution* (New York: Routledge, 2010).

39. For empirical research documenting pathways into prostitution, see Janice G. Raymond, *Not a Choice, Not a Job: Exposing the Myths About Prostitution and the Global Sex Trade* (Potomac Books: Washington, DC, 2013); R. Matthews, H. Easton, L. Reynolds, J. Bindel, and Lisa Young, *Exiting Prostitution: A Study in Female Desistance* (New York: Palgrave MacMillan, 2014).

40. Farley et al., "Garden of Truth: The Prostitution and Trafficking of Native Women in Minnesota," available at http://www.prostitution-research.com/Garden_of_Truth_The%20Prostitution%20and%20 Trafficking%20of%20Native%20Women.pdf

bottom of the hierarchy within prostitution. Age and disability status are further inequalities that function as push
factors into prostitution.

Advocates of legalization or decriminalization admit
all of these facts of inequality. So, for example, a German
government report, written by a committee that supports
continued legalization, states: "This group [prostitutes]
suffered considerably more childhood violence, sexual violence, violence in relationships and violence in the workplace."[41] And in aiming to glamorize and glorify pimping,
infamous American brothel owner and pimp Dennis Hof
reveals an important truth in his biography, *The Art of the
Pimp*. A woman, who at one point was prostituted at one of
Hof's brothels, as a part of her testimonial meant to honor
Hof, writes: "Girls don't show up at the Bunny Ranch because their life is rosy. They're knocking on that door because they're in debt or because something else is wrong
and they are looking for a quick, easy fix. There is no easy
fix, though. You end up staying. You get used to the money,
to the lifestyle. For lots of girls it's just easier to be at the
BunnyRanch than it is to deal with the real world."[42]

Perhaps obvious to some, but nonetheless worth
making explicit, is the fact that women (or men) with
the most power, prestige, opportunities, and security are

41. "Report by the Federal Government on the Impact of the Act
Regulating the Legal Situation of Prostitutes (Prostitution Act),"
[Hereinafter "The German Report] Federal Ministry for Family Affairs,
Senior Citizens, Women and Youth, German Government, p. 11, avail-
able at https://www.bmfsfj.de/blob/93346/f81fb6d56073e3a0a80c442
439b6495e/bericht-der-br-zum-prostg-englisch-data.pdf

42. Dennis Hof, *The Art of the Pimp: A Love Story, One Man's Search for
Love, Sex and Money* (New York: Regan Arts, 2015), 126

simply not "choosing" to be in prostitution. As MacKinnon has forcefully pointed out: "If prostitution were a choice, one would think that more men would be found exercising it."[43] And further, she notes: "No one fights to become a prostitute against all the odds. She is prostituted when the odds beat her."[44] Inequality, in a range of forms, is a precondition to entry.

Once there, exit is difficult and sometimes impossible. The barriers to exit are widely understood, even by advocates of legalization or decriminalization. For example, the authors of the German government report assessing the "success" of legalization write: "When prostitutes make the decision to leave prostitution, they often find themselves confronted by a multitude of problems. Along with financial and/or family problems, health problems linked to prostitution and stress and violence, in some cases experienced early in life, nearly half those wanting to leave prostitution find themselves in a situation that is further compounded by the fact they have little school education or vocational training. The preconditions for leaving the profession are not favorable."[45] A recent study in England documents the barriers to exiting prostitution as including "drug dependency, homelessness, lack of skills training or low educational levels, together with poor employment histories. Other barriers frequently cited include financial issues and problems with physical and mental health."[46] The study also documents coercion to remain in prostitution by pimps, partners, and family members as an additional

43. MacKinnon, "Trafficking, Prostitution, and Inequality," 292.
44. Ibid.
45. The German Report, p. 33.
46. Matthews et al., *Exiting Prostitution*, p. 45

barrier to exit. Such coercion is similarly documented in
a Netherland's governmental report, assessing the situation of prostitutes five years after the lift of the brothel
ban: "A complicating factor in combating the exploitation
of involuntary prostitution is that policy, issue of licenses,
and enforcement are all mainly targeting the owners of
sex businesses. Although owners might use coercion, such
force is chiefly exercised by pimps who operate more in the
background, and of whose existence the owners are not always aware. *Pimps are still a very common phenomenon.* . . .
[T]he fact that the number of prostitutes with pimps has
not decreased is a cause for concern."[47]

What all this helps to bring to light is that whether
someone's "choice" is a genuinely free choice depends on
the background conditions against which it is made. The
vectors of evaluating whether "choices" constitute genuinely free choices include the range of available options
in light of which choices are made, the relative position
of social power one is in, as well as the social norms that
channel people into certain choices. Concerning the latter,
the way social norms shape choices, the fact that it is overwhelmingly women who are "choosing" prostitution certainly highlights that gendered norms and expectations
about what women are for is central to any analysis of prostitution.[48] When layers of inequality function to channel

47. "Prostitution in the Netherlands since Lifting the Brothel Ban,"
available at https://repository.tudelft.nl/view/wodc/uuid:a0ca309e-9739-
49a9-a803-9820a8de0fa5/ (Hereinafter "The Netherlands Report"), p. 4.
48. For a trenchant critique on liberal appeals to choice as a "normative transformer," see Clare Chambers, *Sex, Culture, and Justice: The Limits
of Choice* (University Park: Pennsylvania State University Press, 2008).

certain groups of people (in this case women) into certain "choices," calling such "choices" free serves to erase the inequalities and power structures in the background that serve as coercive pressures. The European Parliament Briefing Paper emphasizes this point effectively in its assessment of prostitution: "In this sense, poverty and bad economic and employment situations are seen as strong push-factors forcing women into prostitution, and which call into question whether their consent can be assumed to have been voluntarily given."[49]

It is also crucial to underscore that the "choice" argument alone isn't sufficient to establish any claim about whether we should respect, facilitate, or permit such choices. There are a lot of "choices" that we think should be prevented, regulated, or even punished. In other words, even if advocates could tell a compelling story that would justify believing that most women in prostitution freely chose to be there—and, again, the empirical facts simply don't support this—that alone is not enough to establish that legalization or decriminalization is justified. More premises are needed. Such advocates need to argue in addition that such "choices" are consistent with other important values, like equality, or justice, or liberty. We generally recognize that "choices" made from circumstances of inequality that exploit the vulnerability of persons in unequal conditions are "choices" that the state should prevent for the sake of equality. For example, the selling of bodily organs, such as kidneys, is a decision some make from desperate economic circumstances and foreclosed opportunities, yet it is widely recognized that markets in organs are

49. EU Parliament Report, p. 7.

premised on inequality in which persons with power (and money) can exploit the vulnerability of others to their own benefit. Similarly, those exploited in sweatshops are often referred to as "modern day slaves." The widespread practice of such slave-like labor has led to serious initiatives from both specific nation-states and the international community to combat forced labor, recognizing it as a human rights violation.

Thus, the central question is not in fact about whether prostitution is a "free choice." Rather, the central question concerns how we should address inequality that channels some persons into prostitution and the resulting exploitation.

1.6 EXPLOITATION

Not everyone agrees that the kind of exploitation present in practices such as the sale of bodily organs, or sweatshops, or prostitution is something states or international bodies should discourage or prohibit. Most often, people understand exploitation as taking unfair advantage of another's vulnerability to gain a benefit. Some advocates of legalization or decriminalization argue that even if prostitution is exploitative, we should nonetheless legalize it for it may be the "best" option available to vulnerable persons under current circumstances. There is a version of this claim in harm reduction arguments in favor of legalization or decriminalization of prostitution. As noted, sometimes it is said that prostitution is inevitable (it will always exist) and so the question is how to make it less bad for the women (people) in it. Although not always explicit, the underlying assumption here is that prostitution will be the best option for some people, notably women.

Recent philosophical work on the concept of exploitation by Matt Zwolinski aims to distinguish cases of wrongful exploitation from cases of mutually beneficial exploitation.[50] The latter, Zwolinski argues, should be permitted because prohibiting such exploitation makes the exploited persons worse off. In other words, even if exploitation means taking advantage of another's vulnerability, this isn't necessarily a wrong we should aim to prevent insofar as the exploitation may make the exploited better off than doing nothing. He considers sweatshops as a primary example of mutually beneficial exploitation and argues that sweatshops should be permitted, even though exploitative, because the laborers within sweatshops are better off than they would be if denied this form of work. Central to this argument is the recognition that those working in sweatshops are in desperate poverty, lacking meaningful alternatives for meeting their basic needs, and driven to sweatshop labor as the only realistic option for survival.

This argument can be made in the case of prostitution as well. As we have already noted, persons in prostitution have few or no alternative options to prostitution to earn an income sufficient to meet their basic needs. There are additional inequalities that channel persons into prostitution, of course. There are reasons that overwhelmingly women, and not men, are the persons in prostitution, even when men similarly face extreme poverty. There are reasons that

50. Matt Zwolinski, "Structural Exploitation," *Social Philosophy and Policy* 29, no. 1 (Winter 2012): 154–79; and Matt Zwolinski, "Sweatshops, Choice, and Exploitation," *Business Ethics Quarterly* 14, no. 4 (2007): 689–727.

women of color, younger women and girls, women with histories of violence and abuse, including sexual abuse, are overrepresented in prostitution, as explained earlier.

As well, there are reasons that men, and not women, are overwhelmingly the buyers of sex—"the johns." Primary among these reasons is the way that masculinity and femininity are socially defined. As described previously, masculinity and femininity are defined, socially, as power relations, each constructed in relation to the other. Constitutive of social constructions of masculinity is the belief that to be masculine is to exercise power, control, and force over others. In short, to experience enculturation into the norms of masculinity is to be taught that dominating others is part of what it is to be a man. To experience enculturation into the norms of femininity is to be taught that part of what it is to be a woman is to be submissive relative to exercises of male power. Norms of heterosexuality are built upon the dichotomy of masculine and feminine sexuality, in which masculine sexuality is about exercising domination, and feminine sexuality about subordination to that domination.[51] Nothing about this analysis implies that men or women, males or females, or sexuality itself is essentially (biologically) structured, inescapably, in terms of domination and subordination. Rather, this analysis is about the social meanings of masculinity, femininity, man, woman, and heterosexuality. Thus, masculinity and femininity are social relations of inequality, something that any analysis of prostitution must confront.

51. Catharine A. MacKinnon, *Toward a Feminist Theory of the State* (Cambridge, MA: Harvard University Press, 1990), Chapter 7 "Sexuality," pp. 126–54.

Applying the "mutually beneficial exploitation" argument to prostitution in absence of explicit recognition of the way in which gender inequality functions to channel primarily women and girls, and not men, into prostitution comes dangerously close to assuming that the sexual use of women, by men, is a fact that is either acceptable or unchangeable. Sometimes boys, men, and gay men, are used in prostitution in the way that women are used in prostitution. As noted previously, precise statistics are difficult to come by, as even in legal markets brothels selling men are non-existent.[52] Estimates of boys and men in prostitution hover around 10%. They, too, are bought by men. Nothing about that fact challenges the analysis of gender as expressed in relations of domination and subordination just given. Rather, it just underscores that gender is social, and not biological.

Extending "mutually beneficial exploitation" analysis to prostitution looks like this: if the state were to prohibit markets in sex (prohibit the buying and selling of sex), then vulnerable persons (largely women) could be worse off than they are at present because selling sex, at least, allows them to meet some of their economic needs. The first thing to note in evaluating this argument as it applies to either sweatshops or prostitution is that it analyzes exploitation in terms of only two options: permit sweatshops (or prostitution) as it exists now or prohibit sweatshops (or prostitution) as they now exist. However, this is a false dichotomy. Those are not our only two options. There is a range of

---

52. There are no brothels with male prostitutes in Nevada. Attempts have been made to open such establishments, but none have survived. Presumably, this is in large part due to lack of demand.

other options and policy decisions available to us. The state could adopt policies to alleviate the poverty and the desperate economic circumstances of those that see various forms of exploitation (sweatshops or prostitution) as their best option given their poverty or other circumstances of inequality.

Zwolinksi and Flanigan argue for a universal basic income, an unconditional guaranteed minimum cash grant for all citizens in a given nation-state. The universal basic income proposal is meant to replace current welfare-state entitlements like Medicaid, low-income housing vouchers, food stamps, and so on. Providing a universal basic income might go some way toward alleviating the crushing poverty that leads vulnerable persons to "agree" to exploitative bargains such as working in a sweatshop or prostituting. How effective such a universal basic income would be in bringing people up to a threshold of economic security depends, of course, on how much it is and whether it is sufficient to meet their basic needs such as health care, affordable housing, education, and training to pursue other opportunities, and so on. And even so, a universal basic income only addresses one manifestation of inequality that pushes women into prostitution: economic inequality. While economic inequality is a central push factor, other layers of inequality similarly structure the lives and choices of people who enter into prostitution, as previously documented.

The central question for those sympathetic to the argument in favor of permitting "mutually beneficial exploitation," however, is what we should do now under present circumstances in which nothing like a universal basic income is available in most places (the Nordic countries do provide a much richer set of social services and resources than the United States and other countries). Arguing that states should permit exploitation of the vulnerable on the grounds that this may be the "best deal" persons at the bottom of various social hierarchies can get serves to justify the status quo.

Moreover, the argument ignores the way in which states have been and continue to be sources of the inequality that function to make particular groups of persons vulnerable to exploitation. States have played an important role in sustaining various forms of inequality both through their direct actions and inaction. Discrimination in employment, education, and housing on the basis of race and sex were permitted by the United States, for example, until only recently. Colonialism has operated in much of the world to benefit members of conquering nations at the expense of indigenous populations, including through laws stripping original inhabitants of property and rights and underwriting their second-class political standing. These practices of inequality occurred both in the form of failing to expressly forbid discrimination and through permitting and thus sanctioning discrimination such as through upholding laws that expressly denied access, opportunity, and equal consideration for members of socially subordinated groups, thus formally entrenching their subordination.

Even where formal political equality has been extended to groups previously denied such equality, substantive inequality is maintained by state policies or lack of policies. Thus, for example, state policies on taxation, programs to benefit persons in poverty, and health care are all examples of state actions that determine the structure of persons' lives in profound ways, and depending on the substance of these policies they may ameliorate or further inequality. To argue that the state should legalize prostitution on the grounds that prostitution is the best option, the best deal, that some people can get, ignores that the state itself is a primary source of structuring the options available to its citizens.

In the context of defending "mutually beneficial exploitation" as acceptable, analogies with rescues of helpless victims are often invoked.[53] If you are stranded in a sinking boat, and a stranger comes along and offers to rescue you for a hefty price, they are exploiting your vulnerability to their benefit, but if the options are death or such "mutually beneficially" exploitation, surely you are going to pick rescue at the hefty price. If we reconstruct this analogy to account for the role that states play in sustaining inequality (including vulnerability to inequality), it looks more like this: Someone maroons you on an island. They return to offer you use of their boat to get off the island, but only if you pay a grossly unfair price. They then justify their actions by saying, "Well, this is the best deal you can get," all the while never acknowledging that their actions partly explain why you are on the island in the first place.

Defenders of the Nordic Model refuse to accept that prostitution is the best deal some women can get and hold states responsible for adopting policies that secure the substantive equality of all persons, including women. Failure

---

53. Matt Zwolinski, "Structural Exploitation," 165–66, imagines a motorist coming upon a stranded person in a snowstorm being charged an exorbitant sum, though Zwolinski challenges the analogy insofar as the snowstorm rescue constitutes a non-competitive market, and he claims sweatshop labor markets are not non-competitive in an analogous sense.

to address sex inequality as such, acceptance of the status quo, makes states complicit in inequality.

1.7 RIGHTS TO MARKETS IN SEX?

A final initial objection to consider is the claim that persons have rights to markets in sex. Some object to restrictions on prostitution on the grounds that there is nothing *inherently* wrong with selling sex; it is just like selling other goods or services. A version of this claim is often advanced in the context of arguments that claim "sex work is work just like any other form of work." That specific claim and the arguments offered in defense of it will be thoroughly evaluated and criticized in the next chapter. This section simply aims to address the argument that there is nothing wrong, in itself, with selling sex compared to other services and goods and that for this reason restrictions on markets in sex violate persons' rights. Flanigan argues that restrictions on markets in sex violate both buyers and seller's rights. She argues that persons have moral rights to consensual sex with others, and that includes a right to exchange sex for money.

Jason Brennan and Peter M. Jaworski offer a similar argument, claiming that many criticisms of prostitution, and other practices like kidney and baby selling, are misguided insofar as they are focused on whether the economic exchange of the goods and services involved is wrong. According to Brennan and Jaworski, markets are morally neutral. In other words, they argue that exchanging some goods or service in a market isn't determinant of whether the exchange is wrong. The moral permissibility or impermissibility of certain exchanges depends on factors other than whether money is used to facilitate the exchange. Thus, they argue that if some kind of exchange is permissible, like giving someone a good or service (a kidney or sex, for example), then that exchange is not morally transformed from permissible to impermissible simply because money conditions the exchange. In their words, "if you may do it for free, you may do it for money."[54]

Nonetheless, they do argue if the underlying exchange is morally wrong, then markets in that good or service are morally impermissible. For example, consider the trade in "shrunken" human heads (tsantsa), which has been outlawed in many countries.[55] When Westerners first encountered shrunken human heads, they prized them as an object to acquire. This creation of a market fueled murders so as to supply the demand. Since murder is wrong, and murder is the means to supply the market, presumably Brennan and Jaworkski would support prohibition of markets in shrunken heads. Though perhaps they would argue once the heads are separated from their owners, the heads themselves are permissibly exchanged while agreeing that murdering for the purpose of selling shrunken heads is wrong.

This raises a relevant point for thinking about markets in sex. The demand for buying sex is the driver of the market. The greater the demand, the greater the number of women is needed to fill the demand. Even if we accept

54. Jason Brennan and Peter M. Jaworski, *Markets Without Limits: Moral Virtues and Commercial Interests* (New York: Routledge, 2016), 10.
55. Thanks to M. M. P. for the example.

the assumption that some prostitution is voluntary, the demand is far greater than that pool of people/women. We know this because sex trafficking, forced prostitution as it is sometimes called, is a huge, global business. Global estimates are that 25 million people are trafficked each year, 80% of whom are women and girls trafficked for purposes of sexual exploitation, as understood under more restrictive definitions.[56] Thus, the market creates the conditions for forced prostitution to be profitable. In other words, allowing markets in sex, at all, creates the conditions for sex trafficking. Just like allowing markets in human shrunken heads created the conditions for murder for the purpose of entering the market—namely, selling shrunken human heads. I will explore the distinction between sex trafficking and so-called voluntary prostitution in chapter 3, and argue that the distinction as generally drawn relies on impoverished conceptions of force and coercion. Some of that argument has been foreshadowed already: inequalities can function as forms of coercion. The point here is simply that permitting open markets in sex can and does create conditions for persons to be coerced into those markets, and this can be seen with even restrictive definitions of sex trafficking.

Those sympathetic to Brennan and Jaworski's position might well reply along the following lines. All markets create conditions for morally wrong behavior. After all, theft of property depends on there being property, and markets involve exchanges of property. Property ownership itself

---

56. "Human Rights and trafficking in persons," United Nations Human Rights Office of the High Commissioner, available at https://www.ohchr.org/EN/Issues/Trafficking/TiP/Pages/Index.aspx

isn't wrong even if it creates the conditions for persons to steal. Any exchange market will create the conditions for illicit exchanges. But in the case of shrunken heads, the underlying act—murder—is wrong, so the market in human shrunken heads is wrong. (Although it is not clear that Brennan and Jaworski would accept that argument.) What about in the case of prostitution? Brennan, Jaworski, and Flanigan each believe the underlying act—exchanging sex for money—is not wrong, and thus a market in sex is not wrong.

Their analysis rests on moving from consideration of the exchange (sex for money) to thinking about broader markets and their permissibility. However, if we think through the issue from the other direction, from the existence of a market to the kinds of exchanges it promotes, the analysis shifts. What does a market in prostitution do? What does the demand fuel in the case of prostitution? It fuels a class of women for sexual use on men's terms. That class of women consists of the most unequal women, those in conditions of extreme poverty and subject to other forms of layered inequality (age, race, trans status, nationality, and so on).

Under such conditions of inequality, sex is exchanged for economic survival. The money functions as the means for coercing women into sex. Yet Flanigan rejects this analysis, in part, because she does not think that constrained options, and various forms of inequality combined, should be understood as coercive conditions that undermine meaningful choices.

We have already examined some of the evidence that those who are prostituted (the sellers of sex) lack meaningful options, face severely restricted choice sets, and face significant barriers to exit. At the very least, these facts demonstrate that sellers do not stand in reciprocal relations of equality with buyers. Buyers have significantly more freedom and power than sellers. Thus, one way to reject Flanigan's argument is to reject the antecedent to the conditional. This means denying the claim that the terms of the exchange (sex for money) and the conditions under which persons are driven to such exchanges are not meaningfully free or voluntary. Neither are they equal exchanges.

A number of important philosophical arguments are available to challenge the claim that markets are morally neutral as argued by Brennan, Jaworski, and Flanigan. Scholars who investigate the moral limits of markets often frame their inquiry in terms of whether there are certain goods or services that should not be "commodified."[57] Although there is no uniform agreement about how to define commodification, there are general features across accounts that can be enumerated so as to frame the discussion that follows. Simply put, a commodity is a "thing" that is an object of economic exchange. In principle, any "thing" that people are willing to buy and sell could be a commodity, an object of economic exchange. "Commodification" is a term that is used to discuss the social process in which "things" or persons become commodities. More specifically, it is most often used in a critical way to describe the turning of persons, or aspects of persons, into goods or services for

---

57. See, for example, Elizabeth Anderson, *Value in Ethics and Economics* (Cambridge, MA: Harvard University Press, 1993) and Debra Satz, *Why Some Things Should Not Be for Sale* (New York: Oxford University Press, 2010).

exchange in a market. Thus, sometimes commodification is described as "the reduction of persons to things."[58]

In this framework, a primary question is whether there are certain "things," including persons or aspects of persons that should not be permissibly commodified. An example will help to clarify: many people think that human babies should not be permitted to be bought and sold—that is, human babies are not appropriately thought of as commodities. Allowing human babies to be bought and sold would be to commodify them, namely, reduce them to a "thing." Those who object to markets in babies then would claim the commodification of babies is wrong and should not be permitted.

Some of those who argue against markets in sex (prostitution) argue that part of what is wrong or bad about prostitution is that sex is one of those "things" or areas of life that should not be commodified. Both Margaret Radin and Elizabeth Anderson argue that markets in sex (prostitution) should be prohibited because markets in sex degrade the value of non-commodified sex. Though Radin and Anderson's arguments vary somewhat and they ultimately defend different policy positions on prostitution, each emphasizes that markets in sex undermine human flourishing. In particular, they each argue that markets in sex, i.e., prostitution, have consequences for non-market sexual relationships. The argument is some human goods, and relationships, cannot be realized in market-based terms. And, further, that in contexts in which markets in similar goods are prevalent, the existence of such markets can, and

---

58. Martha M. Ertman and Joan C. Williams, *Rethinking Commodification* (New York: New York University Press, 2005), 9.

often does, eliminate the possibility of the realization of the non-market good. In other words, the argument is that the prevalence of transactional sex (markets in sex) degrades the value or possibility of non-transactional sex. Once sex becomes a commodity, as it were, the social meaning of sex is transformed such that other forms of sexual connection (based on love or shared connection, for example) become more difficult to realize for those who value sex as a non-economic good.

This argument raises an important conceptual point against Brennan and Jaworski's claim that markets are (morally) neutral. This point aligns with but is not identical to Anderson's view. The view defended by Flanigan (and Brennan and Jaworski) fails to acknowledge the way that market forces can transform how we understand particular goods or interactions between persons. This point, as it stands, is just a conceptual point. As such, it is not a moral claim. Further premises will be required to show that the transformation in question raises moral concerns. But, to demonstrate the way in which introduction of some good into a market can change conceptually what that good is, consider the following example of the meaning of friendship. For two persons to reciprocally enjoy the status "friends" certain things have to be true about their connection. Each must freely and voluntarily engage with the other. A friendship cannot be forced. But, also, neither can it be conditioned on money. Payment for an ongoing association, even if it has some of the features of friendship like participating in shared activities, listening to one another's needs, and so on, just isn't friendship. It is something else. It doesn't follow from this conceptual point that paid associations are morally wrong or bad in some way. It is just that they are not friendships. The point is that even if the association mirrors the activities and behaviors we associate with friendship, the fact that the association is conditioned on the exchange of money makes it a different kind of thing. Call it paid companionship.

The conceptual point is that paid companionship and friendship are not the same thing even if they involve the same activities and behaviors because the economic exchange that forms the basis for paid companionship is a transformative feature of an association. Now if we imagine that market in paid companionship develops (actually, websites advertising and facilitating these relationships do exist) and is widely adopted, it could happen that the practice of friendship (as an unpaid and free association) disappears or that persons who practice free-companionship (i.e., friendship) are judged to be foolish in some way (why do for free what you could get paid for?). If either of those things were to occur, or be easily predicted to occur, we would have grounds for saying that the practice of paid companionship is morally bad because it leads to a social world in which friendship (as we now know and value it) is not practiced. Anderson makes a similar point about sexual relationships—namely, that widespread commodified sexual relationships can undermine the possibilities for others to experience and live out other kinds of sexual relationships, especially those who value sexual relationships as a shared good.[59] From this observation, Anderson argues that the state has a reason to restrict markets in sex, in part, to protect the rights of others to live out their conception of the good of sex. The point of

59. Anderson, *Value in Ethics and Economics*, 141.

my argument here is not to support Anderson's conclusion, but rather, to make the point that markets can be normatively transformative, contrary to Brennan, Jaworski, and Flanigan's claims.

One can also make the conceptual point in the reverse fashion by drawing on the practice of buying brides (historically this was widely practiced, and though less frequent than it once was, this practice still exists). There the removal of market norms, the move away from purchasing women for marriage, transformed the social meaning and practice of marriage. When and where women have been bought for marriage, the payment has typically gone to their fathers. Thus, the economic exchange occurred between two men (the husband and the father) or in some cases two families. The important point for our discussion is that the fact that the bride was purchased both set and followed expectations about who had the power in the marriage, what the wife's role was (subservient), and what the husband's entitlements were. As societies have moved away from the practice of economically arranged marriages and "bride-prices," marriage norms and the inegalitarian gender roles within them have changed. To be sure there is not one single causal story one could tell as to the ways in which marriage norms have shifted over time; gender roles are not solely a product of economic forces. Nonetheless, the ways in which the practice of purchasing brides shaped the inegalitarian norms and expectations within marriage can be understood, in part, as a result of the fact that women were bought and sold.

The point with these two examples is that markets have the power to shape and determine social meanings. The impacts of markets on social practices, in determining the meanings of human behaviors, means that markets are not "morally neutral." Markets are not independent of the full range of human activities; and human activities are not independent of markets. Both are deeply intertwined, and careful consideration of the ways in which markets shape and define human relationships, including, importantly, whether they facilitate or undermine equality, is essential to evaluating whether some markets are pernicious or not. Debra Satz makes this kind of argument.

Satz argues that "if prostitution is wrong it is because of its effects on how men perceive women and how women perceive themselves."[60] And she goes on to argue that, in fact, "prostitution is a theater of inequality; it displays for us a practice in which women are seen as servants of men's desires."[61] The inequality at stake is not just limited to women in prostitution but, according to Satz, women as a class are impacted by being marked with the negative image of sexual servants to men. Thus, Satz favors a legal approach to prostitution aimed at addressing these negative effects. She doesn't draw the conclusion from this argument that prostitution is wrong, or must be limited, across all time and circumstances. Were it the case that exchange of sex for money occurred without background inequalities, was fully free and voluntary, and did not have negative effects on women as a class, Satz says there is no reason to find prostitution more troubling that other kinds of labor markets.[62]

As I write elsewhere, "Despite framing her analysis of prostitution as an "egalitarian approach," Satz emphasizes

---

60. Satz, *Why Some Things Should Not Be for Sale*, p. 146.
61. Ibid., p. 147.
62. Ibid., p. 153.

that "[o]verall my argument tends to support decriminalization in contexts such as the United States and Western Europe, where prohibitions on abuse can be enforced and there is a social safety net to protect women from entering into prostitution under conditions of extreme vulnerability."[63]

Satz's suggestion that a system of deregulation can address the structure of gender inequality she argues for is peculiar. She doesn't explain how regulating prostitution through the principles she suggests avoids the problem she identifies with prostitution as creating a class of women as sexual servants to men. Nor does she explain how decriminalization can be effective for addressing the abuses and health and safety risks within prostitution. Satz's view is undertheorized and overly optimistic about the conditions in the United States and Western Europe acting as safeguards against the channeling of vulnerable persons into prostitution. The empirical evidence simply contradicts Satz's claims in this regard."[64]

Much of the dispute canvassed in this section can be understood in light of the ideal theory/non-ideal theory distinction drawn earlier in the chapter. Brennan, Jaworski, and Flanigan's defense of markets relies on ideal theory (as discussed in section 1.1) as a basis for policy prescriptions in our current, very non-ideal and unequal world. Prostitution is structured and shot-through with inequality, unequal bargaining power, unequal social and political power, unequal vulnerability to harm, and, as a matter of practice, depends

63. Ibid., p. 136.
64. Lori Watson, "The State of the Question Philosophical Debates about Prostitution," *Southern Journal of Philosophy* 57, no. 2 (June 2019): 165–193..

on such inequalities. Failure to situate any analysis of prostitution and policy proscriptions in the material, grounded facts of inequality that give rise to, structure, and follow from it amounts to a defense of the status quo—pervasive and unjust inequality. As the facts of sex inequality and the facts of prostitution, provided throughout my contribution, show, the status quo is not compatible with the substantive equality of women.

The full grounds for rejecting the arguments in favor of full, unfettered markets in sex depend on showing that selling sex is not, in fact, like selling other goods and services, or other forms of work. The next chapter makes this argument.

Why "Sex Work" Cannot Be Understood as Just Another Form of "Work"

2.1 INTRODUCTION

Chapter 1 presented the initial case for the Nordic Model and responded to various objections. Additionally, there I laid out two important desiderata for arguments concerning how to develop legal frameworks for prostitution: (1) That such arguments do not rest on controversial moral claims about the value of sex or a moralized view about the "proper" ways in which one should treat one's own body. Thus, arguments must not rest on moralism or paternalistic justifications. (2) Arguments should address the reality of how prostitution is structured and functions as a form of sex inequality. That is, a non-ideal methodology is the appropriate framework from which to develop arguments and policy positions concerning prostitution.

This chapter offers critiques of legalization and decriminalization that meet these two desiderata. The arguments given here neither invoke moralism nor rely upon paternalism. Also, they evaluate the actual empirical conditions

Debating Sex Work. Lori Watson, Jessica Flanigan, Oxford University Press (2020). © Oxford University Press.
DOI: 10.1093/oso/9780190659882.001.0001

of prostitution in legalization or decriminalization regimes. In evaluating the positive arguments for legalization and decriminalization and showing their flaws, this chapter further lays the ground work for a full defense of the Nordic Model as the best policy position on prostitution. That full defense will be offered in the following chapter.

The main conclusion of this chapter is that positions that rest on understanding prostitution as "sex work" do not succeed on their own terms. The argument is structured so as to carefully think through our shared understandings of "work" and employment relations to examine the ways in which so-called sex work cannot be understood as like any other form of work. A key argument advanced here is that basic human rights guarantees for workers cannot be met in the context of prostitution (where "the work" is selling sex). Occupational health and safety standards that are considered basic human rights simply cannot be met in prostitution. In the course of making this argument, the claim that legalization/decriminalization are effective "harm reduction" strategies will be shown to be untrue.

The second half of the chapter explores the various ways in which persons in prostitution might be thought of as "workers." In most places in which prostitution is either legalized or decriminalized, persons in prostitution are not considered employees, in any traditional sense. Rather, they are classified as independent contractors. The reason for such classification is that independent contractors are thought to be subject to less control than employees, and so the claim is that this model of "employment" is the best way to secure more autonomy for persons in prostitution. However, the empirical evidence refutes the claim that the independent contractor model is autonomy-enhancing.

Moreover, whether persons in prostitution are classified as employees or independent contractors, they are, if understood as engaged in "work like any other," subject to various laws, like civil rights laws that guarantee nondiscrimination. Requiring persons in prostitution to comply with civil rights laws (for example, holding them responsible for discrimination for refusing to have sex with someone on the grounds that they are a member of a protected group) is incompatible with respecting their sexual autonomy. Exempting persons in prostitution from such laws shows that "sex work" is not work like any other form of work.

The final section of this chapter explores the consequences of contractualizing sex. If "providing sex" to a "client" is considered "work like any other form of work," the contract model of exchange ought to govern the agreement between sellers and buyers, as it does in non-sexual exchanges. The German government recognizes that a contractual model for sex cannot be reconciled with "sexual self-determination" of persons in prostitution.[1] Thus, in Germany, "sex contracts" are defined legally as "unilateral contracts." Though, some German legal scholars object to this intervention, arguing that so-called unilateral contracts are not, in fact, contracts at all. And further, these scholars claim: to the extent that so-called unilateral contracts are legally recognized, they actually undermine the legal standing of persons in prostitution.[2] The aim of

1. "Report by the Federal Government on the Impact of the Act Regulating the Legal Situation of Prostitutes (Prostitution Act)" [Hereinafter "The German Report"], Federal Ministry for Family Affairs, Senior Citizens, Women and Youth, German Government, p. 15, available at https://www.bmfsfj.de/blob/93346/f81fb6d56073e3a0a80c442 439b6495e/bericht-der-br-zum-prostg-englisch-data.pdf.
2. The German Report, p. 15.

the argument in this section is to show that sex cannot be contractualized without violating rights of persons in prostitution and also absurd consequences follow from the idea of "contractulizing sex." Thus, the conclusion is drawn that selling sex is simply not like other forms of work or exchange relationships.

The upshot of this chapter, then, is that prostitution cannot be thought of as "sex work." The argument that "sex work is work like any other form of work"—a claim many defenders of legalization or decriminalization rest their arguments upon—is indefensible.

2.2 OCCUPATIONAL HEALTH AND SAFETY

A. Health

One of the most often repeated claims by those who defend legalization or decriminalization is that both allow for the state to develop and enforce occupational health and safety standards and these standards will effectively reduce many of the harms women in prostitution face. The primary legal "occupational health and safety" requirements defended include requirements of condom use for vaginal and anal sex (sometimes oral sex as well) and a formal right of refusal. Beyond these legal standards, there are a variety of recommendations offered in "sex worker" produced occupational health and safety manuals. Such recommendations include suggestions about how to deal with abusive "clients," additional cautions and considerations for protecting oneself against sexually transmitted infections, and "tips" for personal safety. These recommendations are not legal standards and are not officially monitored or enforced.

Two questions arise for thinking through the purported benefits of occupational health and safety standards for persons in prostitution. First, can the kinds of occupational health and safety standards deemed to be essential to human rights, in every other work context, be met in prostitution? The second question is whether the standards defended as appropriate to "sex work"—primarily condom use and a formal right of refusal—are effective "harm reduction" strategies. Since a key claim of defenders of legalization and decriminalization is that one or the other is more effective at reducing harms than other options like criminalization or the Nordic Model, whether such harms are reduced is an important matter for evaluating those approaches on their own terms. However, it is worth emphasizing that tolerating harms as an inevitable feature of the lives of women in prostitution is itself a troubling point of view.

As to the first question raised—namely, whether occupational health and safety standards constitutive of basic human rights can be met in prostitution—it is important to underscore that the same kinds of protections deemed necessary to protect workers in other contexts are not compatible with the sex acts constitutive of prostitution.[3] Every other form of work in which workers may be exposed to bodily fluids and potential blood-borne pathogens is

3. See Lori Watson, "Why Sex Work Isn't Work," *Logos: A Journal of Modern Society and Culture* 14, no. 1 (2015), available online at http://logosjournal.com/2014/watson/

strictly regulated regarding the use of personal protective equipment. Some acts are strictly forbidden, even with personal protective equipment, as they are deemed incompatible with human rights of workers. So, for example, US OSHA regulations prohibit "mouth pipetting/suctioning of blood or other potentially infectious materials."[4] The purpose of this prohibition is prevention of acts that entail a high risk for exposure to and transmission of infectious diseases. This is regarded as necessary to protect worker human rights and equality in work contexts that do not involve sex.

This safeguard, deemed critical in non-sex work contexts, is incompatible with prostitution. This regulation could not be made compatible with blow-jobs and other forms of oral sex. The regulation doesn't say the activity is permitted with a barrier; it says it is prohibited. One reason for the prohibition is that the mouth is more susceptible to transmission of potentially infectious substances than are other more protected body parts (though, skin-to-skin contact is also risky for sexually transmitted infections [STIs]). Condoms may provide some barrier to exposure to sperm (a potentially infectious substance), however, exposure to many other forms of sexually transmitted infections is possible during oral sex. Herpes, genital warts, syphilis can all be transmitted in oral sex, even when a condom is used, as the sores which transmit the diseases are located all around the genital area.

4. See Occupational Safety and Health Standards, Code of Federal Regulations, Standards, Part 1910, Toxic and Hazardous Substances, Blood Borne Pathogens [Hereinafter "OSHA regulations"], available online at https://www.osha.gov/pls/oshaweb/owadisp.show_document?p_table=STANDARDS&p_id=10051

Similarly, US OSHA standards mandate gloves, facemasks, eye protection, and other protective bodily clothing (such as gowns and aprons) for workers that may encounter exposure to infectious diseases.[5] Requiring adherence to such standards in the context of "sex work" would rule out the very acts constitutive of prostitution. Thus, the kinds of worker health and safety standards that are justified on the basis of human rights protections in non-sex work cannot be applied in contexts where sex is the job.

Critics will, no doubt, claim that the specific regulations cited here were drafted for particular kinds of work, medical and laboratory work, for example. Similarly, they will suggest that specific occupational health and safety standards for "sex work" can be developed; and, in fact, various such occupational health and safety manuals specific to prostitution already exist. The plausibility of such "sex work" specific regulations will be considered in what follows with special attention to whether they can indeed function to secure worker health and safety as demanded by various human rights documents and nation-state specific standards for employee safety. However, for the moment the important point is that standards that are regarded as essential to the protection of the human rights of workers in non-sex work contexts would not allow the acts constitutive of prostitution. Thus, if sex work is to be considered "work," it cannot be considered "just like any other form of work." Some argument for developing exemptions for the standards of worker health and safety applicable to every other form of work in which exposure to infectious diseases

5. OSHA regulations.

must be given by advocates of treating "sex work" as work. I will return to this point, but for now it is important to gain an understanding of the basis for occupational health and safety standards.

The basis for occupational health and safety regulations is the claim that the right to a safe and healthy work environment is a human right. For example, the United Nations Universal Declaration of Human Rights states: "Everyone has a **right . . . to just and favourable conditions of work**."[6] The United Nations ILO (International Labor Organization) Convention on Occupational Health and Safety (1981) states:

1. Employers shall be required to ensure that, so far as is reasonably practicable, the workplaces, machinery, equipment and processes under their control are safe and **without risk to health**.
2. Employers shall be required to ensure that, so far as is reasonably practicable, the chemical, physical

---

6. "Universal Declaration of Human Rights," United Nations, Article 23(1) (my emphasis in text). The full text of Article 23 states:

(1) Everyone has the right to work, to free choice of employment, to just and favourable conditions of work and to protection against unemployment.

(2) Everyone, without any discrimination, has the right to equal pay for equal work.

(3) Everyone who works has the right to just and favourable remuneration ensuring for himself and his family an existence worthy of human dignity, and supplemented, if necessary, by other means of social protection.

(4) Everyone has the right to form and to join trade unions for the protection of his interests.

Available online at http://www.un.org/en/universal-declaration-human-rights/

and biological substances and agents under their control are **without risk to health when the appropriate measures of protection are taken**.

3. Employers shall be required to provide, where necessary, adequate protective clothing and protective equipment to prevent, so far as is reasonably practicable, risk of accidents or of adverse effects on health. [7]

Nation state specific interpretations of these human rights vary. For example, in New Zealand, where prostitution is decriminalized, Occupational Health and Safety Standards require that "all workers, no matter what industry they work in, have the **right not to suffer harm** through carrying out normal requirements of their work."[8] And in the United States, the Occupational Health and Safety Act of 1970 says, "The law requires employers to provide their employees with working conditions that **are free of known dangers**."[9]

Substantial risks to health and safety through exposure to STIs and other infectious diseases cannot be eliminated to the degree required by present OSHA standards in the

---

7. Article 6 (my emphasis in text). Available online at http://www.ilo.org/dyn/normlex/en/f?p=NORMLEXPUB:12100:0::NO::P12100_ILO_CODE:C155

8. "A Guide to Occupational Health and Safety in the New Zealand Sex Industry," [Hereinafter "NZ OSH Guide"] Published by the Occupational Safety and Health Service, Department of Labour, New Zealand, June 2004, p. 17, available at http://www.worksafe.govt.nz/worksafe/information-guidance/all-guidance-items/sex-industry-a-guide-to-occupational-health-and-safety-in-the-new-zealand/sexindustry.pdf

9. United States, the Occupational Health and Safety Act of 1970, available at https://www.osha.gov/law-regs.html (my emphasis in text).

United States as required for all other forms of work. Nor can the international human rights instruments' specification of worker safety enumerated previously be met in the context in which sex is the work. The present standards for "personal protective equipment" in the sex industry, where it is legal, include mandatory condom use for penetrative sex, and in some cases for oral sex, including dental dams for vaginal oral sex (though compliance with the latter is reported as next to nil), and recommendations for gloves for some sexual acts (though gloves are not legally required anywhere). However, neither condom use nor the use of other protective "equipment" is sufficient to protect against all STIs, as is commonly known. The sex acts that constitute "sex work" necessarily involve exposure risk that is more than minimal. Men who buy sex are not required to undergo or provide any evidence of their STI status. Whether men have any transmittable infectious diseases is unknown to the women. The numbers of men serviced each week or day varies, but the volume of men required to earn sufficient income for survival (or to meet brothel minimums) means repeated exposure to potentially infected persons.

It is crucial to underscore here that the concept of "safe sex" or "safer sex" as it applies to personal (i.e., non-commercial) sex cannot be simply appropriated for as an ideal of "safe sex" in a commercial setting.[10] The United

10. Moreover, it is worth nothing that the World Health Organization offers a fairly robust definition of "sexual health" that is not merely reducible to common notions of "safe sex." The WHO defines sexual health as "a state of physical, emotional, mental and social well-being in relation to sexuality; it is not merely the absence of disease, dysfunction or infirmity. Sexual health requires a positive and respectful approach to sexuality and sexual relationships, as well as the possibility of having pleasurable and safe sexual experiences, free of coercion, discrimination

States Center for Disease Control (CDC) recommends, among other things, that reducing the number of sex partners one has and mutual monogamy are two ways in which individuals can reduce their risk of exposure to sexually transmitted infections.[11] Yet neither of these is possible in commercial sex settings. Analyses of women in brothel prostitution, for example, estimate that it is common for them to "have sex" ten to fifteen times a day or more, five days a week or more, with different people each time. That adds up to over a 1000 sex acts a year.

For the "sex work" model to be plausible at all, a conception of "safe sex" that takes into account the commercial nature of the exchange is needed. Simply extrapolating from tenets of "safe" or "safer" sex in the context of individuals lives is inadequate. However, this is precisely what many sex work OHS manuals do. Consider the following excerpt from New Zealand's occupational health and safety guide developed specifically for prostitution: "Each person must accept responsibility for preventing themselves and others from becoming infected with sexually transmissible infections . . . Syphilis and blood-borne viruses such as HIV and Hepatitis B and C can be transmitted by means other than penetrative sex and other sexual activity."[12] It

and violence. For sexual health to be attained and maintained, the sexual rights of all persons must be respected, protected and fulfilled" (WHO, 2006a), "Defining Sexual Health," World Health Organization, available at http://www.who.int/reproductivehealth/topics/sexual_health/sh_definitions/en/

11. "Safer Sexual Behaviors," Center for Disease Control, available at https://www.cdc.gov/actagainstaids/campaigns/pic/talks/safer-sex.html

12. "NZ OSH Guide," p. 39.

is important to underscore the risk for STIs is significant, for example, the risk of HIV infection is "13.5 times higher for women selling sex than the general population."[13] In Nevada, where prostitution is legal in some counties, "Las Vegas Metro police report a 5% rate of HIV among women arrested for prostitution."[14] Although this report is from Las Vegas, where prostitution is technically illegal, many of the women in Vegas also work in the rural brothels. There is movement between legal and illegal prostitution in Nevada, as well as other places.[15]

The responsibility for one's health and safety falls upon the worker, in the context of "sex work"; this includes negotiating for appropriate condom use with individual "clients," visually surveying their bodies for signs of infections (as recommended by New Zealand's OHS Guide) despite the fact that many infectious diseases remain invisible to the naked eye, not to mention the need to assess them for potential indicators of violence (more of which Section B). Moreover, some legal brothels in Germany explicitly advertise for condom-less sex for an increased price. Women at the bottom of the hierarchy within prostitution are more vulnerable and less likely to be in a position to insist on condom use.

13. European Parliament Briefing Paper: "Sexual Exploitation and Prostitution and Its Impact on Gender Equality" [Hereinafter "EU Parliament Report"] (January 2014), available online at http://www.europarl.europa.eu/RegData/etudes/etudes/join/2014/493040/IPOL-FEMM_ET(2014)493040_EN.pdf

14. Melissa Farley, Prostitution & Trafficking in Nevada: Making the Connections (San Francisco, CA: Prostitution Research and Education, 2007), 43.

15. Ibid.

While much of the focus of "sex worker" health and safety is placed on STI prevention, there are other significant health and safety risks beyond STIs. Obviously, pregnancy is another known risk of having sex, for some women, even with a condom.[16] They are not foolproof. "Sex work" is unique in this regard; it is the only "occupation" in which pregnancy, for women capable of becoming pregnant, is a known hazard of fulfilling the requirements of the "job." (Surrogacy is a "job" in which pregnancy isn't a hazard but a condition of the "work.") Other injuries commonly occur in "sex work," such as repetitive stress injuries especially to the genitals and anus, bladder infections, chronic cystitis, and kidney infections.[17] In addition, female "sex workers" are at increased risk of cervical dysplasia and cervical cancer.[18] These injuries and increased risk of cancer are a result of sexually servicing dozens or more men a day or weekly.

All of these facts document exposure to known risks and dangers to health and safety; they are intrinsic to the job and are not minimal. The basic human rights protections concerning occupational health and safety cannot be met in the context of "sex work."

---

16. The NZ OHS Guide for sex workers states: "Unintended pregnancy may be a consequence of working in the sex industry" (p. 40).

17. NZ OHS Guide discusses repetitive stress injuries and advises sex workers to change positions or activities in order to avoid them (p. 41).

18. Ansuska Van Der Veen and Nick Goiran, "The Inherent Failure of Current Occupational Health And Safety Legislation in Prostitution," *Curtin Law and Taxation Review*, available at http://nickgoiran.com.au/wp-content/uploads/2014/12/The-Inherent-Failure-of-Current-OHS-Legislation-in-Prostitution.pdf

B. Safety

Violence is endemic to prostitution, a known "occupational health and safety risk" of engaging in "sex work." Defenders of legalization and decriminalization claim that both are effective "harm reduction" strategies. In part, they are claiming that legalization/decriminalization will effectively reduce violence for persons in prostitution.

Violence against persons in prostitution is a fact whether prostitution is criminalized, decriminalized, or legalized. Both the German and New Zealand governmental reports, written by advocates of decriminalization/legalization, state that neither has and cannot reduce violence. The German Report emphasizes the prevalence of violence women in prostitution continue to experience even though it is legal there: "[O]ne cannot ignore the empirical findings that show that those working in this industry are subject to considerable, empirically verifiable, psychological and physical threats."[19] The report continues: "Prostitution is generally a physically and psychologically demanding, risky and dangerous business in which particularly vulnerable groups frequently engage. This was confirmed by a survey of subpopulations of prostitutes during a study into the situation, safety and health of women in Germany that was commissioned by the Federal Ministry of Family Affairs, Senior Citizens, Women, and Youth. This group suffered considerably more childhood violence, sexual violence, violence in relationships and **violence in the workplace**."[20] And

19. The German Report, p. 11.
20. Ibid. My emphasis.

further they note, "All forms of prostitution carry a risk of attack by the client."[21] An additional study conducted by the German government in 2007 (after legalization) found: "92% of women working as prostitutes . . . had suffered sexual harassment, 87% physical violence and 59% sexual violence, 41% of prostitutes had experienced violence in the context of performing sexual services."[22] The same study states that "half of the interviewees showed symptoms of depression, and a quarter had contemplated suicide."[23] A New Zealand Government report evaluating the Prostitution Reform Act five years after its passage surveyed women in prostitution about the effects of the Act, and reports "A majority of sex workers interviewed felt that the PRA could do little about violence that occurred."[24] A paper reviewing the official assessments of the impacts of legalization in the Netherlands states: "The KLPD [the national police force] report stressed that legalization had not ended abuse in the prostitution section. Monitoring and regulation were no guarantee that women do not work under threat of coercion . . . 'It is an illusion that a clean normal sector has emerged.'"[25] This quote emphasizes

21. Ibid.

22. EU Parliament Report, p. 44.

23. Ibid.

24. New Zealand Report, "Prostitution: A Review of Legislation in Selected Countries, Background" (Paper by Occupational Safety and Health Service, Department of Labour, New Zealand), p. 14, available at https://lop.parl.ca/Content/LOP/ResearchPublications/2011-115-e .pdf.

25. Outshoorn, Joyce, "Policy Change in Prostitution in the Netherlands: From Legalization to Strict Control," *Sexuality Research and Social Policy* 9 (2012): 233–43, 240.

abuse and coercion from brothel owners, but that too is a part of the systemic violence women in prostitution face.

A European Parliament report that provides a comprehensive analysis of different approaches to prostitution within the EU states: "While some argue that legalization or prostitution aims at improving the working conditions of women selling sex and should enable them to bring violent clients to court, the experiences in the two Member States which have fully liberalized the prostitution business prove that the situation has not changed."[26] The situation refers to both violence within prostitution and the likelihood of pursuing criminal complaints against violent clients.

Further evidence from Australia, where prostitution is legalized in some states and decriminalized in others (New South Wales): "In New South Wales 85% of prostituted women experienced extreme violence while working including physical assault at 65%, rape with a weapon at 40%, rape without a weapon at 33%, with over half reporting severe depression, and three quarters confirming that they had considered suicide."[27] Mary Sullivan citing a report submitted by the Prostitute's Collective of Victoria, states that the Collective was receiving "an average of 20 reports of violence against sex workers each week."[28] The report also

26. EU Parliament Report, p. 15.

27. Farley, "Pornography, Prostitution, & Trafficking: Making the Connections," Prostitution Research & Education, San Francisco (August 2015), available at http://prostitutionresearch.com/wp-content/uploads/2015/07/Pornography-prostitution-trafficking.pdf

28. Mary Lucille Sullivan, *Making Sex Work: A Failed Experiment with Legalized Prostitution* (North Melbourne, Vic., Australia, 2007), 312.

stated that they believed that number was an "under representation" of the actual levels of violence.[29]

"Sex worker" produced OHS manuals emphasize violence
and rape *as occupational hazards*. "Sex worker" OHS manuals
in Australia, for example, recommend acquiring "de-escalation
negotiation skills" and "maintaining the first strike advantage," phrases that Mary Lucille Sullivan likens to training in
hostage negotiate methods as a means of providing some "protection" against the violence women are likely to experience in
prostitution.[30] In order to address the "occupational hazard"
of violence, legal brothels engage in various forms of surveillance such as closed-circuit TV, listening devices, peepholes,
and many include panic buttons, all in the name of "reducing"
potential violence or stopping it once it has started. Yet as just
documented, such violence persists at significant rates.

Rape and violence are inherent risks in prostitution.
Consider that the New Zealand OHS manual blithely
states: "Unfortunately, incidents occur where workers are
forced by clients to have sex without a condom against their
will (i.e. rape)."[31] A German governmental report similarly
concludes: "As regards improving prostitutes' working
conditions, hardly any measurable impact has been
observed in practice. There are as yet no viable indications
that the Prostitution Act has reduced crime." [32] The fact
that violence, including sexual violence, is endemic to "sex
work" means that "sex workers" will be exposed to *known*

29. Ibid., p. 312.
30. Ibid., p. 294.
31. NZ OHS, p. 37.
32. The German Report, p. 79.

dangers and fail to have their right not to suffer harm guaranteed as required by human rights instruments.

The experience of violence against women in prostitution has physical and mental consequences. Melissa Farley reports: "Symptoms of emotional distress among those in sex businesses are off the charts: depression, suicidality, posttraumatic stress disorder, dissociation, substance abuse. Two-thirds of women, men and transgendered people in prostitution in 9 countries met diagnostic criteria for posttraumatic stress disorder. This level of emotional distress is the same as the most emotionally traumatized people studied by psychologists—battered women, raped women, combat vets, and torture survivors."[33] Neither decriminalization nor legalization have effectively reduced these harms. In fact, in the Netherlands such harms have increased since the lift of the brothel ban. In a 2007 governmental report in the Netherlands that aimed to assess the success of legalization five years after the lift of the brothel ban, investigators found that "prostitutes' emotional well-being is now lower than in 2001 on all measured aspects, and the use of sedatives has increased."[34] The German Report assessing the impact of legalization notes: "However, all in all, the results of the empirical study show that only little has been done up until now to improve working conditions."[35] They note that unless such improvements foster the financial interests of brothel owners, there is no incentive for them to change. The report

33. Farley, "Pornography, Prostitution, & Trafficking: Making the Connections."

34. "Prostitution in the Netherlands Since the Lifting of the Brothel Ban," available at https://english.wodc.nl/onderzoeksdatabase/1204e-engelse-vertaling-rapport-evaluatie-opheffing-bordeelverbod.aspx

35. The German Report, p. 63.

also notes that "violence represents a stress factor for women working in prostitution,"[36] and this observation, put mildly, is in the context of legal prostitution.

The evidence does not support the claim about the reduction of violence under legalization or decriminalization. The nature of the "work" places women in prostitution in a structural position of vulnerability in which rape and violence cannot be prevented. Prostitution puts people, women, in a position to forfeit control over their bodies in ways that increase the risk of rape, violence, and other forms of abuse that make them extremely vulnerable to trauma responses. This is not an argument that rests on a particular vision of what sex ought to be or what good, or moral, sex is. Rather, it says, whatever you think about those questions, recognize that bodily integrity is a necessary condition for basic psychological well-being. And that as a matter of empirical fact, prostitution, whether legal, illegal, or decriminalized, enables violence against women.

Legalization and decriminalization confer legitimacy, the authority of law, upon an institution, which systematically exposes women ("the workers") to the risk of violence that we do not, and would not, tolerate in any other work context. The fact that rape and violence are illegal is immaterial to the fact that nonetheless the level of risk is structural. Under legalization/decriminalization regimes, the structural conditions that place "sex workers" at high risk for sexual assault and violence are tolerated and normalized. This raises the question of the value of sex workers as equal citizens. Permissive prostitution policies tolerate the inequality, the sex inequality, of some workers as a condition of "work."

36. Ibid., p. 12.

C. Sex Work Is Not Like Other Forms of Work

The evidence offered so far shows that it is simply not possible to both meet the legal regulatory standards for worker safety that apply to all other industries while permitting the acts that constitute "sex work." The "personal protective equipment" available, including condoms and gloves, is insufficient to protect against known dangers. Even more, such "equipment" fails to address the physical stresses on the body through repetitive sex acts in a commercial setting. And even further, violence, including sexual violence, is a known danger—not an incidental or infrequent aberration.

Some, as Flanigan does, may object that there are clearly other professions in which it is not possible for employers to provide a working environment "free of known dangers." Two examples that make this point are police officers and some medical personnel. There are other "risky" occupations. I focus here on police officers and medical personnel because the dangers they face are most similar to those in prostitution (violence and exposure to infectious diseases), following which I will consider other risky occupations. Police officers are subjected to known risks as a matter of daily routine. For example, in responding to criminal violence, police officers are exposed to the risk of being shot, or stabbed, or assaulted in any number of ways. Medical personnel that come into contact with persons with infectious diseases are required to treat those persons and as such are at risk for exposure to such diseases.

Are there relevant differences between these occupations and prostitution such that the exposure to risk is acceptable in the former and not the latter? One important difference is that police officers and medical personnel provide a public good. Public goods are products of social cooperation that are intended to benefit all persons equally. Moreover, each is a necessary public good. Guaranteeing public safety is a primary reason for the state in the first place. Providing medical care, in some form, is also an essential good and necessary for meeting the basic interests of citizens. In practice, of course, police presence does not live up to this expectation. And, given the mixed system of public and private medical services in the United States, medical services and access are distributed unequally, often to the detriment of the least well off.

Both of these observations are cause for reform, but they don't undermine the general point that police protection and medical services are public goods (or ought to be understood as such). In contrast, the services provided by persons in prostitution are private goods; access to such "goods" is neither a part of the basic justification for the state nor are such goods a part of citizens' basic interests. The fact that police and medical personnel provide public goods serves as a rationale for tolerating the increased risk for exposure to some forms of harm persons in those professions face. However, the fact of increased risk for persons in such professions means that the choice to enter them needs to be fully voluntary and free conditions of exit guaranteed. Additionally, appropriate training and provision for personal protective equipment is essential.

A second relevant difference is that both police officers and medical personnel have extensive training in the use of personal protective equipment to minimize exposure to risk and, most significantly, they have exclusive control over their personal protective equipment. In the case of medical personnel, the individual employee has control over their use of gloves: they put them on their own body, they can double glove, etc., if appropriate. They have control over facemasks: they put them over their own face, and similarly, with other personal protective equipment such as gowns or in cases of severe infectious diseases hazmat suits, and so on. Police have weapons that they are authorized by the state to use in self-defense. They also have bulletproof vests, Kevlar helmets, and other forms of protection. And they work in teams; they have backup support for confronting violent criminals.

In contrast, the primary piece of personal protective equipment in prostitution is the condom. Although I have already noted that condoms are insufficient protection against STIs and other infectious diseases, consider that the client/john is the one to wear this piece of personal protective equipment. To the extent that condoms provide some layer of protection, their efficacy depends on cooperation from the buyer. The ability of women in prostitution to use personal protective equipment depends upon being able to negotiate effective compliance with the buyer. And, we know that buyers frequently insist on not using a condom use or attempt to negotiate a higher payment for not using them or often remove them without the consent of the woman they are using.[37] "Sex worker" produced

37. Melissa Farley documents the both the refusal to use condoms by some johns and the pressure to forgo condom use for larger pay across a range of contexts (Canada, India, Nevada) in *Prostitution & Trafficking in Nevada: Making the Connections* (Prostitution Research & Education,

OHS manuals and state produced OHS manuals for "sex workers" emphasizes that condoms may break or slip or that customers may remove them; all such manuals offer advice about how to "minimize" these events but treat them as inevitable. As stated earlier, New Zealand's "Guide to Occupational Health and Safety in the New Zealand Sex Industry" notes: "Unfortunately, incidents occur where workers are forced by clients to have sex without a condom against their will (i.e. rape). Sex without a condom can result where the client removes or breaks the condom during the service without the worker's knowledge."[38]

A third and significant relevant difference between occupations such as doctors, nurses, or police officers and prostitution is that people are not lead into these occupations as a result of systematic inequality on the basis of their group membership. Some groups are certainly overrepresented in these professions (privileged men, for example), but their overrepresentation is a result of a history of *exclusion, devaluation,* and *discrimination* against minorities and women. Privileged white men, for example, are not forced into the medical profession for lack of other options, from a position of severe economic deprivation, or because of a social expectation that that is what such men are good for. In contrast, women in prostitution are there

2007), see esp. pp. 43–45. "Eighty-nine percent of Canadian customers of prostitutes refused condoms in one study." "In another study, 47% of women in US prostitution stated men expected sex without a condom; 73% reported men offered to pay more for sex without a condom; and 45% of women said that men became abusive if they insisted that buyers use condoms" (p. 43). This is true even in the legal brothels of Nevada, and enforcement of condom use is up to the individual women.

38. NZ OHS Guide, p. 37.

as a result of lack of options, economic deprivation, and cultural beliefs about women's status and sexuality which includes the belief that femininity involves servicing men's sexual wants.

There are, of course, other risky occupations. Athletes such as boxers, football players, or mixed-martial arts (MMA) fighters are in occupations in which persons are at a high risk of serious injury such as traumatic brain injury (TBI) or chronic traumatic encephalopathy (CTE). Are there relevant differences between these kinds of occupations and prostitution? It is worth noting that the evidence regarding football and CTE has started a national conversation about the "morality" of watching and supporting professional football. The evidence suggests that these occupations carry very significant risk for permanent brain injury. This provides a reason to look carefully at those occupations and their specific risks and the opportunities for eliminating those risks. And if such risks cannot be eliminated or reduced to an acceptable level, that is an argument against permitting such forms of work, not an argument in favor of permissive prostitution policy. Nonetheless, there are important dissimilarities between risky professions, such as professional football, and prostitution. Importantly, both the pathways to entry and the relative range of realistic exit options are strong relevant dissimilarities. And an even more significant dissimilarity is that the violence (tackling and hits on the football field or being punched in boxing/MMA fighting) is constitutive of the activities. Violent attacks against persons in prostitution are not, so to speak, what they signed up for, and yet the prevalence of such violence is significant.

Even if one agrees that football and boxing can be effectively distinguished from prostitution in terms of risk of injury or violence, there are other occupations with increased risk for injury or death. Fishing and logging are each identified as among the most risky occupations.[39] Yet comparably the risks in each are significantly less than in prostitution. In 2016, there were 135 deaths per 100,000 persons in logging, and 84 per 100,000 in fishing. The Bureau of Labor Statistics data here is only assessing fatal injuries on the job. Nonetheless, the risk of fatal injuries in prostitution is much greater. A long-term cohort study in Colorado, determined the mortality rate of women in prostitution to be 391 per 100,000.[40] This mortality rate covers various causes of death, not just murder. Death by murder of clients is still a grave concern in legal markets, like Germany. Anna Zobnina writes: "In the period between 6 October and 11 November 2016, four women in prostitution in Germany were murdered (Sex Industry Kills, 2016). They were murdered in private sex clubs, brothel-apartments and what the Germans euphemistically call 'love mobiles,' i.e. caravans in a remote unprotected location of a city, 'managed' by pimps and visited by sex buyers. At least three of the victims were identified as migrant women (from the Dominican Republic

39. Logging and fishing are listed as the top two most dangerous jobs in a recent *Time* article, as measured by the number of deaths per 100,000 persons. See http://time.com/5074471/most-dangerous-jobs/. The Bureau of Labor Statistics Data is here: https://www.bls.gov/news.release/pdf/cfoi.pdf

40. John J. Potterat, Devon D. Brewer, Stephen Q. Muth, Richard B. Rothenberg, Donald E. Woodhouse, John B. Muth, Heather K. Stites, Stuart Brody, "Mortality in a Long-Term Open Cohort of Prostitute Women," *American Journal of Epidemiology* 159, no. 8 (April 15, 2004): 778–85, https://doi.org/10.1093/aje/kwh110

and Hungary), and all four are suspected to have been killed by their male 'clients.'"[41] A meta-study of 340 articles examining correlates of violence against "sex workers" found that the prevalence of violence described as "ever or lifetime of any combined workplace violence, physical workplace violence, and sexual workplace violence ranged from 45% to 75%."[42] It is starkly clear that the risk of injury and violence is significant for persons in prostitution, and that risk is significantly higher than any other occupation.

One could still object to the argument thus far presented in one of two ways: (1) One could argue that regulations for health and safety are too onerous on individual freedom and should not apply to any form of work (we can imagine a libertarian making this argument). (2) One could argue that while such regulations are appropriate in certain contexts (machinery should be safe, buildings should be free of toxic fumes, and the like), such regulations are not appropriate in the context of "sex work" (of course, one need to give an argument as to why and not merely make an unsupported assertion).

To make this latter argument, one would need to argue that there is something special and unique about "sex work" that makes it different from other occupations, and so requires a different set of standards for occupational health and safety. In effect, one would need to argue that either (a) standards for "sex worker" occupational health

41. Anna Zobnina, "Women, Migration, and Prostitution in Europe: Not a Sex Work Story," *Dignity: A Journal on Sexual Exploitation and Violence* 2, no. 1 (2017): Article 1. DOI: 10.23860/dignity.2017.02.01.01

42. Kathleen N. Deering et al., "A Systematic Review of the Correlates of Violence Against Sex Workers," *American Journal of Public Health* 104, no. 5 (May 1, 2014): e42–e54. DOI: 10.2105/AJPH.2014.301909

and safety should allow a greater degree of risk borne by the individual than we think permissible in other work contexts or (b) "sex work" is unique in some way that makes exemptions from generally applicable laws appropriate.

Legal scholar Adrienne Davis, a proponent of legalization, also agrees that those who attempt to assimilate "sex work" to other forms of work are deeply mistaken.[43] Davis agrees with many of my arguments here that "sex work" cannot be treated like any other form of work. However, she moves from that claim to arguing for legal regulations designed specifically for "sex work." Such a system of legal regulations would require a series of exemptions from generally applicable laws (laws that apply in all other work contexts). There are good reasons for thinking that even with such exemptions, persons in prostitution will face much higher risks and fail to be protected on a basis of equality with other workers, as I have argued earlier. Thus, to get this argument off the ground, one would have to argue that persons in prostitution do not warrant the same levels of protections that we regard as essential to human rights, including equal rights.

It is hard to see what argument one could provide in favor of claiming that sex workers should not have the same level of occupational health and safety protections considered fundamental to human rights. The kinds of arguments that indirectly serve to support a claim like this are generally framed as harm reduction arguments. Such arguments assume that prostitution is inevitable, and thus claim

---

43. Adrienne D. Davis, "Regulating Sex Work: Erotic Assimilationism, Erotic Exceptionalism, and the Challenge of Intimate Labor," *California Law Review* 105, no. 5 (2015): 1195–1275.

the best we can do is to make it less bad or less harmful. Defenders of the Nordic Model reject the belief that prostitution is inevitable and aim to provide a substantive policy proposal to abolish it because they believe sex equality is a realizable ideal.

2.3 WORKER AUTONOMY

A further prominent argument for legalization or decriminalization of prostitution claims that one or the other will reduce or minimize exploitation of "sex workers" and also increase their sexual autonomy by giving them greater control over their working conditions, including choice of client. Again, this is a comparative claim that says legalization or decriminalization offers *more* (sexual) autonomy for persons in prostitution than places in which commercial markets in sex are partially or wholly prohibited. This claim must be assessed in light of the empirical evidence that we have from in places where selling and buying sex is legal or decriminalized.

As a matter of practice, in places where prostitution is either legalized or decriminalized, significant restrictions are in place concerning who can operate or own a brothel. These restrictions often charge significant licensing fees that, in effect, exclude single operators or those without such resources. Moreover, zoning restrictions, also common, severely curtail the places in which "sex work" is permitted. These laws further eliminate single proprietors or small businesses in a variety of places. Thus, in effect, legalization or decriminalization are structured to funnel the "benefits" to a very small and narrow set of persons involved in prostitution—primarily, brothel owners (pimps).

These facts are raised as caution against the claim that legalization is an effective way of increasing the autonomy of women, and men, now in prostitution, as big money and political clout are often required for entry into "the legal business" of selling sex. Of course, one can say such regulations are silly and overly intrusive and appropriate reform measures should eliminate them. However, my argument here aims, in part, to assess the comparative claim that defenders of legalization/decriminalization make—namely, that legalization/decriminalization (as it now stands) increases the autonomy of sex workers compared to places in which markets in sex remain partially or wholly illegal. The fact is that under current circumstances, everywhere that prostitution is legalized/decriminalized, part of the political compromises necessary involved passage of various regulations about who can get a brothel license, zoning restrictions, and who can legally work in prostitution.

Another feature of legalization/decriminalization which is touted by advocates as a method for increasing the autonomy of women in prostitution is that legalization/decriminalization gives persons in prostitution legal rights as workers. To examine this claim, consider that there are two ways in which the "employment" status of persons in prostitution is recognized. They can be classified as independent contractors; this is the most frequent model and is the status of sex workers in Nevada in the United States, the Netherlands, and New Zealand.[44] The other possible

44. EU Parliament Report, discussing the Netherlands since the lift of the brothel ban, states: "The overwhelming majority of prostitutes

employment model is to classify sex workers as employees of the particular brothel or agency for whom they work.

Where classification as "an employee" is available, women in prostitution refuse that status, even though it provides opportunities for healthcare and social security benefits. The German law allows for employee contracts, but "the overwhelming majority of prostitutes had not signed a contract of employment and thus continued working on a freelance basis."[45] Less than 1% of women in prostitution had employment contracts in Germany.[46] Neither the women in prostitution nor the brothel owners want employment contracts. Brothel owners reject them because they see such contracts as an economic risk, which would reduce their profits. Women in prostitution don't want to be more controlled (the report cites women in prostitution as objecting to employment contracts for fear of losing "sexual autonomy" and the "ability to determine when and where they work").[47] Brothel owners in the Netherlands argue against conceiving of the sex worker–brothel relationship as an employee–employer relationship precisely on the grounds that doing so would eliminate the right to refuse sex on the part of the sex worker.[48]

Yet even where women in prostitution are considered independent contractors, the level of control exerted

worked without a contract (95%) and considered themselves self-employed, despite the fact that there was a high level of control of their work by brothel owners," and "Given the lack of contracts, the majority of prostitutes were not entitled to any social service benefits" (p. 34).

45. EU Parliament Report, p. 41.
46. The German Report, p. 19.
47. Ibid.
48. "Prostitution in the Netherlands Since the Lifting of the Brothel Ban."

by brothel owners is extensive. In 2007 the Netherlands commissioned a governmental report to assess the impacts of lifting the brothel ban five years after the passage of the law. In that report, the vulnerabilities of women working as independent contractors is highlighted: "Towards the Tax Administration, prostitutes and owners stubbornly maintain that prostitutes are self-employed, but at the same time the involvement of the owners in the prostitutes' activities takes on such forms, that these are in fact, employer-employee relations. The legal position of the prostitutes is not good."[49]

Also, where women in prostitution are considered independent contractors, their ability to refuse clients is sometimes nonexistence and otherwise tenuous. The New Zealand report assessing the "working conditions" of women in prostitution, after legalization, highlights the control that some brothel owners exert over women in prostitution denying them any right to refuse particular clients. As documented in the report, a brothel owner stated: "If they do refuse we need an explanation. We won't allow nationality to be the reason—they don't have a right to discriminate. If the client is intoxicated or abusive, they don't have to if they don't want."[50] Another says: "One 18-year-old worker had just finished a job. A big Samoan guy was waiting who she had not even had the chance to check out. He was really rough with her, held her down by the throat. She went out to complain to the manager who told her to 'go back in.'"[51] The authors of report summarize that

49. Ibid.
50. The New Zealand Report, "Prostitution" p. 45.
51. Ibid., p. 45.

there is "good" and "bad" management concerning whether they would permit women to refuse a client. But the report notes that even the "good" ones required a "good" reason, meaning a reason "the management" will accept, on the part of the women to refuse.[52] Overall, the New Zealand report concludes that coercion and exploitation by brothel owners has not been eliminated by the Prostitution Reform Act, though they claim "some improvement."[53]

Moreover, the right to refuse any particular client is difficult to exercise under brothel conditions. One sex-worker in Nevada writes of her experience:

> Even though the brothels consider prostitutes to be independent contractors (convenient and less costly to them than employee status), the prostitutes do not have the control or freedom that independent contractors or sole proprietors have. If they decide to refuse a customer, management must be provided with what it deems an acceptable reason. Some "customers" should certainly be avoided at all costs. They might be rude, rough, or drunk, want too much for their money, have an attitude problem, or just simply be jerks. I don't think anyone should have to provide sexual services to men like that. Yet, many of the brothels put the burden of proof on the prostitute. She must justify her right to refuse business, even though she loses money herself by doing so. The prostitute is the best judge of who is eligible for her services, and she should be able to decide that without feeling pressured by a third party.[54]

52. Ibid., p. 45.
53. Ibid., p. 17.
54. http://www.bayswan.org/Laura.html

In spite of a formal legal right to refuse brothel owners' instructions or demands, or to refuse particular clients or their demands, in practice this right is often ignored. For example, a New Zealand Government Report, reviewing the Prostitution Reform Act 5 years after its passage writes: "Over 60% of sex workers in each sector felt that they were more able to refuse to provide commercial sexual services to a particular client since the enactment of the PRA."[55] Several things are worth noting here: First, the members of the committee are advocates of the Prostitution Reform Act. Second, this sentence is written as a positive statement, consider the alternative way it might be expressed "40% of sex workers did not feel more able to refuse." Third, it says "more" able to refuse, not able to refuse, so it is a comparative claim. Fourth, it says "services to a particular client" not refuse to engage in prostitution at all. The Committee authoring this report goes on to note that they are "very concerned that it appears that there are still some managed sex workers who are being required by brothel operators to provide commercial sexual services against their will on occasion."[56] In Victoria, Australia, a woman working for an agency explained to interviewers that refusing a client was difficult, because they would be fined A$300 for refusing.[57]

In Nevada, women who work in the brothels are classified as independent contractors, and as such denied the legal protections that only accompany the status of "employee."[58] For example, women working in brothels

55. "The New Zealand Report," p. 17.
56. Ibid., p. 14.
57. Sullivan, *Making Sex Work*, p. 296.
58. http://www.bayswan.org/Laura.html

in Nevada are not provided health insurance (employee based), their compensation is taxed at a higher rate, they must tip out to other staff, they must pay remittances (or a percentage) to club owners or brothel owners, and pay for room and board and other necessities. Remittances and rent typically amount to 50% of compensation including tips and gifts. Furthermore, while such independent contractor contracts explicitly state "the Company shall exercise no control over . . . choice of clients, number of clients, or schedule of the Independent Contractor,"[59] they also contractualize "non-compete agreements."

Such non-compete agreements state the independent contractor "will not provide services with Company customers, other than Independent Contractor's spouse or domestic partner, outside of the Premises." The motivation for such non-compete clauses is to control "the product." Brothel owners don't want women "giving away" their services to customers on the side, nor do they want women to "steal" their customers.

In addition, in Nevada and elsewhere women in prostitution are required to undergo weekly medical exams (for which they are responsible for payment). Clients, johns, customers, whatever you want to call them, nowhere are similarly subjected to medical vetting. Thus, under legalization prostituted women's bodies are subject to state surveillance, control, and discipline. Legalization comes with a serious cost to women in prostitution: state regulation and surveillance of their bodies.

59. This is the language from an actual contract in Nevada, run at that time by Denis Hoff. See, http://tmz.vo.llnwd.net/o28/newsdesk/tmz_documents/1222-jimi-lynn-bunnyranch.pdf.

Maintaining status as an independent contractor may appear to give the veneer of autonomy, but it fails insofar as economic burdens associated with this status place "workers" in a position of vulnerability not simply with respect to buyers/clients/johns but also the persons in charge of the club or brothel. Moreover, it "preempts" certain forms of employer liability: worker compensation isn't available to independent contractors nor are a host of other Federal worker protections. Moreover, one contract I inspected (which appears to have boilerplate language in many of its clauses) included an indemnification against "any and all claims, demands, and actions, and any liabilities, damages, or expenses resulting therefrom, including court costs and reasonable attorney's fees, arising out of or relating to Services." Further, there was a clause requiring agreement to binding arbitration for any dispute with the brothel, which required waiving the right to jury trial.

Under US law no business or service provider, including those operated by independent contractors, has a legal right to refuse services when the basis for refusal is membership in a protected class. To refuse service based on membership in a protected class (under Civil Rights laws) is to unlawfully discriminate. Thus, refusing service to persons because of race, sex, nationality, religion, age, and disability, for example, is unlawful discrimination. Unless there is a specific and carefully crafted exemption for "sex workers," refusing a client for say reasons of age would constitute a civil rights violation of the person being refused.

Persons with disabilities and certain medical conditions are protected classes. If we accept the claim that "sex work is work, like another form of work," and so treat "sex work" just as other forms of employment, a right to refusal on the basis of the medical condition of a prospective client is not secure. Arguing that a "sex worker" can refuse a client on condition of their medical status, such as having an STI, requires treating "sex work" differently than other forms of work.[60]

Persons with disabilities, including STIs, are covered under the Americans with Disabilities Act (ADA) and the standard for refusal of service as explained by the Department of Justice is: "In almost every instance, the answer to this question is no. Persons with disabilities may be excluded from the activities or services of a private or public entity because of a health concern only if they pose a significant risk to the health or safety of others, known as a "direct threat," that cannot be **eliminated or reduced to an acceptable level by reasonable modifications** to the entity's policies, practices, or procedures. The determination that a person poses a significant risk to the health or safety of others may not be based on generalizations or stereotypes about a particular disability; it must be based on an individualized assessment of the person with the disability that relies on current medical evidence."[61] All the arguments in favor the legalization/decriminalization of prostitution rely on the claim that the risks of contracting an STI can be reduced to an acceptable level so as to protect worker health and safety, though we have seen this isn't so. Nonetheless, if we accept that claim, then why would we create an exemption for refusal of clients/johns who are HIV positive?

60. Thanks to Craig Agule for discussion on this and the following points.

61. http://www.ada.gov/qahivaids_license.pdf

Moreover, the prohibition on discrimination on the basis of disability raises questions as to the permissibility of refusing to allow sex workers with STIs, including HIV, to work under the "sex work" model. In Nevada, it is presently a felony in Nevada for a woman with HIV to continue to work in prostitution.[62] However, it is arguable that this is inconsistent with nondiscrimination laws for persons with disabilities, and if a reasonable accommodation is available, which is her entitlement under the law, this law and the prohibition might reasonably be legally challenged. Moreover, if the "sex worker" advocacy position on condoms as being sufficient personal protective equipment to guard against transmission of STIs is accepted, then prohibitions on HIV positive women in prostitution has no rationale. If condoms are purportedly sufficient to protect persons in prostitution from STIs, then why aren't they also sufficient to protect clients? In fact, they are not sufficient to protect either. The point is that insofar as defenders of "sex work is work like other forms of work" want to insist on the claims (a) the claim that condoms are sufficient protection for "workers" and (b) "sex work" should be treated like other forms of work, including relevant standards for all other

---

62. NRS 201.358: Engaging in prostitution or solicitation for prostitution after testing positive for exposure to human immunodeficiency virus: Penalty; definition 1. A person who: (a) Violates NRS 201.354; or (b) Works as a prostitute in a licensed house of prostitution, after testing positive in a test approved by the State Board of Health for exposure to the human immunodeficiency virus and receiving notice of that fact is guilty of a category B felony and shall be punished by imprisonment in the state prison for a minimum term of not less than 2 years and a maximum term of not more than 10 years, or by a fine of not more than $10,000, or by both fine and imprisonment.

employment contexts (like the ADA), then there should be no special exemptions or exclusions for either HIV positive "workers" or "clients." Perhaps a few defenders of the sex work position would accept this conclusion. However, if one wants to, at least, grant the right of persons in prostitution to refuse a "client" on grounds of HIV status or any other reason, then "sex work" cannot be treated like other forms of work.

Some argue that concern for persons with disabilities should warrant an either full scale legalization or, at least, permissive policies that create access to persons in prostitution for their sexual needs.[63] Thomsen makes an argument to this effect, arguing that while prohibition of purchasing sex is generally justified, an exemption for persons with disabilities is warranted. He claims, "some disabled persons are partially or entirely incapable of satisfying this need [for sexual relations] except through the purchase of sexual services from a prostitute."[64] This argument is presented as if it is an advocacy position for persons with disabilities. However, it conceals some fairly significant assumptions that reflect hostile attitudes towards persons with disabilities. First, it trades on the assumption that some persons with disabilities are sexually undesirable to any others—that the only way any one might have sexual contact with such persons is to be paid to do so. That is a degrading assumption. Second, even if it is true that some persons with disabilities are unable to find willing sexual partners, the fact of their disability isn't relevant to that

63. Thomsen, Frej Klem, "Prostitution, Disability and Prohibition," *Journal of Medical Ethics* 41 (2015): 451–59.
64. Ibid., p. 455.

fact per se. Plenty of people struggle to find sexual partners.[65] Insofar as people with disabilities are stigmatized
in ways that others fail to consider them as a potential
partner is a serious social problem. However, the solution
to that problem is not to create a class of women (or men)
to sexually service them on the grounds that is the only
possible access to sex they may have. That is doubly stigmatizing, both to persons with disabilities and to the persons
whose purpose it is to "service" them. Third, and finally,
the proposal for exemptions for persons with disabilities is
practically likely to be unadministrable. What constitutes a
disability for purposes of such an exemption would have to
be legally defined, and likely so broadly defined that, in effect, it would be to legalize prostitution full-scale. In effect,
the argument is a work around by appealing to the relative
(unjust) social powerlessness of persons with disabilities to
justify the imposition of powerlessness on another socially
subordinated class (women).

Assimilation of "sex work" into a work model raises
unique problems that are under theorized by advocates
of legalization or decriminalization, as this section has
shown. Standard employment law, if applied directly to
"sex work," undermines arguments for strong rights to refusal, whether one is an independent contractor or formal
employee. Civil rights protections for persons seeking
services, in other areas of life, prohibits refusal of service
on grounds of protected class membership. Employee-
employer relationships are asymmetrical relationships in

65. Brian Earp and Ole Martin Moen make this point against Klem's
argument, see their "Paying for Sex—Only People with Disabilities?"
Journal of Medical Ethics 42, no. 1 (2016): 54–56. Although, they argue
for legalization with some regulations.

which employers have legal entitlements to exercise control over both the working conditions and the employee. Independent contractors are vulnerable in many ways vis a vis those that funnel clients to them, and often have seriously reduced economic standing due to those relationship. Moreover, they are also required to comply with civil rights laws. The claim that "sex work is work like any other form of work" alongside a claim that treating it as such increases the autonomy of "sex workers" is simply indefensible in the context of any knowledge of how employment law actually works.

2.4 SEX CONTRACTS

The obvious reply is to suggest that there is something unique and different about sex that entails strong rights of refusal even in employment contexts (or when provided from independent contractors). Defenders of decriminalization and legalization of prostitution, however, hang much of their argument on the claim that "It is vital that [sex workers] are seen as being engaged in work and therefore have the same rights as other workers."[66] The important point they make here is the insistence that sex work be seen—treated—like other forms of work. To the extent one wants to insist on that point, the arguments that claim legalization/decriminalization increases sexual autonomy are simply undermined. If one wants to insist on the primacy

66. "Submission to the Senate Standing Committee on Education, Employment and Workplace Relations: Fair Work Bill 2008." The Sex Workers Union Australian Sex Workers Industrial Rights Network: A Member of Scarlet Alliance, the Australian Sex Workers Association.

of sexual autonomy as an inviolable right in the context of legalized/decriminalized sex work, then one is forced to admit that selling sex is different than other forms of work. And if one wants to continue to argue for legalization/decriminalization, one will have to argue for carve outs in the law that treat prostitution as unique and unlike any other form of work. At a minimum, such carve outs will have to include a right to refuse for any reason—irrespective of civil rights laws that prohibit discrimination on the basis of membership in a protective class. Presumably too, under an employee–employer model, one will have to insist that refusal "to do one's job" is not sufficient grounds for dismissal. Thus, employee contracts will effectively be unenforceable.[67] As noted earlier, independent contractor status doesn't resolve the right to refusal question, especially as many effectively are managed within brothels. So we need a legal carve out there too.

Germany aims to address these kinds of concerns by legally declaring prostitution "contracts" are as unilateral contracts, where women in prostitution have a unilateral right to claim payment for "services," but "clients or brothel owners do not have any enforceable claim to the performance of (specific) sexual services based on any agreement reached."[68] Although this phrasing leaves open

67. Section 17 of the PRA (New Zealand) gives every sex worker the right to refuse to provide, or continue to provide, a commercial sexual service to any person. The fact that the person has entered into a contract to provide commercial sexual services does not limit the sex worker's ability to withdraw his or her services or consent. http://www.business.govt.nz/worksafe/information-guidance/all-guidance-items/sex-industry-a-guide-to-occupational-health-and-safety-in-the-new-zealand/sexindustry.pdf

68. The German Report, p. 14.

the possibility of other forms of contractual remedy, as it simply denies a right to specific performance. It does not rule out claims for breach altogether.

Not everyone supports treating prostitution contracts as unilateral contracts: the report states that some legal specialists argue that prostitution contracts must be mutually binding: "It is claimed that this [unilateral contracts] creates an imbalance in the prostitutes' legal position vis-à-vis their clients, which leads to inconsistent weighting and to the fact that rule is inconsistent with the legal system."[69] Thus, some legal specialists in Germany insist that exemptions like this (treating prostitution contracts as unilateral contracts) is inconsistent with the basic premises of contract law, where contracts are understood to be bilateral exchanges imposing obligations on both parties.

In defending the decision to make prostitution contracts unilateral, the authors of the German Report emphasize that it is necessary to protect the rights to sexual autonomy, whether refusing brothel owners' instructions or a particular client as well as the right to leave prostitution. They emphasize that this kind of legal carve out excludes the possibility of treating prostitution as a "job like any other."[70]

To fully appreciate the extent to which sex cannot be analogized to any other form of labor, it is worth exploring the plausibility of enforcing sex contracts, as bilateral exchanges, in contexts in which both the selling and buying of sex are fully legal or decriminalized.[71] Typically,

69. Ibid., p. 15.
70. Ibid., p. 16.
71. See Anderson, "Prostitution and Sexual Autonomy," and Hallie Liberto, "Normalizing Prostitution versus Normalizing the Alienability of Sexual Rights: A Response to Scott A. Anderson," *Ethics* 120, no. 1 (October 2009): 138–45.

employment contracts, or contracts for the exchange of services, are bilateral exchanges. Both parties incur duties and responsibilities by entering into the agreement to exchange services for money, or labor for payment.

Treating sex contracts as normal employment or exchange contracts leads to deeply problematic consequences. When one party fails to fulfill their side of a contractual exchange, the aggrieved party can sue for breach of contract. Thus, a critical question is whether it is reasonable to enforce remedies for breach of contract in the context of prostitution. This requires an examination the arguments clients/johns could make to argue a breach occurred. I argue that enforcing such contracts in the face of such arguments for breach by clients/johns leads to seriously absurd consequences. Moreover, enforcing such contracts would serve to legally enforce conditions of inequality and the exploitation of persons in prostitution. The contractual model does offer the opportunity for prostituted persons to make claims against clients for failure to pay. Some may see this as a benefit of a contractual model. However, this is mostly a theoretical possibility. In Germany, for example, despite such legal rights, persons in prostitution rarely exercise them.[72]

First, it is important to note that courts generally don't enforce specific performance in the case of contracts for personal services, with some notable exceptions. Such exceptions include cases concerning "unique goods."[73] Most

---

72. German Report, p. 14.

73. Alan Schwartz, "The Case for Specific Performance," *Faculty Scholarship Series* (1979), 1118. https://digitalcommons.law.yale.edu/fss_papers/1118

relevant to our current discussion, surrogacy contracts are such an exception to the general refusal to enforce specific performance. The personal service in question in surrogacy contracts is gestating a fetus to term, and specific performance is handing over a child to the contracting parents. In places where surrogacy is legal, such as California, specific performance is enforced as per the contract—that is, the surrogate is forced to turn over the child or children produced as per the contract.[74]

The most obvious objection to court ordered specific performance in the case of sex contracts is that requiring specific performance (sex with a john) would be to court order rape. Beyond that grotesque thought, such an order would run afoul of the 13th Amendment and other legal prohibitions of involuntary servitude, in the United States.[75] Thus, it is pretty implausible to think that specific performance would even garner consideration by anyone.

Despite the fact that specific performance is rarely granted as a form of relief for most contracts, plaintiffs

74. See, for example, *Johnson v. Calvert*, 851 P. 2d 776—Cal: Supreme Court 1993 available at https://scholar.google.com/scholar_case?case= 112980646483731250&q=Johnson+v.+Calvert:+KENNARD,+J.,+Disse nting&hl=en&as_sdt=6,31

75. Catharine A. MacKinnon argues that prostitution violates a number of fundamental civil rights, importantly those guaranteed by the 13th and 14th Amendments in the US Constitution. See her "Prostitution and Civil Rights," in *Women's Lives Men's Laws* (Cambridge, MA: Harvard University Press, 2005), 151–61. Margaret Jane Radin makes a similar argument concerning specific performance as a remedy for breach of contract in the context of prostitution. She writes: "If sexual service contracts were to be specifically performed, persons would be forced to yield their bodily integrity and freedom." *Contested Commodities: The Trouble with Trade in Sex, Children, Body Parts, and Other Things* (Cambridge, MA: Harvard University Press, 1996), 135.

have successfully sought injunctions forbidding performers (actors or recording artists, primarily) from offering their services to others for the duration of the original contract.[76] Recall Prince, George Michael, and more recently, Kesha's contract disputes with their record labels. Prince famously wrote "slave" on his face during performances to protest being held to his contract. None of these artists could record music for other record labels during the time they were under contract to the original label. Each pursued lawsuits to void the terms of the original contract.

If this kind of remedy were pursued in the case of a sex contract, and granted, it would amount to a court order that the particular defendant (prostituted woman) in question not "sell her services" for the duration of the original contract. Again, a very unlikely scenario, but is a form of control that brothel owners in Nevada attempt to exert with non-compete clauses. Such contracts explicitly state: "Independent contractor will not provide Services with any Company customers, other than Independent Contractor's spouse or domestic partner, outside of the premises, and will not, either directly or indirectly induce, recruit or encourage any of the Company's customers to cease visiting the Company's premises or to commence visiting the premises of another brothel, or take away such customers, for herself or for third parties."[77]

This certainly challenges the often-claimed benefit of legalization or decriminalization that advocates assert—namely, that women in prostitution are "freer" where

76. http://tmz.vo.llnwd.net/o28/newsdesk/tmz_documents/1222-jimi-lynn-bunnyranch.pdf
77. Ibid.

prostitution is legalized or decriminalized. It is worth underscoring that the clause refers to "the Company's customers," and not the particular brothel's customers. Thus, it covers anyone who has solicited services with any of the parent company's brothels. Potentially, this is a large number of persons whom the prostituted woman is prohibited from having sex with. Given the language in the following clause (the exception clause), this non-compete is not just about who can be charged for sex, but who she can have sex with, for it excludes spouses and domestic partners (presumably men who are not paying for "services"). Thus, the clause excludes her from having sex with anyone who has solicited any of the brothels held by the parent company, not just sex for money. Certainly, part of the motivation is that she not "give away" the product in addition to prohibiting her from making any monies (from prostitution) to which the brothel cannot lay claim.

Non-compete agreements are the subject of much contestation. Many argue that they should not be enforced at all in any context, and only serve to further vulnerabilities of workers writ large. And certainly many of those in favor of decriminalization and legalization will argue that such agreements should not be enforced. However, libertarians, such as Flanigan, support an individual's right to contract with others on whatever terms they commonly agree to, even when the agreement gives more power to one party. The mutually beneficial exploitation argument, explored in chapter 1, asserts that even with bargaining terms that are exploitative to one party, the bargain should be upheld if the exploited party judges it to be the best deal they can get. Thus, where non-competes are in practice and something brothel owners are in a position to demand of persons in prostitution, the libertarian should have no objection to them provided the prostituted person assents (even if such assent is possible only because of an unequal bargaining position).

A further area of contract law that warrants exploration is economic remedies granted to those determined to have suffered an economic loss as a result of a breach. Generally, economic remedies are limited to the economic losses suffered as a direct result of the breach (the failure of the breaching party to fulfill the terms of the contract). Rarely are additional damages awarded.[78]

To think through how claims for breach would work in the case of sex contracts, consider that johns/brothel owners could, in principle, claim economic losses as a result of a refusal of sex (failure to fulfill the contract). Thus, were sex contracts regarded as valid and bilateral exchanges, johns/brothel owners may simply recover the money they paid for "services" not rendered. In other words, in cases of refusal to "complete the contract" to provide "the services" (sex as expected by the buyer), the john can make the case that the contract was breached and recover any economic loss. Economic losses are not just limited to the exact amount of money they would have spent on the sex, they can include money for expenses (travel, missed work, etc.) directly related to the expectation that the contract would be fulfilled. Thus, enforcing breaches open up the possibility for johns to make economic claims upon sex workers beyond simply "returning money." Brothel owners could make similar claims in cases in which they'd spent money to advertise for particular women. Legal recognition

---

78. Blum, *Contracts*, p. 722.

of either kind of claim would further the power asymmetry between prostitutes and johns/brothel owners insofar as they would have a legal avenue for effectively extorting women in prostitution.

Even more importantly, there is an exception to the general rule of limiting remedies to purely economic losses that may be relevant in the context of contracts for sex. That is, where "contracts whose clear and principal purpose is not to satisfy any economic or commercial goal of the plaintiff, but to give her [the plaintiff] an emotional, sentimental, or psychic benefit."[79] In order to argue for punitive damages (damages beyond the economic loss itself) the plaintiff has to demonstrate that the subject of the contract "deeply involve[s] matters of personal concern to the plaintiff" and that the non-economic purpose of the contract is clear and "the defendant must reasonably have realized that a breach would likely inflict serious emotional distress."[80] Could a "john" make a plausible argument that meets these conditions? In other words, could a john plausibly make an argument for punitive damages in the case of a breach, and thus extract financial penalties beyond the mere recovery of their actual economic losses? Attempts have been made. In New Zealand a man tried to sue a woman in prostitution for compensatory damages, though the judge dismissed his particular case.[81] A US citizen filed a suit for breach against a Nevada brothel, seeking $1.8 million in damages.[82] His case was also dismissed. A German man filed a suit against a dominatrix, claiming she was "too

79. Ibid., p. 722
80. Ibid., pp. 722–23.
81. http://time.com/36603/prostitute-sued-by-nz-man/
82. http://www.abajournal.com/files/escort_suit_filing.pdf

dominating."[83] The court dismissed the case on the grounds that both had been using cocaine at the time and thus they could not discern the facts.

Thus, while such suits have not yet been successful, as far as my research shows, nonetheless the conceptual possibility of such suits follows from a "sex work" approach. This is especially true in light of the claim that a primary aim of conceiving of "sex work" as work is to fully normalize it as a form of labor, like any other.

To make a successful argument for breach that included compensatory damages, the john would be required to show that the purpose of the sex contract is not to satisfy an economic goal. It is clear that the purpose of a sex contract is not to satisfy an economic goal of the buyer. They want sex, for which they pay money. But the "benefit" (i.e., sex) received is non-economic. That element is satisfied. Now, additionally, a plaintiff (john) would have to show that they aimed to secure an "emotional, sentimental, or psychic benefit." Many johns claim that their primary purpose in seeking prostitutes is an emotional connection or experience. Whether this is true, of course, is another matter. However, in aiming to capitalize on whatever truth is in this kind of claim, brothels and women in prostitution sometimes offer what they call "the girlfriend experience." As one Nevada brothel advertisement describes "the girlfriend experience":

> At the Chicken Ranch in Pahrump Nevada, our lovely ladies make it easy for you to experience all that you want in a relationship. These beautiful women won't complain to you

83. https://www.thelocal.de/20121010/45473

about their mothers, give you a hard time for wearing that shirt, or check your text messages to see if you are talking to your ex. They take the anxiety out of meeting a "nice girl," the stress out of courting, and the frustration out of being in a relationship.[84]

And it continues,

Once you've decided on a woman to join you for the night (or weekend), break the ice over drinks in the bar and then head to her room for a more private encounter. Your "girlfriend" will treat you to the emotional and physical intimacy you desire. Conversation will flow easily as you get to know each other on a deeper level, sharing stories, laughing with each other and eventually, when the time is right, exploring each other's bodies and learning how to pleasure one another.[85]

Thus, it is not implausible that a john could claim for the purposes of litigation, and breach, that they (from their subjective state) were seeking such emotional or sentimental benefits. Additionally, any john might plausibly claim to be seeking a "psychic benefit"—insofar as sex, and sex on their terms, is an element of their personal well-being. Of course, case law would have to sort out the legitimacy of these claims and we can imagine good defense attorneys challenging their veracity. Nonetheless, such arguments are not (legally) implausible on their face, and courts will have to adjudicate them. In point of fact, common cases in which additional damages are often awarded in the context of personal service contracts include service in cases of funerals

84. https://chickenranchbrothel.com/index.php/blog/the-girlfriend-experience
85. Ibid.

and weddings, both of which are highly meaningful unique interpersonal interactions.[86]

Finally, a plaintiff would have to show that the defendant (the person in prostitution) reasonably realized a breach would inflict serious emotional distress on the plaintiff. This is arguably a higher bar to plausibly satisfy, but not as difficult to satisfy as you might think. Brothels, in particular, regularly advertise specific women with specific "talents" or traits that appeal to men's interests and desires for those specific traits. That is, they are advertising and offering a specific experience with a specific person, not just a general and inchoate sexual experience. Moreover, many of these women gain followings and sometimes have a celebrity-like status among johns. As advertised under "the girlfriend experience" at the Bunny Ranch in Nevada, "The Girlfriend Experience does not stop when the party is over. Most clients requesting the GFE usually become regulars. What I mean by this is we continue to chat over emails, texts and phone conversations throughout my time at the Ranch. We exchange daily photos and silly links to things we are interested in."[87] Under such conditions, it is not hard to imagine that one could plausibly argue that the defendant (the woman in prostitution) reasonably realized a breach would inflict serious emotional distress on the plaintiff.

The upshot of these arguments' potential recognition and enforcement of "sex contracts" raises serious sex equality concerns. Beyond the concern for sex equality are possibilities of dissatisfied, unhappy, or vindictive clients

86. Blum, *Contracts*, p. 725.
87. https://www.bunnyranch.com/blog/girlfriend-experience/

suing women for breach. Such suits raise the potential for johns winning economic and punitive damages against such women for exercising their sexual autonomy—that is, refusing to have sex they don't want, trying to change the conditions of a sexual encounter, withdrawing consent after initially giving it, and so on.

Market mechanisms have emerged that function as informal contract enforcement. Online discussion groups created and frequented by buyers serve as rating sites, where buyers can name, rate, and discuss the "services" of prostituted women. Though not legal enforcement of contractual arrangements, these sites serve as reputational substitutes to litigation, providing "sellers" with strong market incentives to satisfy "buyers" demands to secure reputational standing in the market.[88] "To the extent that buyers can observe sellers reputation and have lower willingness to pay for goods provided by low-reputation sellers, sellers have incentives to keep buyers satisfied in order to protect their reputations."[89] Internet rating sites, such as Ter, have emerged as informal contractual enforcement mechanisms, and function as external pressure on sellers— prostituted women, both in legal and illegal markets—to provide "services" as demanded by buyers. These informal market mechanisms demonstrate that a contractual understanding of the exchange between john and prostitute does not function to improve the power of women in prostitution to effectively exercise their agency. Conceptually sex

88. See Scott Cunningham and Todd D. Kendall, "Examining the Role of Client Reviews and Reputation within Online Prostitution," in *The Oxford Handbook of the Economics of Prostitution*, ed. Scott Cunningham and Manisha Shaw (Oxford: Oxford University Press, 2016), 9–32.

89. Ibid., p. 9.

contracts are an implausible framework for understanding and adjudicating "sexual exchanges." But if "sex work" is work like any other form of labor or exchange relationship, this model should apply. The aim here has been to show that sex cannot be treated, or understood, as "just like" other forms of labor or exchange relationships.

Although there is much evidence that neither legalization nor decriminalization has, in fact, increased (sexual) autonomy for women in prostitution, the considerations raised here aim to show it is not clear that the necessary protections for sexual autonomy, or simply autonomy, can be guaranteed under legalization/decriminalization. The only move available to defenders of legalization is to give up the "sex work is work like any other form of work" argument and acknowledge that sex in the context of work is unique, unlike any other form of work. But once we admit this premise into the conversation, the arguments in favor of legalization look much, much weaker—in part, because the harms associated with and constitutive of sex work are unlike other potential harms in work contexts. These arguments aim to expose the fact that basic human and civil rights that apply to worker health and safety, sexual autonomy, and bodily integrity cannot be adequately guaranteed within prostitution and legalization/decriminalization can do nothing to address these harms. Moreover, arguments for exemptions rest, in part, on refusing equal status to persons in prostitution compared with other forms of employment.

In Defense of the Nordic Model

3.1 INTRODUCTION

The last chapter aimed to show that the "sex work" position is indefensible. Its proponents' claim that sex work is work like any other form of work does not survive scrutiny. Moreover, the claim that either legalization or full decriminalization are effective "harm reduction" strategies is untrue, as argued for in chapter 2. However, full-scale criminalization is not defensible either, as discussed in the Introduction. The Nordic Model offers a solution, a legal approach to prostitution that elevates the status of women, and others, in prostitution while targeting those who harm persons in prostitution, the buyers and third-party profiteers. Thus, the Nordic Model targets demand as a means to abolishing prostitution. This chapter aims to further defend the Nordic Model as the best approach to prostitution.

The Swedish government describes the "Nordic Model" as follows: "Since 1 January 1999, it has been a crime to buy sexual services inside Sweden, and an individual who obtains a causal sexual service relation for compensation is sentenced to pay fines or serve a prison term of up to

Debating Sex Work. Lori Watson, Jessica Flanigan, Oxford University Press (2020). © Oxford University Press.
DOI: 10.1093/oso/9780190659882.001.0001

six months for the purchase of sexual services. In contrast to previous measures against prostitution, the criminalization of the purchase of sexual service targets demand, i.e., the sex buyer or the prospective sex buyer."[1] The Swedish Parliament subsequently passed an Act allowing the penalty to be raised to "a one-year maximum imprisonment."[2] Thus, significant penalties attach to purchasing sex. The law targets the source of demand, the buyers and third-party profiteers, as a means of abolishment of prostitution. As the authors of the report evaluating the Swedish law, 10 years after its passage, write, "if there was no demand there would be no prostitution."[3]

The rationales for this law, including in Sweden at the time of its passage, incorporated the claims that prostitution was intimately related to violence against women and "a lack of gender equality."[4] As documented in chapter 1, intersecting inequalities function as push factors into prostitution and structure it within. The empirical and grounded analysis of pathways into prostitution and the way it actually functions reveal it as an institution of sex-based, and other intersecting, inequalities. Suggestions of reform or "harm reduction" do not address this basic fact.

1. "Selected extracts of the Swedish government report SOU 2010:49: 'The Ban against the Purchase of Sexual Services. An evaluation 1999–2008'" (available at https://ec.europa.eu/anti-trafficking/sites/antitrafficking/files/the_ban_against_the_purchase_of_sexual_services._an_evaluation_1999-2008_1.pdf), p. 2.

2. See Max Waltman, "Prohibiting Sex Purchasing and Ending Trafficking: The Swedish Prostitution Law," *Michigan Journal of International Law* 33 (2011): 133–57. Available at SSRN: https://ssrn.com/abstract=1966130

3. Ibid.

4. "Selected extracts of the Swedish government report," p. 5.

Suggestions for reform or so-called harm reduction that are offered fail to go to the engine of inequality that fuels and structures prostitution, demand.

In addition to targeting demand, the Nordic Model offers social support services to persons in prostitution. These services target what women in prostitution say they need, including access to medical care, "housing, financial assistance, psychosocial support, and more."[5] These services are provided for those who wish to access them. They are free. And no one seeking such services is required to exit prostitution to receive them.[6] As documented in chapter 1, the barriers to exit for most women in prostitution are very difficult to overcome. The provision of social support in a broad fashion is a necessary element of any comprehensive policy on prostitution.

Further, the Nordic Model, specifically as implemented in Sweden, includes education campaigns targeting buyers and the broader public on the harms of prostitution. Sweden also provides counseling services for men who want to stop using women in prostitution.[7] These services are provided on a voluntary basis as well.

Thus, the Nordic Model is a holistic public policy approach to prostitution. Moreover, in targeting demand for sexual services, the Nordic Model contains a unified strategy for combatting both prostitution and sex trafficking. In fact, by focusing on demand, the often

5. Ane Mathieson, Easton Branam, and Anya Noble, "Prostitution Policy: Legalization, Decriminalization and the Nordic Model," *Seattle Journal for Social Justice* 14, no. 2 (Fall 2015): 367–428.

6. Ibid., p. 404.

7. Ibid., p. 407.

invoked illusory distinction between the two is irrelevant from a legal point of view.

3.2 PROSTITUTION AND SEX TRAFFICKING

Prostitution and sex trafficking are often claimed to be distinct as a conceptual, and sometimes legal, matter. Under US law, prostitution is defined as a form of trafficking, though the law distinguishes between trafficking and "severe trafficking." The Victims of Trafficking and Violence Protection Act of 2000 defines sex trafficking as: "The term 'sex trafficking' means the recruitment, harboring, transportation, provision, or obtaining of a person for the purpose of a commercial sex act."[8] Thus, clearly, this definition incorporates what is generally known as "prostitution," as obtaining a person for purpose of a commercial sex act is included with the definition of sex trafficking. However, the Act focuses on "severe forms of trafficking in persons" for purposes of resource allocation to law enforcement, support for victims, and penalties for those found guilty of such trafficking. Severe forms of trafficking are defined as

> (A) Sex trafficking in which a commercial sex act is induced by force, fraud, or coercion, or in which the person induced to perform such act has not attained 18 years of age; or
> (B) The recruitment, harboring, transportation, provision, or obtaining of a person for labor or services, through the use

8. "Victims of Trafficking and Violence Protection Act of 2000," available at https://www.state.gov/j/tip/laws/61124.htm

of force, fraud, or coercion for the purpose of subjection to
involuntary servitude, peonage, debt bondage, or slavery.[9]

While US federal law technically defines prostitution as a
form of sex trafficking, the emphasis on "severe forms of
trafficking in persons" rests on a common assumption that
prostitution and sex trafficking are distinct phenomena
in important ways. Those aiming to distinguish between
them emphasize that prostitution is "voluntary" or a "free-
choice," and contrast sex trafficking as sexual exploitation
through "force, fraud, or coercion."[10] As argued in chapter 1,
the purported conceptual distinction here evaporates with a
material analysis of the realities of layered inequalities that
function coercively to channel women into prostitution.

A brief review of some of the most salient facts will help
structure the argument of this chapter. Recall, economic
vulnerability as well as inequality across class, age, race,
nationality, disability status, or various intersections of all
of these categories constitute substantive inequalities that
function to coerce and channel women into prostitution.
Moreover, it is well documented that within prostitution
there is a racial, ethnic, and nationality-based hierarchy—
both where it is legal/decriminalized and illegal. Race inequality structures prostitution: women of color and First
Nations or indigenous women are at the bottom of the hierarchy in prostitution. Trans women, and trans women of
color, are both overrepresented in prostitution and situated at the bottom of the hierarchy within it.

9. Ibid.
10. MacKinnon, "Trafficking, Prostitution, and Inequality," p. 299.

Age inequality structures prostitution: aside from the fact that many women enter prostitution under the age of 18, women in prostitution, where it is legal, are overwhelmingly under 30. According to the European Parliament Report, 75% of persons (mostly women) in prostitution "are between 13 and 25 years old."[11] Youth is an indicator of vulnerability to control and manipulation; thus, it is a "desirable" trait for pimps and brothel owners seeking to recruit women into prostitution. Youth is also prized among men who buy sex.

Nationality and country of origin are geo-political inequalities that both act as push factors into prostitution and structure inequalities within it. In places where prostitution is legal or fully decriminalized proper papers are required, much like access to non-sex work is structured by citizenship status or access to work visas. The requirements for working papers do not act as a safeguard against trafficking or forced prostitution for vulnerable women. Rather, noncitizens or immigrants without the proper working papers continue to work in the illegal prostitution that thrives alongside legal prostitution. Thus, the claim that decriminalization or legalization is an effective strategy for eliminating "black markets" in sex is simply false.

The EU Parliament report (2014) states, "on average approximately 70% of prostitutes in Western Europe are migrants. In fact, for migrants, the likelihood to engage in prostitution increases compared to the general population. This has been explained with the increased vulnerability of migrant women due to racial discrimination, lack of

11. EU Parliament Report, Executive Summary, p. 6.

knowledge of the language, administrative barriers derived from strict migration policies, and labor segregation which drive migrants to informal labor markets and increase the risk of suffering poverty and marginalization.

Defenders of full decriminalization or legalization argue that opening the market further, by for example eliminating requirements for working papers for immigrants, is the preferred policy position. This policy proposal, however, only further opens markets to men's demand for prostitution, and does nothing to address the substantive inequalities that lead women to enter into prostitution nor does it address the incentives created for pimps and procurers to induce or force women into prostitution for economic gain. Thus, the solution is not simply the removal of requirements of working papers, as working in legal markets neither addresses the underlying inequalities nor does it substantively improve such women's lives.

The living conditions of migrant women, economic refugees, under legalization are vividly described in a popular and important news outlet in Germany. *Der Spiegel* published an article in 2013 titled "How Legalizing Prostitution Has Failed."[12] The article documents the immigration of two Romanian women, Alina and an unnamed friend, to Germany for the purpose of working in prostitution. Alina describes her decision to enter into prostitution as a result of having no job, no money, no opportunities in her native country, and the desire to escape an abusive father. Once working in a brothel called "Airport Pussies,"

12. "How Legalizing Prostitution Has Failed," *Der Spiegel*, available at http://www.spiegel.de/international/germany/human-trafficking-persists-despite-legality-of-prostitution-in-germany-a-902533.html

Alina describes her "working conditions" as follows: she was kept "locked up in the club" only allowed to leave to buy cigarettes and snacks escorted by a guard. The men she serviced did not always use a condom, and the brothel management (the pimps) did not allow her to object. "She says she was hardly ever beaten" but that "they said they knew enough people in Romania who knew where our families lived. That was enough [to keep her there]." The pimps knew the police and knew in advance when a raid might occur; the pimps used their power over the women in the brothel to tell them exactly what to say to police. The article states "65–80% of the girls and women [in prostitution in Germany] come from abroad. Most are from Romania and Bulgaria." In underscoring the failure of legalization to create better working conditions and secure autonomy for women in prostitution, the article states: "Today many police officers, women's organizations and politicians familiar with the well-meaning law is in fact little more than a subsidy program for pimps and makes the market more attractive to human traffickers."[13] Legalization or full decriminalization exploits, cements, and promotes inequalities into and within prostitution.

Those at the bottom of the race and class hierarchy within prostitution, even where it is legal, are often least likely to have the power to insist on so-called safe working conditions as defined within current standards; less likely to be able to insist upon condom use; more likely to agree to not use a condom for an extra fee; and more vulnerable to other forms of exploitation. It's worth noting that 60% of those in legal prostitution in the Netherlands are Latina,

13. Ibid.

though with proper papers.[14] Trans women are also significantly overrepresented in prostitution—the EU Parliament report states that the proportion of trans persons in prostitution ranges from 5% to 25% depending upon the country.[15]

The facts are that overwhelmingly the persons in prostitution are vulnerable along a number of axes of inequality. This fact has been documented throughout my contribution to this volume and is summarized in section 3.1. Knowledge of these facts is critical for showing that the purported distinction between "voluntary prostitution" and "sex trafficking" is illusory and not a distinction to hang one's hat on for thinking through possible policy positions. There are multiple forms of coercion, often ignored, such as the way inequality functions to coerce vulnerable persons into prostitution.

That so-called consent of the exploited, specifically the sexually exploited, is neither conceptually nor practically meaningful for distinguishing prostitution from sex trafficking is explicitly recognized in the United Nations Palmero Protocol, which defines trafficking as

> (a) "Trafficking in persons" shall mean the recruitment, transportation, transfer, harbouring or receipt of persons, by means of the threat or use of force or other forms of coercion, of abduction, of fraud, of deception, of the abuse of power or of a position of vulnerability or of the giving or receiving of payments or benefits to achieve the consent of a person having control over another person, for the purpose

14. "Prostitution in the Netherlands since the lifting of the brothel ban."
15. European Parliament Report, p. 29.

of exploitation. Exploitation shall include, at a minimum, the exploitation of the prostitution of others or other forms of sexual exploitation, forced labour or services, slavery or practices similar to slavery, servitude or the removal of organs;

(b) The consent of a victim of trafficking in persons to the intended exploitation set forth in subparagraph (a) of this article shall be irrelevant where any of the means set forth in subparagraph (a) have been used.[16]

The critical elements of the Palmero Protocol that acknowledge that so-called trafficking and prostitution are largely identical are: "the abuse of power or of a position of vulnerability" and "the giving or receiving of payments or benefits to achieve the consent of a person." These elements capture the facts that persons are pushed into prostitution due to the vulnerability of specific forms of inequality and that payment, in this context, coerces performance of unwanted sex acts. As shown in the analysis in preceding chapters, prostitution is a sex unequal practice of exploitation that rests inequality. Such inequality, in its substantive forms, is coercive. "Consent" gained by such coercion is illusory. The Palmero Protocol is written so as to recognize this, and thus doesn't rest on a conceptual distinction between sex trafficking and prostitution as it is frequently understood.

Defenders of full decriminalization and legalization claim that permissive policies will reduce "involuntary prostitution" and sex trafficking. The evidence refutes this claim. For example, the Netherlands 2007 (5 years after the

16. https://www.ohchr.org/en/professionalinterest/pages/protocoltraffickinginpersons.aspx

lift of the brothel ban) report states: "A complicating factor
in combating the exploitation of involuntary prostitution is
that policy, the issuing of licenses, and the enforcement are
all mainly targeting the owners of sex businesses. Although
owners might use coercion, such force is chiefly exercised by
pimps who operate more in the background, and of whose
existence owners are not always aware. Pimps are still a very
common phenomenon. . . . [T]he fact that the number of
prostitutes with pimps does not seem to have decreased is a
cause for concern."[17] In addition, one year after decriminalization in New Zealand, a government report stated: "35% of
women in prostitution reported that they had been coerced
in prostitution. The highest rate of coercion by johns was reported by women in massage parlor prostitution who were
pimp-controlled (described as 'managed' by the Report)."[18]
The European Parliament's 2014 report on "Sexual exploitation and prostitution and its impact on gender equality"
states that the most conservative estimates suggest "that
1 in 7 prostitutes in Europe are victims of trafficking,
while some Member States estimate that between 60%
and 90% of those in their respective national prostitution
markets have been trafficked."[19] This report includes countries in which prostitution continues to be criminalized.
Two important points require emphasis: first is that even

17. "Prostitution in the Netherlands since the lifting of the
brothel ban."
18. Melissa Farley, "Theory versus Reality: Commentary on Four
Articles about Trafficking for Prostitution," *Women's Studies International
Forum* 32 (2009): 311–15, available at http://www.prostitutionresearch.
com/TraffickingTheoryVsReality2009%28Farley%29.pdf
19. EU Parliament Report, http://www.europarl.europa.eu/RegData/
etudes/etudes/join/2014/493040/IPOL-FEMM_ET(2014)493040_
EN.pdf

in legalized or fully decriminalized locales, sex trafficking, as understood in its more narrow definitions, is still prevalent. Second, legalization and full decriminalization in particular locales impacts neighboring locales, increasing sex trafficking over all.

The often-repeated claim that legalization of prostitution reduces sex trafficking (as defined in terms of "force, fraud or coercion") is simply false. A 2012 study by three economists aiming to determine whether legalization of prostitution increases human trafficking concluded: "Countries with legalized prostitution are associated with higher human trafficking inflows than countries where prostitution is prohibited. The scale effect of legalizing prostitution, i.e. expansion of the market, outweighs the substitution effect, where legal sex workers are favored over illegal workers. On average, countries with legalized prostitution report a greater incidence of human trafficking inflows."[20] The claim that legalization is an effective way to reduce coercion into prostitution and sex trafficking is contradicted by the evidence.[21]

The answer to addressing the inequality that drives and structures prostitution is not to continue the

20. Seo-Young Cho, Axel Dreher, and Eric Neumayer, "Does Legalized Prostitution Increase Human Trafficking?" *World Development* 41, no. 1 (2013): 67–82, available online at http://papers.ssrn.com/sol3/papers.cfm?abstract_id=1986065

21. An additional study by Niklas Jakobsson and Andreas Kotsadam, "The Law and Economics of International Sex Slavery: Prostitution Laws and Trafficking for Sexual Exploitation," *European Journal of Law and Economics* 35 (2013): 87–107, concludes that "trafficking is least prevalent in countries where prostitution is illegal, most prevalent in countries where prostitution is legal, and in between in those countries where prostitution is legal but procuring is illegal."

criminalization of the selling of sex. Criminalization of the selling of sex punishes disproportionately the vulnerable persons in prostitution. Laws are enforced unevenly; women are arrested for selling sex, while buyers are often not arrested or receive lesser charges and punishment.[22] Moreover, women are generally arrested multiple times, creating a legal record that follows them throughout their lives, making exit from "the life" all the more difficult.

Whereas historically, the women in prostitution were blamed, criminalized, monitored, and outcast, and considered to be the "drivers" of an immoral institution, we now understand that what drives prostitution is demand. The Nordic Model has taken root beyond Sweden; it is now law in Norway, Iceland, France, Canada, Republic of Ireland, and Northern Ireland. Many other countries are actively considering passing similar legislation, including Great Britain in 2018. In addition, the European Parliament recently passed a resolution calling for member nations to adopt the Nordic Model. The Nordic Model has two main goals: to curb the demand for commercial sex that fuels trafficking and to promote equality between men and women. As MacKinnon describes the law: "[E]liminating her criminality raises her status; criminalizing him lowers his privilege. This is a sex equality law in inspiration as well as effect."[23]

By decriminalizing the selling of sex, the model removes the legal barriers that further subordinate those already subordinated via prostitution. But it continues to criminalize the buying of sex, since addressing "the demand" side of global sex markets is a necessary condition

22. MacKinnon, "Trafficking, Prostitution, and Inequality," p. 301.
23. Ibid.

for greater equality. And the model has been effective at reducing the number of persons in prostitution and reducing sex trafficking into countries that adopt it.[24]

Within the United States, where prostitution is fully criminalized in most jurisdictions, many law enforcement agencies have nonetheless developed and adopted demand reduction strategies that target buyers over sellers. While these efforts are inspired by the recognition that demand is the problem to be solved, they occur alongside continued enforcement of criminal laws against prostituted persons. As such, these efforts are not a comprehensive solution and are minimally effective.

Such strategies include "John schools," "reverse stings," and public shaming. "John schools" are diversion programs designed for those arrested for solicitation of prostitution. These programs generally provide presentations on the impacts of prostitution on communities, health risks, and impact on survivors. The latter is akin to victim impact panels provided by groups like Mothers Against Drunk Driving to educate those convicted of driving under the

---

24. European Parliament Briefing Paper. "Ekberg estimates—based on various cases reported to the Swedish Ministry of Industry, Employment, and Communications—that the number of prostitutes in Sweden decreased rather substantially from 2500 in 1999 to 1500 in 2002, with street prostitution in particular decreasing by between 30–50% after the prohibition of prostitution." In contrast, both prostitution and trafficking increased in Denmark and Germany after legalization; Cho, Dreher, and Neumayer, "Does Legalized Prostitution Increase Human Trafficking?" See also European Parliament Report, section 3.5.2, discussing Sweden's law "the demand of sexual services seems to have halved." Also, the Report notes, from 1995 to 2008 (the law passed in 1999), there was a 50% decrease in street prostitution. Further, in a 1996 survey, "around 13.6% of men stated that they had bought sex, while in 2008 this number had fallen to 8%" (Sweden).

influence about the impacts of drunk driving related death and injury on survivors and their families. Currently the length of time of these programs ranges from 15 minutes viewing of a video to 6 hours.

Reverse stings are conducted in the context of street prostitution, online prostitution, and brothel prostitution. In each case police officers pose as women in prostitution and arrest those who solicit them. Public shaming aims to stigmatize buyers of sex by publicly revealing their identities. Sometimes this method involves publishing johns' names in newspapers, or websites, or on billboards. Sometimes this method involves a "Dear John" letter sent to the home of a person whose car license plate was recorded by police observing them in locations known for street prostitution. Other demand reduction strategies include: community service, suspension of driver's licenses of persons convicted of solicitation, public education and awareness programs, auto seizure, and surveillance cameras as deterrents.

None of these demand reduction strategies are as effective as criminal sanctions for buyers, specifically the threat of jail time and large fines. In empirical research conducted with sex buyers in multiple countries, sex buyers report that the most effective deterrents are being named a sex offender and threat of criminal charges that include incarceration and public exposure.[25]

25. Melissa Farley, Julie Bindel, and Jacqueline M. Golding, *Men Who Buy Sex: Who They Buy and What they Know*, available at http://prostitutionresearch.com/2009/03/01/men-who-buy-sex-london-2009/

3.3 MEN WHO BUY SEX

An empirically informed understanding of men who buy sex is critically important for a full analysis of prostitution as a social practice of inequality. The overwhelming focus of research into prostitution is on the women who are bought and sold.[26] One set of researchers claim that as much as 99% of prostitution research is focused on women in prostitution.[27] However, recently some researchers have turned their attention to the men who buy sex in order to better understand them and their attitudes and behaviors. This research into the demand side of prostitution is necessary for understanding its structure and developing policy proposals to address its harms.

Important results of this research reveal the relationship between sexual violence and buying women in prostitution. Various studies have been conducted, in different cultures and across legal approaches to prostitution (contexts in which it is illegal, legal, fully decriminalized, and in countries who have adopted the Nordic Model). The research into attitudes and behaviors of sex buyers demonstrates that there is remarkable uniformity among the men who buy sex, independent of the cultural milieu (e.g., Phnom Penh and London) and legal approach to prostitution in their location. Buyers of sex are more likely to hold hostile attitudes toward women, more likely to acknowledge having committed acts of sexual aggression

---

26. Melissa Farley, Jacqueline M. Golding, Emily Schuckman Matthews, Neil M. Malamuth, and Laura Jarrett, "Comparing Sex Buyers with Men Who Do Not Buy Sex: New Data on Prostitution and Trafficking," *Journal of Interpersonal Violence* 32 (2017): 3601–25.

27. Ibid.

both against women in prostitution and women not in prostitution, less empathy, are more likely to accept rape myths, and use pornography at a higher rate than non-sex buyers.[28]

One study compared attitudes and behaviors of men who buy sex and men who do not.[29] The studies were designed to measure the relationship between sexual aggression and users of women in prostitution. The social scientific tools used to measure sexual aggression were drawn from Malamuth's Confluence Model of Sexual Aggression,[30] a tool for predicting sexual violence that measures multiple factors that comprise "the characteristics of men likely to commit sexual aggression."[31] Thus the model aggregates a number of factors that together constitute a collection of characteristics that predict men's likelihood of acting in sexually violent ways.

The two strongest predictors of sexual aggression within the Confluence Model are hostile masculinity and impersonal sex.[32] "Hostile masculinity is a personality profile combining hostile-distrustful orientation, particularly toward women, with attitudes supporting aggression

28. A number of studies yield these results. See for example: Victor Markarek, *The Johns: Sex for Sale and the Men Who Buy It* (New York: Arcade Publishing, 2011); Farley et al., "Comparing Sex Buyers With Men Who Do Not Buy Sex"; Farley, Bindel, and Golding, *Men Who Buy Sex*; Melissa Farley, Wendy Freed, Kien Serey Phal, and Jaqueline Golding, "A Thorn in the Heart: Cambodian Men Who Buy Sex" (2012), available online at http://prostitutionresearch.com/2012/07/17/a-thorn-in-the-heart-cambodian-men-who-buy-sex.

29. Farley et al., "Comparing Sex Buyers With Men Who Do Not Buy Sex."

30. Ibid.

31. Ibid.

32. Ibid., p. 4.

against women such as rape myth acceptance, and sexual gratification via domination of women."[33] It also "includes hypersensitivity to rejection by women."[34] Impersonal sex is defined as frequent, causal sexual relationships often with a high number of sex partners.[35] When these two traits are present together they are effective predictors of sexual aggression. The studies that Melissa Farley and her collaborators conducted on sex buyers show that men who buy sex score higher on these two measures—hostile masculinity and impersonal sex—than men do who not buy sex.

Examples of interviewee comments, in the UK study, include: "Prostitution is like masturbating without having to use your hand"; "My favorite experience in prostitution was when she was totally submissive"; "Look, men pay for women because he can have whatever and whoever he wants. Lots of men go to prostitutes so they can do things to them that real women would not put up with." Other comments emphasize the financial nature of the "transaction."[36] In a study of sex buyers in Boston, some of the most striking comments are as follows: "She is just a biological object that charges for services"; "They don't enjoy it at all. They just blank their mind out. Men think they enjoy it, but it's just fake"; "Being with a prostitute is like having a cup of coffee, when you're done, you throw it out."[37] In the Cambodian

33. Ibid.
34. Ibid.
35. Ibid.
36. Melissa Farley, Julie Bindel, and Jacqueline M. Golding, "Men Who Buy Sex and What They Know" (2009), available online at http://prostitutionresearch.com/2009/03/01/men-who-buy-sex-london-2009/
37. Farley et al., "Comparing Sex Buyers with Men Who Do Not Buy Sex."

study, some relevant quotes from buyers: "Prostitution is
the man's heaven but it also those girls' hell"; "All the power
is in the hands of the brothel owners, while prostitutes
were just the machines following orders"; "When we were
at the brothel we negotiated with the brothel owner. It was
like buying a baby pig"; "Seeing gang rape in the movies, the
girl always agreed to it, but in Cambodia, the girl taken for
gang rape was always beaten."[38]

A recent study of brothel reviews by sex buyers in
both legalized (Australia) and fully decriminalized (New
Zealand) locales further reveals the sense of entitlement
and normalization of violence in the attitudes of men who
buy women for sex.[39] The authors of this research reviewed
posts and comments on user run and moderated sites that
host reviews of brothels and particular women in them.
The reviews reveal buyer practices, attitudes, and desires
for particular sex acts, as well as how they "evaluate" the
women that they bought sex from. Jonovski and Tyler
note that the reviews document attitudes of buyers that
reduce women to things (sexual objectification). For example, one buyer posted: "I knew this one was a jizagargler
so I thought I'd add to the collection. Fucked *it* in the arse,
fucked *its* mouth then gave *it* something warm to taste."[40]
They also document men's preference and exercise of pressure for women to have sex without condoms, preference
for power and exertion of force, and expectations that

38. Farley et al., "A Thorn in the Heart."

39. Natalie Jovanoski and Megan Tyler, "'Bitch, You Got What You
Deserved!': Violation in Sex Buyer Reviews of Legal Brothels," *Violence
Against Women* (2018). DOI: i10.177/107780121875737

40. Ibid., p. 9.

because they have paid money, they are entitled to have their desires met on their terms.

Several further observations are worth highlighting: First, and again, the ways in which buyers describe their attitudes and behaviors toward women, and women in prostitution specifically, corresponds to the ways in which women in prostitution describe their experience and the harms they endure. For example, a study investigating women's emotional responses to engaging in prostitution found that 90% of women described their experience with negative emotional terms, such as sad, distraught, hopeless, worthless, disgusting, angry, irritated, numb, detached, scared, fearful, anxious, hurt, degraded, and humiliated.[41] Some women who have left prostitution and now engage in activism against prostitution have expressed the connections between the recent #metoo movement and their experiences in prostitution. Autumn Burris, Founding Director, Survivors for Solutions stated: "Prostitution is #MeToo on steroids due to the hourly sexual harassment, rape, unwanted advances/penetration and aggressive and violent behavior by white, privileged men sexually commodifying our bodies."[42]

The second important observation is, as Farley et al. write: "These findings are more consistent with an understanding of prostitution as sexual aggression rather

41. Lisa A. Kramer, "Emotional Experienced of Performing Prostitution," in *Prostitution, Trafficking, and Traumatic Stress*, ed. Melissa Farely (New York: Routledge, 2010), 187–97.

42. http://prostitutionresearch.com/pre_blog/2018/04/11/metoo-what-prostitution-survivors-say-about-the-links-between-prostitution-and-sexual-harassment-and-rape/

than as sexual labor."[43] Specifically, this statement aims to draw attention to the facts that buyers have greater hostility toward women, including women in prostitution, and have demonstrable aggressive beliefs and behaviors toward women, including the women they use in prostitution. They are not simply buying a sexual "release" as it is sometimes said, they are buying the opportunity to act out on a human being, their masturbation fantasy, which is frequently a sexually aggressive behavior learned from pornography.

Further, a study in South Korea (2018) shows "that buying sex is positively associated with a sex crime and the experience of paying for sex with a minor exacerbates the severity of sex crimes."[44] Prostitution is illegal in South Korea, and the author notes that the data here are restricted to that context. However, insofar as the evidence collected here shows a positive correlation between buying sex and sex crimes, there may be good reasons to reject the claim that decriminalization or legalization will have the effect of reducing sex crimes. Cho's research into the relationship between buying sex and sex crimes aims, in part, to undermine the claim that those who buy sex (use women in prostitution) are deterred from committing sex crimes against non-prostituting women since they use women in prostitution instead. In other words, it is sometimes claimed that if women in prostitution are available to "satisfy" the sexual needs of men, then those same men are less likely to

43. Farley et al., "Comparing Sex Buyers With Men Who Do Not Buy Sex," p. 16.

44. Seo-Young Cho, "An Analysis of Sexual Violence: The Relationship between Sex Crimes and Prostitution in South Korea," *Asian Development Perspectives* 9, no. 2 (2018): 12–34.

commit sex crimes because women in prostitution serve to ameliorate the "need" to commit such crimes. There is no evidence for the argument that prostitution reduces rape rates in the general population.

Cho's research shows that "if a sex offender has visited prostitutes more often in the past year, he was more likely to commit a sex crime."[45] Moreover, "This effect holds for all types of sex crimes in question (sexual assaults, forced sex with a stranger, and forced sex with a partner), as well as for all age groups of prostitutes (adults and minors)."[46] Cho draws the conclusion that "the experience of buying sex has substantial explanatory power over the probability of one committing a sex crime." Part of the larger explanation is the correlation between sex buyers and sex offender's acceptance of rape myths, which Cho's research demonstrates and Farley's larger research on buyers also shows.

Research into and knowledge of the demand side of prostitution is critical for developing effective policy positions that address the institution of prostitution as it actually functions. Legalization and full decriminalization both create the conditions for demand to flourish unabated, and thus provide legal cover for the exploitation and harms that occur through prostitution. The Nordic Model, in contrast, by attacking demand aims to address the root causes of such exploitation and harm. In the final section of this chapter, I turn to consider the criticisms of the Nordic Model and offer suggestions for practical improvements.

45. Ibid., p. 22.
46. Ibid., p. 22.

3.4 CRITICISMS OF THE NORDIC MODEL

Criticisms of the Nordic Model can be divided into two broad sets: those that target the rationale for it and those that claim it leads to bad or unacceptable consequences. Both categories of criticisms were raised during the legislative discussions of the Nordic Model in Sweden, and following its passage. Those who opposed it, and those who continue to oppose it, offer the following criticisms:

1. Criminalizing the buyers is likely to drive prostitution "underground" (Flanigan raises this objection)
2. Street prostitution (often conflated with "underground prostitution") is less safe than brothel or "indoor" prostitution
3. That the Nordic Model would result in an increase in violence against persons in prostitution
4. That the Nordic Model would lead to an increase in "unsafe" sex practices by persons in prostitution
5. That "sex work" is generally freely chosen and persons who "chose" to engage in it have a human right to do so (Flanigan makes a version of this objection)
6. That the philosophical/theoretical framework that underlies the Nordic Model assumes that prostitution cannot be freely chosen, and as such its defenders "deny the agency" of persons in prostitution
7. That the Nordic Model is an unjustifiable form of paternalism.

The first five of these are empirical claims about which we have evidence that contradicts or seriously mutes these criticisms. In 2010, ten years after the passage of the Swedish law, the government of Sweden issued a report evaluating the impacts of the law. The report considers the impacts on prostitution, sex trafficking, as well as the application of the ban on purchase of sexual services by police and other legal administrators.

The empirical findings in the report that bear on these criticisms include the following:

1. A reduction in the number of persons in street prostitution. "Since the introduction of the ban on the purchase of sexual services, street prostitution in Sweden has been reduced by half."[47] The analysis offered in the report attributes this reduction directly to the law banning purchase of sex. This conclusion is drawn, in part, by comparing the levels of street prostitution in Norway, Denmark and Sweden before and after the Swedish law. Prior to the passage of the law, the prevalence of street prostitution in these three places was comparable.[48] As of 2008 (nine years after the law was passed), "the number of people in street prostitution in both Norway and Denmark was estimated to be three

47. Swedish Government Report: "Selected Extracts of the Swedish Government Report SOU 2010:49: The Ban against the Purchase of Sexual Services. An Evaluation 1999–2008," published by Swedish Institute (November 2010), available at https://ec.europa.eu/antitrafficking/sites/antitrafficking/files/the_ban_against_the_purchase_of_sexual_services._an_evaluation_1999-2008_1.pdf, p. 7.
48. Ibid., p. 7.

times higher than in Sweden."[49] The authors of the report go on to note the economic and cultural similarities between these places, and infer that the explanation of the drop in street prostitution in Sweden is a direct result of the law. Moreover, in 2009 Norway passed a similar demand directed law (criminalizing the buying but not selling of sex) and a similar drop in street prostitution immediately followed.[50]

2. Directly addressing the claim that the criminal ban on purchase of sex would "drive prostitution underground," the report states although there is more Internet prostitution in Sweden than previously, there is no evidence that increase is greater than comparative neighboring countries. In other words, if the claim that the ban would drive more prostitution "underground," then you'd expect to see an increase in "indoor" prostitution (of which prostitution via the Internet is one type). But, the empirical evidence doesn't support this prediction. The authors of the report conclude: "This indicates that the ban has not led to a change in arenas, that is, from street prostitution to the Internet, in Sweden. In light of this it should be possible to conclude that the reduction of street prostitution by half that took place in Sweden represents a real reduction in prostitution here and that this reduction is also mainly a result of the criminalization of sex purchases."[51]

49. Ibid., p. 7.
50. Ibid., p. 8.
51. Ibid., p. 8.

Part of the explanation of the decrease in prostitution is the effect of the law on public attitudes including those of buyers. At the time of the report, based on multiple surveys, 70% of respondents indicated they viewed the ban positively. The surveys indicate that the law acts as a deterrent for buyers with some respondents indicating that as a result of the ban they no longer buy sex.[52] Max Waltman, a Swedish political scientist, who conducted extensive analysis of the law in Sweden and "the Nordic Model" more broadly, documents a reduction in demand as well. He writes: "the number of men who reported, in the national population samples, having purchased sex seems to have dropped from 12.7% in 1996 (before the law took effect) to 7.6% in 2008."[53] Apart from the obvious reason that sex buyers are deterred insofar as they do not want to be arrested or convicted for a crime, part of the explanation has to do with a shift in attitudes as a result of the public campaign in favor of the law. The Swedish culture prides itself on a commitment to gender equality and the message that buying sex is not compatible with gender equality and the dignity of prostituted persons was effective.

The law has not only reduced demand, and thus actual purchasing of women, but also has shaped public attitudes toward prostitution. Thus an important, but not frequently noted consequence of the law, is the shift in the stigma associated with prostitution, from women in prostitution to men whose demand as buyers fuels prostitution.[54] One of

52. Ibid., p. 9.

53. Waltman, "Prohibiting Sex Purchasing and Ending Trafficking: The Swedish Prostitution Law." Waltman's work is particularly helpful and informative to English speakers, for he translates many texts that are not available in English.

54. MacKinnon emphasizes this point, "Trafficking, Prostitution, Inequality," p. 302.

the common arguments advocates of full decriminalization or legalization make is that "the problem" with prostitution, sex work in their words, is that it is stigmatized and the harms that persons in prostitution face include stigma and devaluing their "work" as work. They go on to argue that removing such stigma by normalizing or legitimizing sex work is a critical part of improving the lives of persons in prostitution. Defenders of the Nordic Model can readily agree that stigma of prostituted persons is misplaced, harmful, and an instantiation of inequality. Projecting reactive attitudes of disgust and shame onto prostituted persons is a powerful form of devaluing and erasing their status as persons. But the solution is to address the substantive inequalities that asymmetrically situated them as inferior, not to elevate the conditions under which they are bought and sold to "normal" or "legitimate." The Nordic Model in calling out and addressing the asymmetry of power that underwrites practices of prostitution shifts attention from stigmatizing women in prostitution to those that abuse and use their unjust social power and privilege to exploit and coerce sex from persons in prostitution.

A further and important consequence of the ban is a reduction in sex trafficking in Sweden. This is a stark contrast with its neighboring countries. Several studies by economists demonstrate this claim. These studies were discussed earlier, but to repeat: legalization and decriminalization increase persons in prostitution, including persons trafficked for purposes of sexual exploitation, into those locales. The comparison between Sweden and Demark demonstrates this. "In 1999, Demark decriminalized sex buying and sex selling; whereas in 1999, Sweden criminalized sex buying and decriminalized sex selling. After the enactment of this legislation, estimates show between 1999 and 2002 prostitution in Sweden dropped between 30% and 50%. Conversely, in 2008 estimates show that street prostitution in Denmark—with a population size 40% smaller than Sweden—to be three to four times higher."[55]

3. The claims that persons in prostitution would be less safe, face more violence, and engage in "unsafe" sex practices as result of the ban have not been borne out either.[56] And importantly, related claims that women in prostitution would be more likely to have an adversarial relationship with law enforcement are not true. Mathieson et al., conducted interviews in Sweden with women in prostitution and law enforcement, more than after the passage of the law (2013), they report: "The officers also stated that nine-tenths of the women encountered were willing to provide statements against buyers. Many of the women expressed resentment towards the buyers. It can be argued that, since women under the Nordic model are not penalized for prostitution, they have a far more equal relationship with police than women under criminalization regimes. Women identified as victims in prostitution are empowered to speak more fully about their experiences and to know that they have protection under the law."[57]

---

55. Mathieson, Branam, and Noble, "Prostitution Policy."
56. "The Swedish Report," p. 9.
57. Mathieson, Branam, and Noble, "Prostitution Policy," p. 409.

The fact that many of the predictions of bad consequences and objections about the theoretical approach underpinning the Nordic Model turn out to be unfounded does not mean the law is perfect, as it is, or could not be improved. Max Waltman documents some of the obstacles to effective implementation in his research.

Some of the most important challenges have followed from judicial decisions interpreting the law. A 2001 Swedish Supreme Court decision held that whether the person in prostitution "consented" to the acts was relevant for several features of the law.[58] This decision implied that purchasing sex "was primarily a crime against the public order and not primarily against her as a person."[59] This interpretation of the law is not consistent with the legislative findings and intent of the law, for it frames the injury, as so the crime of the buyer, as the diffuse harm of disrupting public order, rather than the injury of exploitation of the women on the basis of sex.

As a consequence, the law was not interpreted to allow damages for persons in prostitution (against those that have harmed them). Waltman argues this decision is misguided for several reasons: the penalties for such crimes are lower than penalties for crimes against persons and so law enforcement subsequently lowered their priority in enforcing the law. Also, interpreting the law as a crime against the person rather than "against public order" is necessary for the award of damages to the injured person. Moreover, the fundamental rationale of the Nordic Model is that

58. Waltman, "Prohibiting Sex Purchasing and Ending Trafficking: The Swedish Prostitution Law," p. 153.
59. Ibid.

asymmetries of power, on the basis of sex, that underwrite and support practices of prostitution are both violations of sex equality and exploitative of particular women (persons). Remedying those violations, and rectifying the social circumstances of inequality that produce them, is central to the purpose of the law. Achieving that purpose requires holding buyers accountable, not only by imposing criminal penalties, but also by requiring restitution to the persons they have injured. The ability to impose "damages on the purchaser creates both an economic opportunity—that the state does not have to pay for—to facilitate the prostituted person's escape, and well as an incentive for the prostituted person to testify against her sex purchasers, an incentive that is currently lacking."[60]

The administration of the Nordic Model could use some improvement. In particular, as Max Waltman argues with regard to Sweden's legal decisions interpreting the law, the decisions just described limit the law's potential for effectively holding buyers accountable and funding the services needed for persons in prostitution. Nonetheless, the basic conceptual approach is sound public policy, both as it aims to elevate the status of persons in prostitution and in targeting those that harm and exploit their vulnerability.

Objections 5–7 were considered in detail in chapter 1. As argued there, they rest on confusions or mistakes of fact and correcting these errors is so important that some repetition of responses is warranted. Objections 5 and 6 are related, but 5 is an empirical claim that most persons in prostitution have, in fact, freely chosen to enter and remain in. We have seen a wealth of evidence contradict this claim.

60. Ibid., p. 156.

As documented throughout my contribution, inequality and vulnerability due to various forms of inequality are push factors into prostitution. Exit, once in prostitution, is very difficult, requires many attempts, and a lot of support.

Objection 6 raises the question as to how to best define "free choice" and "agency." Some critics of the Nordic Model, including Flanigan, claim that those terms should be understood in ways that count choices, under conditions of inequality and severely constrained options, as nonetheless free in a significant sense. Further, they draw the conclusion that if such choices are meaningfully free, then the state should not adopt policies that interfere with those choices. In essence, much of the debate can be focused on the arguments here.

It is worth repeating the empirical facts and observations of persons directly involved with assessing "how free" those in prostitution, in fact, are. The Rapporteur to the European Union Committee on Equality and Non-Discrimination makes this point forcefully when he writes: "In Germany, like elsewhere, I heard different opinions on whether prostitution may or may not be voluntary. Only some sex workers and a few people working in their organisations claimed that prostitution can be the result of free choice. After listening to these people and to those who work in organisations helping victims of trafficking and sex workers who try to leave prostitution, I am inclined to think that voluntary, free and independent prostitution—free from exploitation—is little more than a myth, it applies to a small minority of sex workers."[61]

61. José Mendes Bota, "Prostitution, Trafficking and Modern Slavery in Europe," report by Committee on Equality and Non-Discrimination, Parliamentary Assembly, European Union, 2014, available at http://

Further in that report, in describing the situation in the Netherlands after the lift of the brothel ban, it is noted that the law (of 2000) has "substantially failed to achieve its goals"; "the link between prostitution and trafficking, even in registered establishments, has become increasingly strong"; "A 2008 report of the KLPD, the national police, states that between 50% and 90% of those in licensed prostitution work involuntarily"; and that "the majority of the prostitution industry there remains under the control of organized crime."[62]

Arguments to the effect that even if entry into prostitution is structured by inequality that functions as a form of coercion, notably for a class of persons on the basis of gender, the state should nonetheless adopt a permissive policy (either decriminalization or legalization) effectively abandon principles of sex equality. Abstracting away from the historical and material conditions of women's social and political subordination, including the dominant social norms that situate women, as a class, as the sexual servants of men's needs and desires, abandons women to that status quo.

The paternalism objection was dealt with at length in chapter 1. To repeat: paternalism occurs when someone (including the government) prevents persons from acting in particular ways because those ways of acting are thought to be contrary "to their own good." The Nordic Model neither

semantic-pace.net/tools/pdf.aspx?doc=aHR0cDovL2Fzc2VtYmx5LmNv
ZS5pbnQvbncveG1sL1hSZWYvWDJILURXLWV4dHIuYXNwP2ZpbGV
pZD0yMDU1OSZsYW5nPUVO&xsl=aHR0cDovL3NlbWFudGljcGFjZS5
uZXQvWHNsdC9QZGYvWFJlZi1XRC1BVC1YTUwyUERGLnhzbA==&x
sltparams=ZmlsZWlkPTIwNTU5

62. Ibid.

prevents nor penalizes persons who engage in prostitution. It targets third parties, buyers, pimps, and procurers for the harms inflicted upon persons in prostitution, including channeling and keeping vulnerable persons in prostitution. Moreover, as I note elsewhere "whether some law is paternalistic is a matter of the reasons, the justifications, offered for the law, not the consequences it has. After all, many laws have the consequence limiting behaviors; that fact alone does not establish that laws are paternalistic."[63] The justification for the Nordic Model does not rely on paternalistic reasons. The justification is grounded in a commitment to sex equality principles.

Yet Flanigan objects that even if the justification of the Nordic Model is not paternalistic, it still has the effect of limiting opportunities for women to engage in prostitution insofar as they may have fewer "clients," men deterred by the law. Further, she objects that the Nordic Model violates "sex workers rights" as she argues that persons have a right to engage in sex for any reason, assuming it is consensual. To address the limited opportunities argument first: As documented throughout my contribution, prostitution is the result of foreclosed opportunities, most often "choice" of last resort or the product of force. And again, once there, exit from it is exceedingly difficult. Thus, one way of framing the disagreement between Flanigan and I on this point is to ask: Where should we invest our energies in creating opportunities for women in prostitution? Should we, per Flanigan's suggestion, invest them in

63. Lori Watson, "The State of the Question: Philosophical Debates about Prostitution," *Southern Journal of Philosophy* 57, no. 2 (June 2019): 165–193.

creating open markets in prostitution? Or should we structure our policies such that prostitution is understood as a practice of sex-based exploitation rather than an "opportunity"? Throughout my contribution, I have aimed to make the case for the latter position.

As to Flanigan's claim that the Nordic Model violates the rights of persons in prostitution because it penalizes buyers, the argument is premised on the claim that persons have a moral, natural, or pre-political in some sense, right to sell sex. From this premise, she infers that any state policy that acts as an obstacle to the exercise of that right is unjustified. Aside from the fact that prostitution interferes with the exercise of many other rights of persons in prostitution, this argument moves from the right to engage in some activity to the right to markets in that activity. Flanigan advances this argument from a broader commitment to libertarian political philosophy. A full argument against libertarian political philosophy is beyond the scope of this work. However, what is important to emphasize for the purposes of evaluating libertarian approaches to prostitution is that libertarianism emphasizes freedom over equality. Moreover, libertarians generally emphasize the value of negative freedom—freedom from interference—as the kind of freedom states ought to protect. Securing the basic conditions for exercising freedom involves removing obstacles to individual choices, not empowering individuals to make autonomous choices.

As such, it is fair to say that libertarians, generally, have a fairly impoverished appreciation of the way that social forms of power serve to shape individuals' choice, opportunities, and ability to effectively exercise their rights. Even if particular libertarians have such an understanding of social power, they would deny that the state is the appropriate outlet for redressing such inequalities. Libertarians are avid defenders of "free market principles" thinking the market, and not the state, is the appropriate mechanism for addressing inequality.

As noted in Flanigan's contribution, one way the libertarian commitment to open markets is essential to securing freedom is the argument that whatever is morally permissible to gift to another person is equally permissible to sell to them. The basic claim here is that if we are free to gift something, restricting an economic market to sell the same item, good, or service we can give away is an unacceptable restriction on freedom. Critical engagement with this argument exposes the inadequate theory of power, or the absence of an understanding of the way market forces transform power relations, in libertarian political philosophy.

Before thinking through the argument concerning whether whatever we are free to gift, we ought to be free to sell, it is worth pausing to think about whether sex is properly understood as a "gift" or something persons "give away." Conceptualizing sex as such seems to rest on a particularly heteronormative conception of sex, in which sex is something women "give" to men. Generally speaking, it seems odd to characterize sex as a "gift exchange."

Nonetheless, even if we accept the analogy, the argument that follows is flawed. Gifts are not economic exchanges; they do not introduce reciprocal obligations between gift giver and gift recipient. A gift receiver may owe some form of gratitude, however whether gratitude is an appropriate response will vary contextually and contingently upon the relationship between the giver and receiver. An unexpected and unwanted gift from an acquaintance seeking to ingratiate themselves through a gift may give rise to no obligation of gratitude and may warrant resentment on the part of the receiver. The point is that the practice of gift giving doesn't entail reciprocal obligations between the gifter and receiver. Gifts do not obligate the receiver to reciprocate, nor do they empower the receiver to make further claims upon the gift giver.

In contrast, economic exchanges transform relationships and introduce new obligations in ways that gift giving does not. Contrast two cases: I may offer you my loyalty, as a kind of gift. In so doing, I may announce due to my assessment of your character, commitments, and so on, I will engage you as a loyal ally in our common aims. Consider an alternative scenario in which I offer to sell you my loyalty in exchange for money or some other good. The economic nature of this exchange transforms the meaning of "loyalty" and introduces a distinct set of obligations, demands you can make upon me, should I wish to withdraw my commitment to act as a loyal ally. In the case of the gift of loyalty, an expression of a kind of mutual friendship and alliance, my shift or pronouncement that I can no longer offer my loyalty in good faith, should lead you to reflect on where our shared commitments broke down. Or may lead you to engage in critical self-examination about the ways in which your behavior triggered a breakdown in our alliance, in our shared commitments. In the case in which you have paid for my loyalty, surely an underlying recognition that such loyalty is contingent and not genuine shapes the exchange and interaction. That the loyalty is given in exchange for an economic reward confers powers upon the person paying to make demands. It also suggests there is no real loyalty there. The idea that when something is gifted and when something is bought and sold doesn't fundamentally alter the nature of the thing—such as loyalty or friendship—introduces new and different expectations and obligations is simply implausible. The analysis fails to acknowledge the ways in which markets transform the relationships, and the goods, exchanged, as I argued in chapter 1.

Thus, the move Flanigan wants to make from a right to have sex to a right to sell sex is not at all straightforward. Economic exchanges, and markets more broadly, transform relations between persons and introduce power dynamics that require investigation and evaluation. Economic exchanges and markets can, and do, undermine rights and place persons in unequal power relations that threaten their rights, including the right to equality. This is nowhere more clear than in the case of prostitution, as documented throughout my contribution.

3.5 CONCLUSION

The argument presented here for the Nordic Model rests on a commitment to sex equality. Prostitution as a social practice and institution is premised upon and perpetuates sex inequality. Given the asymmetrical position of persons in prostitution relative to men who buy sex, laws should not target persons in prostitution. Rather, targeting demand, the buyers of sex, is the best way to end sexual exploitation of persons in prostitution.

Defenders of the Nordic Model refuse to accept that prostitution is inevitable and that the best we can do is to attempt to make it "less bad" or "reduce harms." In contrast, the Nordic Model, rests on the understanding "that any society that claims to defend principles of legal, political, economic, and social equality for women and girls must reject the idea that women and children, mostly girls, are commodities that can be bought, sold, and sexually exploited by men. To do otherwise is to allow that a separate class of female human beings, especially women and girls who are economically and racially marginalized, is excluded from these measures, as well as from the universal protection of human dignity enshrined in the body of international human rights instruments developed during the past 50 years."[64]

64. Gunilla Ekberg, "The Swedish Law that Prohibits the Purchase of Sexual Services Best Practices for Prevention of Prostitution and Trafficking in Human Beings," *Violence Against Women* 10, no. 10 (October 2004): 1187–1218. DOI: 10.1177/1077801204268647, quote from Ministry of Industry, Employment, and Communications in Sweden, p. 1189.

PART 2

IN DEFENSE

OF DECRIMINALIZATION

JESSICA FLANIGAN

The Case
for Decriminalization

SEX WORK SHOULD BE DECRIMINALIZED because the criminalization of sex work violates the rights of sex workers and
their clients and it has bad consequences. In the first phase
of the argument for decriminalization, I make the case for
decriminalization directly. In the second phase, I engage
with objections to decriminalization and further consider
arguments in favor of criminalization, legalization, and the
Nordic Model.

The case for decriminalization has three parts. First,
criminalization violates the rights of sex workers and
their clients. Second, decriminalization would be better
on balance for sex workers' and clients' well-being, and
sex markets do not impose morally comparable harms on
others. Third, criminalization is inegalitarian. Laws that
prohibit the sale or purchase of sex subordinate economically vulnerable sex workers and socially marginalized
clients to public officials.

Many scholars, activists, and officials oppose decriminalization. Some people reject the claim that criminalization violates rights. They argue that people do not have
a right to buy and sell sex and that officials may rightly

Debating Sex Work. Lori Watson, Jessica Flanigan, Oxford University
Press (2020). © Oxford University Press.
DOI: 10.1093/oso/9780190659882.001.0001

prohibit consensual choices which are involuntary, exploitative, or degrading. A second set of opponents to decriminalization reject the claim that decriminalization would be better for sex workers' and clients' well-being. One form of this objection relies on the claim that decriminalization would increase the prevalence of sex work, which is worse than other jobs. Another form of this objection asserts that the sex industry has negative externalities, such as increased rates of sexual transmission of disease, human trafficking, rape, or crime. A third group of opponents to decriminalization reject egalitarian arguments for decriminalizing sex work. Instead, they claim that a decriminalized sex industry would exacerbate existing economic or social inequalities. These objections operate at two levels. First, some egalitarian critics may argue that, as an empirical matter, the decriminalization of sex work would make inequality worse. Second, egalitarian critics may argue that, as a conceptual matter, arguments for the decriminalization of sex work implicitly rely on premises that deny the legitimacy of other policies that promote social and economic equality.

Throughout this analysis, I will develop arguments that fall along a spectrum of idealization. At one end of this spectrum are ideal-theoretic arguments. Proponents of criminalization, the Nordic Model, and legalization, sometimes caution that we should evaluate the best version of these policies, rather than looking at how they are actually implemented. In other words, we should evaluate arguments about which policy would be best by imagining which policy we would support if any kind of policy were possible. But I will argue that, if our policy ambitions were not constrained by political feasibility, then the best kind of sex industry policy would be one that permitted people to trade sexual services for money, but which also allowed freedom of movement and provided a reliable social safety net, effective legal representation, and care for dependent children.

Non-ideal theoretic arguments are at the other end of the spectrum of idealization. Proponents of criminalization, prohibition, and regulation, sometimes caution that we should evaluate policies by looking at how they are actually implemented. Here again, the case for decriminalization is stronger than the case for criminalization, prohibition, or even regulation. But the evidence for this claim is fraught on all sides. New Zealand's approach to the sex industry most closely approximates the full decriminalization that I favor, whereas the polices that have been adopted by Canadians, Swedes, and Norwegians most closely approximate the Nordic Model that Watson favors. Yet it is difficult to compare these models as they are actually enforced because New Zealand is very different from Canada, Sweden, and Norway. Different countries have different demographic, social, and economic conditions which would affect whether they would experience the same benefits or difficulties associated with the Nordic Model or decriminalization. To a degree, debates about the merits of each model are explained by different interpretations of the relevant empirical evidence. But these debates do not entirely depend on which interpretation of the evidence is accurate because even in non-ideal circumstances the Nordic Model violates the rights of sex workers and their clients and decriminalization does not.

Of course, even so-called idealized accounts consider some political realities, such as scarcity of resources or people's tendency to act in their own self-interest. And even non-ideal theoretic arguments include some element of idealization in that they prescribe what public officials ought to do rather than just describing what they will likely do. In general, empirical claims about the health effects of decriminalization, or its effect on crime and trafficking, or arguments that cite evidence from New Zealand are generally aimed against the set of arguments in favor of the Nordic Model as it is actually enforced. Arguments that appeal to concepts like rights, voluntariness, relational equality, or economic justice are generally addressing ideal-theoretic arguments in favor of the Nordic Model.

A final word on the use of empirical evidence in this argument. Watson and I both compare the effects of decriminalization to the effects of the Nordic Model, legalization, and criminalization by citing the available evidence, while acknowledging that the available evidence is often weak. Many of the relevant studies of different policies are either inconclusive qualitative analyses, such as ethnographic research, or correlational analyses that provide only limited evidence of causation. In places where sex work is criminalized or heavily regulated, researchers who study the effects of these policies struggle to distinguish the negative effects of law enforcement from the negative effects of participating in the industry more generally. It is also difficult to know the extent that the negative aspects of the sex industry can be explained by broader cultural forces, economic inequality, patriarchy, or stigma associated with sex work. Making matters worse, there is a great deal of research on both sides that is financed and presented as part of a broader effort at advocacy for particular policies. This alone does not discredit the research, which includes some rigorous and large studies, but it makes it difficult to impartially evaluate the balance of available empirical evidence on questions related to the sex industry.

In light of this empirical uncertainty, I think the burden of proof should rest with proponents of prohibition (in all its forms) to establish that their favored policies would be beneficial to sex workers or beneficial on balance. By this I mean that in cases where the evidence is weak, there should be a presumption against criminalization, prohibition, or regulation. There are three reasons in favor of this presumption, which relate to the arguments I will develop in the next sections. First, prohibitive policies are enforced with coercion. In general, people should use coercion as a last resort. This principle applies to public officials. If coercion is not clearly necessary to achieve a goal, and it is also not clear that coercion will effectively achieve a goal, officials should favor non-coercive approaches instead. So since the necessity or effectiveness of enforcing laws against sex work are uncertain, it is better to avoid wrongfully coercing sex workers and their clients.

Second, the moral risk of enforcing a prohibitive policy exceeds the moral risks of decriminalization for public officials.[1] Say I am correct about decriminalization and yet officials nevertheless wrongfully enforce a prohibitive policy. If so, then officials will cause unjustified harm and violate their moral duty to respect the rights of all participants and potential participants in the sex industry. On the other hand, say I am wrong about decriminalization and yet officials wrongfully nevertheless enforce a

1. For a further explanation of moral risk, see Dan Moller, "Abortion and Moral Risk," *Philosophy* 86, no. 3 (2011): 425–43.

permissive policy. If so, officials still will not necessarily have violated a duty to respect people's rights, at best they would have failed in their more general duty to protect the health and safety of people, which they fail to live up to in all sorts of other ways already.

The third reason in favor of a presumption in favor of decriminalization is specific to the contrast between decriminalization and the Nordic Model. Proponents of the Nordic Model grant that criminalization is harmful, stigmatizing, and counterproductive because subjecting sex workers to criminal penalties makes them even worse off. But many of the reasons against criminalizing the sale of sex are also reasons against criminalizing the purchase of sex. For example, criminalizing the purchase of sex also forces sex workers to operate in black markets, perpetuates stigma against the industry, and exposes sex workers to potential police abuses and interference. So in the absence of clear empirical evidence that establishes that subjecting some people in the sex industry to criminal penalties is good but subjecting other people in the sex industry to criminal penalties is bad, the same general reasons to think that criminalization is mistaken are also reasons to doubt the effectiveness of the Nordic Model. Or, if proponents of the Nordic Model reject the claim that criminalization is presumptively harmful, stigmatizing, and counterproductive, then they must defend the middle ground against proponents of criminalization. Either way, where fine-grained evidence about the comparative effects of different policies is lacking, it is especially difficult to defend the intermediate position advanced by proponents of the Nordic Model on empirical grounds.

These arguments are second-order, meta-normative arguments. By this I mean that these are arguments about how we should approach and assess the evidence about what we should believe, in contrast to arguments about what we should believe. As I make the case for decriminalization, I will focus on the first-order normative arguments for decriminalization, which respond to Watson, and others' first-order normative arguments for the Nordic Model or criminalization. Some readers will be convinced by the first-order normative arguments for decriminalization or for the Nordic Model. For those who remain uncertain though, I propose that there are second-order moral reasons to at least provisionally support decriminalization instead of the Nordic Model.

I begin in this chapter with the strongest argument in favor of decriminalization, as I see it, which is that criminal penalties violate the rights of sex workers and their clients. Adults have rights to have consensual sex with each other for any reason, even if that reason is money. People have these rights because they have rights to decide what to do with their bodies, rights to choose who they associate with, rights to form intimate relationships, and rights to choose their occupation. Implicit in this argument is the assumption that people can have moral rights that are broader than their legal rights. On my view, existing legal regimes that prevent people from buying sexual services or selling sex fail to respect workers' and clients' rights.

The rights-based argument for decriminalization is the strongest argument in that the success of this argument does not depend on contingent empirical facts about whether decriminalization would promote the interests of sex workers, whether it would promote the general welfare, or whether it would achieve social and economic equality. These consequentialist and egalitarian arguments depend more on facts about how markets in sex work actually function under different policy regimes. If sex workers' and clients' rights do not justify decriminalization, then the case for decriminalization rests with these empirically contingent considerations. Yet a close look at the evidence about the effects of criminalization, prohibition, and regulation suggests that decriminalization likely has better consequences for sex workers and their clients relative to these other polices, and better consequences overall as well. Moreover, egalitarian considerations also do not clearly justify criminalization, prohibition, and regulation, especially if we grant that subordination to public officials is as much of an affront to egalitarian ideals as social and economic subordination.

4.1 SEX WORK AND RIGHTS

As I am using the term, to say that someone has a right to do something means that it is permissible for her to do it and that it would be presumptively wrong for someone else to interfere with her freedom to do it. On my view, it is not wrong for people to sell or buy sexual services and it would be presumptively wrong for people to interfere with people on the grounds that they were selling or buying sex. Some people make a further distinction between basic liberties and non-basic liberties. On this view, basic liberties are those that merit strong institutional protections and must not be violated, even for the sake of the greater good.

Non-basic liberties are those that there is a presumption in favor of protecting but which officials may limit in order to achieve other social aims. Elsewhere, I've argued against the distinction between basic and non-basic liberties, on the grounds that all rights should merit strong institutional protections.[2] But for the purposes of my argument in favor of a right to buy and sell sex, I will show that even if one does accept a distinction between basic and non-basic liberties, paradigmatic basic liberties entail a right to sell sexual services.

I present three arguments in favor of rights to sell and pay for sex. First, it is permissible to exchange sex for money because it is permissible for people to have sex for any reason. If a choice is permissible, a pecuniary motivation or reason for making that choice does not transform the choice into an impermissible one. Given that buying and selling sex is permissible, it would be wrong for anyone, even a public official, to interfere with a person's choice to buy or sell sexual services.

These reasons establish a right to sex work. But these arguments rest on the premises that if a choice is permissible then it is permissible to make that choice for money, and that it is wrong for public officials to interfere with people's permissible choices. Many people deny these premises. My second argument is that even if there were some choices which could only be permissibly made without involving money and even if public officials had the authority to interfere with some permissible choices, sex work would still be permissible and officials should not interfere with the

---

2. Jessica Flanigan, "All Liberty Is Basic," *Res Publica* 24, no. 4 (2018): 455–74.

choice to sell or buy sex. To show this, I argue that a right to sell sex is entailed by other basic liberties.

My third argument addresses the Nordic Model. Proponents of this approach may affirm a right to sell sex but deny that there is a right to purchase sexual services. In response, I briefly make the case that there is a right to pay for sex. But even if there is not such a right, if there is a right to sex work then in virtue of sex workers' rights it is wrong to prohibit clients from purchasing sexual services from sex workers.

4.1.1 Permissible Exchanges

The first argument for a right to buy and pay for sex is, as a first pass, that it is permissible to have sex with someone, it is permissible to give money to someone, and it is permissible to accept money from someone. Of course, not all conjunctions of permissible acts are themselves permissible. It could be permissible to promise to lend your car to Joe on Friday, and permissible take your car to work on Friday, but impermissible to do both. But the reason that the conjunction of promising to lend your car on Friday and using your car on Friday is impermissible is because promise-breaking violates Joe's right against being deceived. In sex work, though, the conjunction of having sex and accepting money or having sex and giving money does not constitute an additional rights violation in the way that the conjunction of two permissible acts in Joe's case did.

Begin with the claim that it is permissible to have consensual sex. Assuming that they are not breaking a promise or wrongfully harming someone in some other way, people can permissibly have consensual sex for any reason.[3] It is permissible to have casual sex just for fun. It is permissible to have sex with someone because you hate them and you think hate-sex is a turn on. It is permissible to have sex out of pity. It is permissible to have sex to feel powerful. It is permissible to have sex with someone in order to make an ex jealous. It is permissible to have sex with the brother of someone who borrowed your favorite shoes and threw up on them in order to get revenge against her. In some of these cases, there may be moral considerations against having sex for these reasons, but it is still within a person's rights to choose consensual sexual partners, even if for bad reasons.

It is also generally permissible to pay someone for services or to ask for money for services, assuming that the service itself is permissible. While it would be impermissible to pay someone to cut down your neighbor's tree because you don't like the leaves, it would also be impermissible to ask someone to do it for free. On the other hand, it's permissible to pay your local arborists for their services on your own property, and they may also do it for free. Or, while it would be impermissible to accept money for beating up someone's business rival, this is because beating up people's rivals is impermissible. It's not the presence of payment that makes these exchanges wrong.

---

3. This characterization allows that it can be wrong to have sex for bad reasons in some cases. For example, if having sex consists in one day of fun but it damages a lifelong friendship, and if people have duties to maintain their friendships even at moderate cost to their own well-being, then it could be wrong to have sex in this case but the wrongful action is "damaging a friendship" not sex.

Following this line of reasoning, Jason Brennan and Peter Jaworski develop a more general argument for the permissibility of exchanges that includes a defense of sex work. Essentially, their claim is that "if you may do it for free you may do it for money."[4] There are some qualifications. For example, there may be some acts which are permissible but obligatory, such as rendering a fair judicial verdict. In these cases, a person must do it for free, so if they are doing it for money then it may indicate that they were tacitly threatening to violate a duty. But in general, and at least in the case of sex work, if an act is permissible but not obligatory then it is permissible to do it only on the condition of payment.

But some philosophers argue that even if an act is permissible but not obligatory, it could still be wrong to explicitly request money for it. One reason for this claim is that the introduction of market incentives could change the meaning of some acts in ways that violate the rights of third-parties. If so, then a permissible but not obligatory act may be impermissible if done for money on the grounds that it is impermissible to do things that violate the rights of third-parties. Elizabeth Anderson's arguments against sex work take this form. Anderson argues that a market in sexual services would crowd out the values of voluntary sexual intimacy. She writes, "prostitution is the classic example of the debasement of a gift value through its commodification."[5] On her account, the sex industry is

4. Jason F. Brennan and Peter Jaworski, *Markets without Limits: Moral Virtues and Commercial Interests*, 1st ed. (New York; London: Routledge, 2015).

5. Elizabeth Anderson, "The Ethical Limitations of the Market," *Economics and Philosophy* 6, no. 2 (1990): 179–205.

incompatible with the norms of sexual intimacy in personal relationships such as altruism, mutual appreciation, and reciprocity, which currently characterize sexual intimacy.[6] In contrast, she claims that because sex work is a market exchange, it is inherently self-interested, impersonal, and non-reciprocal.

In response to this argument, I grant the premise that in some cases external harms do require further justification, and can even merit regulation. If a person's car pollutes the air, that person may violate people's rights not to be exposed to lead and other toxins. In this way, driving a car would be impermissible and environmental regulations could be justified on these grounds. But Anderson's argument relies on two other premises which I contest—that the commodification of sex debases the gift value of sex and that debasement of a gift value through commodification is impermissible.

The commodification of sex does not debase the gift value of sex any more than the commodification of any other service debases its gift value. The commodification of housekeeping does not debase the gift value of a person cleaning up after her family. The commodification of food service does not debase the gift value of a homemade meal. Housekeepers can still lovingly clean their own homes and professional cooks can generously prepare home-cooked meals. And in some cases, a service can include both

6. Similarly, Jeppe Von Platz argues that sex work is morally objectionable because it causes people to relate to each other in ways that are inappropriate and invites people to treat each other in ways that are disrespectful. Jeppe von Platz, "Person to Person: A Note on the Ethics of Commodification," *Journal of Value Inquiry* 51, no. 4 (December 1, 2017): 647–53.

gift-values and market values without one crowding out the other. For example, imagine a retail worker who helps customers pick out flattering outfits. Part of the reason she provides the service is because she is paid to be in the store. But she may also find it meaningful to help people look their best and choose to altruistically spend time helping customers when she could just as easily sit at the register and ignore them without penalty.

Nor does commodification necessarily crowd out recipient's perceptions of the gift-value of services. People who pay housekeepers, order food, and go shopping can still appreciate it when their spouses do the dishes, when their neighbors stop by with dinner, or when their friends give them advice about dresses. Similarly, sex workers and clients do not lose their ability to have reciprocal altruistic sex in other contexts because they also are paid or pay for non-reciprocal sexual services.

And it's not clear that there is a gift value intrinsic to sex anyhow. An activity has a gift value if it is characterized by altruism, mutual appreciation, and reciprocity. Some sex outside of the marketplace is like this, but sometimes people have sex for selfish reasons with people they don't like and they don't reciprocate. Granted, selfish, acrimonious, and non-reciprocal sexual encounters are also not ideal, but they don't occur only in places where sex is protected from the market. Historically, people's actual sexual practices have always fallen short of our ideals whether markets in sex work were legal or not. And critics of sex work who are concerned about the commodification of sex through the sex industry also will struggle to explain why other kinds of sexual relationships are not similarly objectionable. The boundary between sugaring and sex work is unclear, even to those who are engaged in it. For example, consider the following account of people who form sugar daddy- sugar baby relationships:

> [They] embrace the economic underpinnings of their instrumental uses of intimacy, but they also invoke romantic discourses of chemistry, connection, and personal choice and the morality of economic exchange, demonstrating a refusal to see their relations as work and solely driven by market logic.[7]

In some ways sugaring is a form of sex work, but in other ways sugaring resembles romantic relationships that form outside of the marketplace. Other romantic relationships that are uncontroversially isolated from the labor market can nevertheless be sensitive to pecuniary incentives too, such as one's desire for housing or an expensive lifestyle. Perhaps sexual norms and practices are deficient when characterized by pecuniary motivations, but even if this were so, this critique would fail to apply uniquely to the explicit forms of commodification that sex work involves.

And even if there were some valuable goods that were instantiated in non-commercial sexual encounters and even if the commodification of sex did crowd out those values, this still would not establish that participating in sex markets is impermissible on the grounds that it has negative externalities associated with crowding out the value of non-commercial sex. To establish that participating in sex markets is impermissible on these grounds, one would not only need to show that some people are made worse off by

7. Kavita Ilona Nayar, "Sweetening the Deal: Dating for Compensation in the Digital Age," *Journal of Gender Studies* 26, no. 3 (2017): 335–46.

the commercialization of sex, but also that they had an entitlement against being made worse off in that way.

Returning to our previous examples of impermissible exchanges, it is impermissible to pay someone to cut down your neighbors' tree or to beat up your business rivals because your neighbor had a right to that property and your business rival had a right against assault. Do people have rights to maintain the gift value of non-commercial sex? People are not morally required to preserve the gift value of activities that exist outside of the market. Even if some valuable norms were lost by commodifying an activity that was previously part of a gift relationship, other values could be gained. Consider childcare as an illustration of this point. Say that women joining the workforce and paying for nannies and daycare changed the nature of mother-child relationships, even for women who continued to watch their own children without payment. We might imagine stay-at-home mothers objecting to the commodification of daycare on the grounds that it corrupted the gift-value of their labor. Now instead of viewing motherhood as its own sacred calling, stay at home mothers would feel the need to justify their choice to stay at home and isolate themselves from the market.

This example shows two things about gift value arguments against sex work. First, say it were true that the introduction of a market changed practices and institutions in ways that made some people worse off by changing the nature of their relationships and people's perceptions of their relationships. Even then, those who were made worse off still would not have been harmed in a way that could justify violating other people's occupational rights in order to prevent that harm. It is not enough to say that a practice or institution makes people worse off in order to establish that it is impermissible or that other people can interfere with those who participate in it.

Second, this example shows that gift norms are often not that valuable in the first place. In this case, isolating the value of an activity from the value it could have in the marketplace entrenches sexist historical expectations that women will perform labor without pay. But if the alleged value of a practice derives from the gendered provision of unpaid labor, then those who claim that the practice has such value must explain why paying women for this labor undermines its value while at the same time paying men for similar labor (such as paying men to be caregivers in hospitals or classrooms) would not undermine the value of the practice. More generally, arguments in favor of pre- serving gift values on the grounds that they constitute so- cially valuable practices or institutions, such as the family or a marriage, often implicitly assume that those practices' value derives from the fact that participants in them don't get paid but do not explain why whatever value is inherent in the practice is incompatible with payment. If the value inherent in these practices is related to the provision of free labor, then I am skeptical that it is valuable to have social practices that necessarily require everyone to participate for free or not at all.

Another example—the practice of letting people choose who they marry makes some people worse off than they would fare if partners were chosen by matchmakers or parents. But that observation does not establish that unarranged marriages are impermissible or that people should not be permitted to choose their partners on the grounds that the practice makes some

worse off than they would be. In order to establish that
an occupational choice or an intimate choice has externalities that make it impermissible, one must establish
not only that third parties are made worse off by it but
that permitting these choices violates third parties' enforceable rights.

We can extend a similar argumentative strategy to
other arguments against the sex industry that cite third-
party harms and externalities. In order for the presence
of an externality to establish that the work is impermissible or to justify interference, one must show that third
parties have an entitlement to not be made worse off in
that way. Some people argue that the sex industry harms
all women by degrading their status in society, or that
it exposes communities to higher crime rates, or that it
limits women's sexual autonomy in the workplace. I will
return to all of these arguments, but for now it is worth
noting that in each of these cases it is insufficient to
merely cite some third parties who are made worse off by
others' choices to buy or sell sex in order to establish that
buying and selling sex is impermissible. To justify legal
intervention, one must also show that buying and selling sex violates someone's enforceable rights such that
those who buy or sell sex are liable to be interfered with
by public officials.

If sex work is a permissible choice, then it would be
presumptively wrong for someone else to interfere with a
person's freedom to do it, even if that person is a public
official. Michael Huemer poses the following thought experiment to illustrate this point: Huemer firsts asks that we
imagine that two people, Jon and Mary, consensually trade
money for sex. Huemer writes,

Later, one of their neighbors, Sam, finds out about what happened. Sam thinks people should only have sex for procreation or sensory pleasure. The thought of people having sex for money makes him angry. So Sam goes over to Mary's house with his gun. He points the gun at Mary and orders her to accompany him to his house. Once there, he locks her in his basement for the next six months. As it turns out, Mary was not from the neighborhood. Jon had convinced her to travel from out of town to have sex with him. When Sam learns of this he is incensed. He kidnaps Jon at gunpoint and locks him up in the basement for the next 20 years.[8]

In this story, Sam is clearly the villain. On Huemer's (and my) view, if Sam wore a Sheriff's badge or a Mayor's sash, it wouldn't change the fact that he did something seriously wrong by imprisoning Mary or Jon, because Mary and Jon were not doing anything wrong to make them liable to be interfered with.

Huemer's argument relies on the view that if it is presumptively wrong for anyone else to interfere with someone's freedom to do something, then it is also presumptively wrong for public officials to interfere with that choice by enforcing criminal penalties. Many people reject Huemer's argument that public officials may not interfere with people's permissible choices as a general matter, but accept that public officials may not interfere with certain permissible choices. On this more moderate view of political authority, public officials can often interfere with people for the sake of the public interest or even for the benefit

8. Michael Huemer, *The Problem of Political Authority: An Examination of the Right to Coerce and the Duty to Obey*, 1st ed. (Houndmills, Basingstoke, Hampshire; New York: Palgrave Macmillan, 2013).

of those who they are interfering with. But some choices, basic liberties, are protected from this kind of interference. Because Huemer's argument is relatively controversial, it is worth addressing whether those who reject Huemer's view and support strong institutional protections for basic liberties should also acknowledge a right to sell sexual services.

4.1.2 Basic Liberties

Political philosophers often distinguish between basic and non-basic liberties. Some mean the distinction to just refer to rights that are especially important or in need of constitutional protection. In the United States, the Bill of Rights may be viewed as a list of basic liberties, in contrast to the other freedoms, which are not explicitly enumerated in the constitution. Others, most notably philosophers whose work engages with the scholarship of John Rawls, define basic liberties as those rights which are necessary for the adequate development of citizens' moral powers, including their ability to develop and pursue a conception of the good life and a sense of justice that recognizes other people's ability to the same. [9]

However we define basic liberties, they generally include freedoms such as the right to express oneself freely, bodily rights, the right to make intimate and personal decisions, the right to associate freely, privacy rights, and a right to at least some personal property. Other candidate basic liberties include economic and occupational rights. Many critics of sex work argue that the freedom to buy or sell sex is not a basic liberty and implicitly suggest that

9. John Rawls, *A Theory of Justice: Original Edition*, Reissue ed. (Cambridge, MA: Belknap Press: An Imprint of Harvard University Press, 2005), 61.

public officials are authorized to interfere with non-basic liberties for the sake of the greater good or for the sake of people whose rights they are limiting. For this reason, they maintain that the criminalization or regulation of the sex industry is morally acceptable.

Even if we grant the distinction between basic and non-basic liberties and grant the assumption that public officials may interfere with the exercise of people's non-basic liberties, the right to sell sex is entailed by paradigmatically basic liberties so public officials still ought not criminalize or regulate the industry for the sake of the greater good or for the sake of sex workers. Return to the list of paradigmatically basic liberties—freedom of expression, bodily rights, the right to make intimate and personal decisions, freedom of association, privacy rights, and personal property rights. To a basic liberties theorist, these rights merit strong institutional protection from government interference. It is on these grounds that people have the right to publish subversive literature, refuse lifesaving medical treatment, marry people of different races, form a union, to evade surveillance or to refuse to quarter soldiers in their homes. These basic liberties merit protections even if censoring subversive literature would promote the greater good by ensuring political stability, if forcing people to accept lifesaving treatment saved their lives, if prohibiting interracial marriage reflected the values of the political community at the time, if union-busting facilitated economic growth, and if surveillance and citizens' quartering soldiers was good for national security.

These basic liberties also entail a right to engage in sexual performance and to choose one's sexual partner. Sexual performance is a form of expression, sex involves the exercise of one's authority over one's body, it is an intimate and personal decision that involves associating with another person in a private context. Since the right to engage in sexual performance and to choose one's sexual partner is entailed by basic liberties, it merits the same strong institutional protections as other basic liberties, even when limiting these freedoms would promote the greater good or the well-being of people whose rights were limited.

In response, one may reply that while the right to engage in sexual performance and to choose one's sexual partner is entailed by basic liberties, the right to engage in sexual performance or choose a partner *for money* is not. This is because many basic liberties theorists think that economic choices are non-basic, even if the very same choice would be basic outside of the marketplace. For example, on this view, personal artistic expression may be a basic right but corporate speech and advertising is not.

There are three ways of addressing this response. First, some philosophers reject this response on the grounds that economic rights are basic too. They argue that the same reasons that support protecting other basic liberties are reasons in favor of protections for economic choices such as occupational freedom.[10] Some sex workers conceive of their profession in this way. Consider for example, Annie Sprinkle, a sex worker who defends her profession as a legitimate occupational choice, analogous to the choices that many other workers make when choosing a difficult and

---

10. John Tomasi defends the claim that economic freedoms, including occupational freedom, are basic rights that merit strong institutional protection. John Tomasi, *Free Market Fairness*, Reprint ed. (Princeton, NJ: Princeton University Press, 2013).

risky occupation.[11] If economic freedoms are basic, then the right to sell sex is not only entailed by the traditional list of basic liberties which protect rights of sexual expression and rights to choose one's partners, it's also entailed by basic economic freedoms.

Second, even if we do not grant that economic freedoms are basic; the basic liberties framework still supports a right to sell sex. Here the analogy to freedom of expression is instructive. Many forms of protected expression are done for profit. Artists and journalists express themselves for money, and a law that prohibited the sale of paintings or opinion writing would violate these professionals' freedom of expression. Many sex workers, especially pornographic actors and strippers, conceive of their work as a form of artistic expression or political speech as well. And the sex industry is relevantly similar to other for-profit industries which are protected as permissible forms of expression. For example, many films depict graphic sex scenes, like pornography. It is morally arbitrary to claim that sexual performance is permissible outside of the sex industry but not within it. It is perhaps for this reason that the US state of Oregon's state constitution protects nude dancers' rights as a form of protected expression just as nudists' rights are protected on similar grounds.[12] Likewise, it is morally

11. Peter de Marneffe describes Sprinkle's defense of sex work in these terms. Peter de Marneffe, *Liberalism and Prostitution* (London: Oxford University Press, 2012), 25.

12. The Associated Press, "Oregon Judge Rules Limit on Nude Dancing Is Illegal," *The Seattle Times*, May 7, 2005, sec. Local News, https://www.seattletimes.com/seattle-news/oregon-judge-rules-limit-on-nude-dancing-is-illegal/; Marlena Williams, "Stripping in Oregon," Oregon Encyclopedia, October 15, 2018, https://oregonencyclopedia.org/articles/stripping_in_oregon/#.XCo8ks9KiV4.

arbitrary to claim that sexual performance is permissible for the purposes of making pornography, but that the very same acts would be impermissible if only one actor received payment and was not being filmed.

Third, public officials should not consider certain rights to be basic when exercised in private but non-basic when exercised in public. Such a view would entail that the moral status of an action can be transformed in virtue of the exchange of money after the fact. Imagine that Martha's neighbor Jeff owns a landscaping company. During the winter, Jeff uses his snow-blower to clear his clients' sidewalks and driveways. One day, with Martha's consent, he clears her driveway after a snowstorm. While sitting inside, sipping cocoa and watching him work, Martha decides to pay him for his services. When Jeff is finished clearing the driveway Martha approaches him with payment, which he accepts. In this case, Martha transforms an altruistic act into a market exchange when she pays him. But she does not change the normative significance of the act in virtue of her subsequent payment.

Now imagine that Julie, a sex worker, goes on a date with Matt. Julie has consensual sex with Matt. At this point, Julie is exercising her rights to make intimate and personal choices about her body and to choose her partners. Say that Julie and Matt, after sex, decide that they would rather see each other as a provider and a client rather than as romantic partners. Matt decides to pay Julie for that night, which she accepts. If Julie accepts payment, doing so would not retroactively render a previously permissible sexual encounter impermissible because nothing changes about the previous consensual encounter, which is protected by both Julie's and Matt's rights. And if Julie's initial choice to have consensual unpaid sex is protected as a basic right, to say that such a right exists only in private contexts and not in the marketplace would seem to imply that exercising one's rights of sexual intimacy precludes the future exercise of other rights. On such a view, a person may have a basic right of sexual intimacy and a right to voluntarily transfer or acquire personal property, but exercising the former right rules out the right to exercise the latter right under certain conditions.

Summing up, people have a right to sell sex, meaning that it is permissible to sell sex and it would be presumptively wrong for public officials, or anyone else, to interfere with workers' freedom to do it. It is permissible to sell sex because it is permissible to have sex for any reason, and concerns about the externalities of the sex industry cannot justify interference with sex workers' choices. Even if one has the view that it is sometimes permissible to limit non-basic liberties for people's own sake or for the greater good, paradigmatically basic liberties entail a right to sexual intimacy, which should include a right to make intimate sexual choices for money.

4.1.3 Clients' Rights

Just as sex workers' decision to sell sex ought to be protected by their basic liberties to sexual intimacy, clients' decision to pay for sex is protected on the same grounds. Just as sex workers have a right to express themselves through sexual performance and to choose intimate partners without governmental interference, clients also have rights to view workers' performances and to choose sex workers as intimate partners. For some clients, the preference to see sex workers is a part of their sexual identities. For others, paying sex workers is the only way that they can experience sexual intimacy. If sexual freedom and intimacy are important liberties worth protecting, protections for the right to pay for sex is required for the sake of clients' sexual freedom and intimacy.

The justifications for free expression illustrate this point. One justification for protecting free expression appeals to speakers' rights or interests in expressing themselves. This justification appeals to the benefits of protecting free expression for sex workers. But a second justification for freedom of expression as a basic right is that members of the public have an entitlement to or interest in accessing different kinds of speech and expression. This justification explains why it would be wrong for officials to censor controversial political texts or subversive art after the writers or artists are diseased.[13]

If this justification for protecting free expression succeeds, it establishes that sex workers' clients have rights and interests in viewing or experiencing what amounts to a protected form of performance art. So just as officials would violate citizens' rights if they censored socialist newsletters or sacrilegious artwork, officials also violate citizens' rights when they censor sexually explicit content and prohibit sexual performance. It may seem counterintuitive to think of clients as analogous to people who have an interest in accessing controversial political texts and subversive art. But in all these cases, the listener-based justification for freedom of expression

---

13. Eugene Volokh, "Speech Restrictions That Don't Much Affect the Autonomy of Speakers," *Constitutional Commentary* 27 (2010): 347.

shouldn't take a stand on the content of the expression because it is also important that people determine for themselves which kinds of speech they have an interest in accessing.

Proponents of the Nordic Model may be sympathetic to the foregoing arguments in favor of sex workers' rights while rejecting my claim that clients have a right to pay for sex. They may then argue that unlike prohibition, the Nordic Model does not violate sex workers' rights because sex workers are not subject to criminal penalties under the Nordic Model. Rather, the Nordic Model only restricts clients' freedom to pay for sex, which on this view they have no right to do.

For the sake of argument, say we deny that clients have rights to view and participate in sexual performances and rights to choose their intimate partners. This would entail denying a right to pay for sex. Even if clients had no such rights, granting that sex workers have rights to sell sex would still rule out the Nordic Model on the grounds that the Nordic Model violates sex workers' rights.

Consider an analogy to abortion. If women have bodily rights, rights to make intimate and personal decisions, and privacy rights, these rights jointly entail the right to have an abortion. A critic of abortion may grant that these rights exist, but then deny that anyone has the right to provide women with abortion. They may then support a policy that prohibits people from providing abortions but which does not prohibit women from accessing abortions. Such a policy would clearly violate women's' abortion rights though, even if abortion itself were not straightforwardly prohibited. Similarly, if sex workers have a right to sell sex, in virtue of other basic liberties, but no one may legally pay for their services, then such policies would violate sex workers' basic liberties as well.

4.1.4 Summary

As I see it, the most compelling reason in favor of decriminalization is that criminal penalties violate the rights of sex workers and their clients. Even the Nordic Model, which only criminalizes the purchase of sex, violates the rights of sex workers in practice and in principle by limiting workers' and clients' access to intimate partnerships and occupational choices. For these reasons, a society that truly takes women's' rights seriously would be a society with decriminalized sex markets.

4.2 SEX WORK AND WELL-BEING

Some readers may be unpersuaded by my arguments that people have rights to buy and sell sex, either because they are unimpressed by rights-based arguments generally or because they think that sexual rights are not as morally significant as I have claimed. The foregoing argument for sex workers' and clients' rights is in some ways revisionary. Many people reject the claim that if an act is permissible then it is permissible to do it for money. Others reject the claim that it's presumptively wrong for public officials to interfere with citizens' permissible choices. And while many people support protections for basic liberties such as freedom of expression and association, bodily rights, privacy rights, and rights of sexual intimacy, few have explicitly argued that these rights entail rights to buy and sell sex. In this section I argue that even if one rejects the foregoing arguments for rights to buy and sell sex, public officials should also decriminalize sex work because decriminalization has better consequences than alternative policy regimes.

This argument relies on a series of empirical claims about the costs and benefits of decriminalization relative to other polices. As I mentioned in the introduction, empirical research that compares the effects of various sex work policies is often inconclusive. In this section I will make the case for decriminalization in three parts. First, I will argue that decriminalization is more likely to promote workers' interests than other policies because workers have a better understanding of their interests than public officials. I also present evidence that suggests that many of the negative effects that workers experience from participating in the sex industry are exacerbated in black markets. Second, I argue that decriminalization is also good for sex workers' clients, and that proponents of the Nordic Model should not overlook the benefits of decriminalization for clients. Third, I argue that decriminalization is good for communities, including people who do not participate in the industry at all. Even if the sex industry has some negative externalities, decriminalization is better for communities on balance.

In discussing whether decriminalization has better consequences than alternative regimes I focus on whether decriminalization promotes the general well-being of sex workers, their clients, and other citizens who are subject to the law better than alternative policies, such as criminalization, the Nordic Model, and regulation. This argument is not committed to a particular theory of well-being, nor is it committed to the view that officials should maximize well-being.

4.2.1 Workers' Well-Being

The first consequentialist argument for decriminalization is that it promotes sex workers' well-being. Before turning to the evidence, there are epistemic reasons to think that this is true. In general, workers are in a better position to know whether a profession will promote their overall well-being than police or public officials. Sex workers know better than public officials whether selling sex is a good occupational choice, given their other options. Yet some critics of the industry suggest that unlike other workers, potential sex workers face distinctive challenges related to knowing what the profession will be like.[14] Even if this is true, and even public officials had a legitimate interest in addressing these distinctive epistemic challenges, they could do so by making quality information about the profession freely available and easily accessible, rather than restricting access to the profession for all workers on these grounds. Moreover, once individuals are sex workers, they surely have a better understanding of whether the job promotes their interests than police or public officials do.

So when workers choose to sell sex, it is often because they judge that sex work is preferable to other forms of employment. Though sex work is riskier than many other jobs, like workers in other risky professions they may value aspects of the job that don't appear in public health or crime data, such as flexible hours, excitement, higher wages, workplace

14. de Marneffe, *Liberalism and Prostitution*.

autonomy, or socialization. Surveys of sex workers support this claim. For example, in New Zealand 80% of workers report that they appreciate the high wages and flexible hours of their industry, and others cite the community, recreational benefits of sex, independence, and contact with clients.[15]

And the same epistemic reasons in favor of the claim that sex work is better for sex workers than their other occupational options also weigh in favor of the claim that decriminalization is better for sex workers than other policies. Sex workers and sex worker advocacy organizations overwhelmingly favor decriminalization over criminalization, the Nordic Model, or even strict regulation.[16] Regarding regulation, Krusi et al. observe, "for many participants the enforcement of clients forced them to spend longer hours on the street to earn an income."[17] Many sex workers choose to work in the industry because it offers flexible hours and financial independence, but legal restrictions prevent workers from accessing these benefits.[18]

15. Gillian Abel, Lisa Fitzgerald, and Cheryl Brunton, "The Impact of the Prostitution Reform Act on the Health and Safety Practices of Sex Workers" (Department of Public Health and General Practice, University of Otago: Report to the Prostituon Law Review Committee, November 2007), https://www.otago.ac.nz/christchurch/otago018607.pdf. Jan Jordan, "The Sex Industry in New Zealand: A Literature Review" (Ministry of Justice, New Zealand Government, March 2005), https://www.justice.govt.nz/assets/Documents/Publications/sex-industry-in-nz.pdf.

16. Sally Howard, "Better Health for Sex Workers: Which Legal Model Causes Least Harm?," *BMJ* 361 (2018): k2609.

17. A. Krüsi et al., "Criminalisation of Clients: Reproducing Vulnerabilities for Violence and Poor Health among Street-Based Sex Workers in Canada: A Qualitative Study," *BMJ Open* 4, no. 6 (June 2, 2014).

18. Sufia Begum et al., "Sex Workers Talk about Sex Work: Six Contradictory Characteristics of Legalised Sex Work in Melbourne, Australia," *Culture, Health & Sexuality* 15, no. 1 (January 1, 2013): 85–100.

Decriminalization also benefits sex workers in more measurable ways. Specifically, decriminalization is better for workers' safety and health than criminalization, the Nordic Model, and strict regulations because decriminalization avoids the health and safety risks associated with black markets. Consider first the benefits of decriminalization relative to a prohibitive regime. In New Zealand sex workers report that their working conditions became safer after decriminalization in 2003.[19] Today in New Zealand, being a legal sex worker is safer than being an ambulance nurse.[20]

One of the main reasons that decriminalized sex work is safer than criminalized sex work is that sex workers are less likely to call the police when they fear criminal sanctions for selling sex. Sex workers therefore have fewer institutional protections from violence in more prohibitive contexts.[21] If sex workers can confidently threaten to call the police if their clients threaten, deceive, assault, or steal from them, then clients are less likely to mistreat them. But when the option to call the police is available to sex workers, they have more reason to be confident that they can safely refuse to provide services without fear of violence. In New

19. "Prostitution Law Reform in New Zealand," Parliamentary Library Research Paper, May 2012, https://www.parliament.nz/resource/en-NZ/00PLSocRP12051/c62a00e57bd36e84aed237e357af2b7381a39f7e.

20. New Zealand Accident Compensation Corporation, ACC Levy Rates Guidebook 2010/2011. Wellington: New Zealand, 2010:118. As cited in Ole Martin Moen, "Is Prostitution Harmful?," *Journal of Medical Ethics*, January 1, 2012, medethics-2011-100367.

21. Kathleen N. Deering et al., "A Systematic Review of the Correlates of Violence Against Sex Workers," *American Journal of Public Health* 104, no. 5 (March 13, 2014): e42–54.

Zealand, 70% of sex workers reported that they were more likely to report workplace violence after their country decriminalized the industry.[22]

Criminalization also decreases workers' power to negotiate about their clients' experiences and about condom use because women who refuse a clients' conditions may face implicit or explicit threats of being reported to the police. The criminalization of sex work not only endangers sex workers by subjecting them to the threat of criminal penalties, because it is an illegal industry officials may not investigate and punish violence against sex workers as effectively as they would punish violence against workers in decriminalized industries.[23] For example, in several US states rape shield legislation, which excludes evidence of a rape complainant's sexual history from being used as evidence in trials, does not apply to sex workers or complainants with a previous conviction for sex work.[24]

Policies that criminalize the sale of sex also increase the probability that sex workers will be sexually assaulted by police officers. For example, several recent reports published by Amnesty International document sex workers' experiences with extortion and rape by police officers,

22. Elaine Mossman, "Brothel Operators' and Support Agencies' Experiences of Decriminalization," in *Taking the Crime Out of Sex Work: New Zealand Sex Workers' Fight for Decriminalisation*, ed. Gillian Abel et al. (Policy Press, 2010).

23. Michael L. Rekart, "Sex-Work Harm Reduction," *Lancet (London, England)* 366, no. 9503 (December 17, 2005): 2123–34; "Violence against Sex Workers and HIV Prevention," Information Bulletin Series, Number 3 (World Health Organization, 2005).

24. Karin S. Portlock, "Status on Trial: The Racial Ramifications of Admitting Prostitution Evidence under State Rape Shield Legislation," *Columbia Law Review* 107 (2007): 1404–36.

highlighting that in some contexts police actively targeted sex workers.[25] Tawanda Mutassah, the senior director for law and policy at Amnesty International writes, "criminalization enables the police to harass [sex workers] and not prioritize their complaints and safety."[26] And a synthesis of 40 qualitative studies concludes that,

> In contexts of any criminalization, repressive policing of sex workers, their clients, and/or sex work venues disrupted sex workers' work environments, support networks, safety and risk reduction strategies, and access to health services and justice . . . policing within all criminalization and regulation frameworks exacerbated existing marginalization . . . Sex workers' relationships with police, access to justice, and negotiating powers with clients have improved in decriminalized contexts.[27]

Police violence against sex workers is an international occurrence, but in the United States more general racial

25. "Policy on State Obligations to Respect, Protect, and Fulfil the Human Rights of Sex Workers (International Board)" (Amnesty International, August 11, 2015), https://www.amnestyusa.org/press-releases/policy-on-state-obligations-to-respect-protect-and-fulfil-the-human-rights-of-sex-workers-international-board/. Amnesty International, "The Human Cost of Crushing the Market: Criminalization of Sex Work in Norway" (Amnesty International, n.d.).

26. "Amnesty International Publishes Policy and Research on Protection of Sex Workers' Rights," May 26, 2016, https://www.amnesty.org/en/latest/news/2016/05/amnesty-international-publishes-policy-and-research-on-protection-of-sex-workers-rights/.

27. Lucy Platt, Pippa Grenfell, Rebecca Meiksin, Jocelyn Elmes, Susan G. Sherman, Teela Sanders, Peninah Mwangi, and Anna-Louise Crago, "Associations between Sex Work Laws and Sex Workers' Health: A Systematic Review and Meta-Analysis of Quantitative and Qualitative Studies," *PLOS Medicine* 15, no. 12 (December 11, 2018): e1002680.

disparities in exposure to police violence extend to sex workers' experiences. For example, following the death of Freddie Gray, a black man in Baltimore, a US Department of Justice investigation of the Baltimore report found that Baltimore police also extorted sex from alleged sex workers and when women complained about sexual assault by police "the women's complaints were poorly and partially investigated, if at all, with little or no consequences for the officers involved."[28]

In light of these problems with criminalizing the sale of sex, many people favor the Nordic Model, which ostensibly does not subject sex workers to criminal penalties. Yet decriminalization is also better for workers' health, safety, and well-being than the Nordic Model. Even though *in principle* the Nordic Model only prohibits people from paying for sexual services, *in practice* the Nordic Model exposes sex workers to many of the same harms associated with criminalization.

The Nordic Model does make some progress toward the goal of preventing violence against sex workers, but it does not protect workers' from violence as well as decriminalization does.[29] Even in places that permit the sale of sex, workers may be reluctant to contact the police because there are other negative consequences for participating in

28. Andrea J. Ritchie, "Two Years After the Uprising, Black Women's Experiences of Policing in Baltimore Still Under the Radar," Truthout, accessed July 17, 2017, http://www.truth-out.org/opinion/item/40395-two-years-after-the-uprising-black-women-s-experiences-of-policing-in-baltimore-still-under-the-radar.

29. Ann Jordan, "The Swedish Law to Criminalize Clients: A Failed Experiment in Social Engineering, Issue Paper 4," *Center for Human Rights and Humanitarian Law: American University Washington College of Law*, 2012.

criminalized industry, such as deportation or arrests related to other offenses such as drug possession or parole
violations.[30] Sex workers face the potential loss of their custody rights in countries that enforce the Nordic Model as
well.[31] And the Nordic Model also puts sex workers at risk
because police retain the power to criminally punish people
who "promote prostitution" and sex workers who report
violence are subject to eviction or loss of employment for
being associated with a criminal industry, even if the sale
of sex is not itself a criminal offense.[32] In contrast, decriminalization eliminates these harms that are associated with
working in an illegal industry.

Proponents of the Nordic Model may reply that these
considerations arise in non-ideal circumstances, but that
the best version of the Nordic Model would still be preferable to decriminalization. For example, proponents of the
Nordic Model clearly would never condone sexual assault
by police officers, so they may reject my citing the fact that
all policies that involve law enforcement in the sex industry

30. In some cases, even sex workers who are citizens of countries
in the European Union faced deportation within European countries that enforce the Nordic Model. Don Kulick, "Sex in the New
Europe: The Criminalization of Clients and Swedish Fear of Penetration,"
Anthropological Theory 3, no. 2 (2003): 199–218; Charlotta Holmström
and May-Len Skilbrei, "The 'Nordic Model' of Prostitution Law Is a Myth,"
The Conversation, accessed September 25, 2017, http://theconversation.
com/the-nordic-model-of-prostitution-law-is-a-myth-21351.

31. Michelle Goldberg, "Should Buying Sex Be Illegal?," *The Nation*,
July 30, 2014, https://www.thenation.com/article/should-buying-sex-
be-illegal/.

32. Jay Levy and Pye Jakobsson, "Sweden's Abolitionist Discourse
and Law: Effects on the Dynamics of Swedish Sex Work and on the
Lives of Sweden's Sex Workers," *Criminology & Criminal Justice* 14, no. 5
(2014): 593–607.

4. THE CASE FOR DECRIMINALIZATION | 205

potentially expose workers to potential police violence as a reason against the model.

But proponents of the Nordic Model cannot sustain their reply without undermining their case for it. In evaluating the merits of a policy, we can either evaluate it as it is actually enforced or as it would be enforced ideally. As the Nordic Model is actually enforced, it does not promote workers' health or safety or well-being, it perpetuates the stigmatization of sex workers and limits their occupational freedom. Ideally, places that enforced the Nordic Model would also work to destigmatize sex work, punish police violence, and ensure that people have access to a wide range of occupations that are more flexible and sustaining than sex work. But in such an ideal society, the rationale for the Nordic Model would be undermined by its own ideal implementation. After all, such a society would ensure that all workers were able to meet their basic needs, thus undermining the argument that clients exploit conditions of economic deprivation. And in an idealized society that did not stigmatize female sex workers, we may imagine that people's attitudes toward women were more progressive more generally, thus undermining the argument that the Nordic Model is necessary to establish egalitarian relations between the sexes and genders.

The case for the Nordic Model cannot have it both ways. I have argued that the Nordic Model is not better for sex workers in practice. One may concede this point and argue for the Nordic Model as a policy ideal, but if effective enforcement of these policy ideals were available then the Nordic Model could not be justified either, because if the ideal Nordic Model were possible then other ideal policies would also be feasible and these other policies, such policies that provided a strong social safety net or robust employment options with flexible hours and high wages, would eliminate the most compelling justifications for the Nordic Model.

Another concern is that decriminalization would not promote safety better than the Nordic Model as long as the stigma associated with sex work persists. Yet decriminalization and destigmatization go hand in hand because decriminalization reduces the stigma associated with working in a criminal industry. The Nordic Model also threatens workers' safety relative to full decriminalization by weakening workers' bargaining power with respect to their clients because their clients are already taking a risk by purchasing sex.[33] It is for these reasons that sex worker advocacy groups recommend decriminalization, which not only enables them to safely access the police but destigmatizes the industry as well.[34]

4.2.2 Decriminalization versus Regulation

In light of this evidence, one may wonder whether regulation is preferable to decriminalization. The case for regulation is that it could provide sex workers with many of the same health and safety benefits of decriminalization while promoting health and safety further through regulations.

---

33. For example, such policies may also impair workers' ability to negotiate in favor of condom use. "UNAIDS Guidance on HIV and Sex Work" (Joint United Nations Programme on HIV/AIDS, 2012), http://www.unaids.org/sites/default/files/sub_landing/files/JC2306_UNAIDS-guidance-note-HIV-sex-work_en.pdf, p. 12.

34. "Failures of Justice" (Budapest, Hungary, 2015), available athttp://www.swannet.org/files/swannet/FailuresOfJusticeEng.pdf.

Several countries and the US State of Nevada currently regulate the sex industry. These regulations include expensive registration requirements, health checks that take time to complete, advertising restrictions, and restrictions on the location and content of sex workers' labor, licensing requirements, and age restrictions that prohibit some adults from becoming sex workers.

If the call for regulation is a call for these strict occupational licensing requirements or burdensome health and safety standards, then there is good reason to be skeptical of this solution. The first reason for skepticism about regulation is that it violates the rights of sex workers in the same way that prohibition would, assuming they have occupational freedom to sell sex without a license. In addition, sex workers themselves oppose these forms of regulation. For example, Juno Mac argues against regulating the industry on the following grounds:

> It's not a great model for human rights . . . sex workers are made to comply with special restrictions like registration and forced health checks. Regulation sounds great on paper, but politicians deliberately make regulation around the sex industry expensive and difficult to comply with . . . Rich well-connected brothel owners can comply with the regulations but more marginalized people find those hoops impossible to jump through . . . In this two-tiered system, the most vulnerable people are forced to work illegally, so they're still exposed to all the dangers of criminalization.[35]

35. Juno Mac, "Transcript of 'The Laws That Sex Workers Really Want,'" accessed September 29, 2017, https://www.ted.com/talks/juno_mac_the_laws_that_sex_workers_really_want/transcript.

Sex-worker advocacy organizations echo Mac's concerns about what they call "backdoor criminalization" through regulation and favor decriminalization, along the lines of New Zealand's policy approach.[36]

To illustrate sex workers' concerns about extensive industry-specific regulations, consider proposals to require pornographic actors to use condoms and subscribe to regular health checks overseen by public officials. These health regulations may seem like a good idea, but people with industry specific knowledge oppose them.[37] Condoms are cumbersome and uncomfortable, especially over the course of a long day of filming. Pornography with condoms is also less popular and incompatible with certain acts like group sex scenes, so workers and studios that use condoms are disadvantaged in the market. And even if condom requirements

36. See e.g. Katherine Margaret, "Sex Workers to Amnesty: Vote YES on Decriminalization!," *Sex Workers Outreach Project*, accessed September 29, 2017, http://www.new.swopusa.org/2015/08/04/sex-workers-to-amnesty-international-vote-yes-on-decriminalization/ ; Global Network of Sex Work Projects (NSWP), "We Call on the Amnesty International Council to Stand Firm and Support Decriminalization of Sex Work and Protect the Human Rights of Sex Workers," *Change.org*, August 2015, https://www.change.org/p/amnesty-international-secretary-general-amnesty-international-board-amnesty-international-council-we-call-on-the-amnesty-international-council-to-stand-firm-and-support-decriminalisation-of-sex-work-and-protect-the-human-rights-of-sex-workers; International Committee on the Rights of Sex Workers in Europe, "For Decriminalization and Justice: Sex Workers Demand Legal Reform and Social Change," *Open Democracy*, February 29, 2016, https://www.opendemocracy.net/beyondslavery/sws/international-committee-on-rights-of-sex-workers-in-europe/for-decriminalisation-and-j.

37. Maria L. La Ganga, "Why a Porn Star Is Fighting California's Condom Law: 'It's a Women's Rights Issue,'" *The Guardian*, October 18, 2016, sec. US news, https://www.theguardian.com/us-news/2016/oct/18/porn-tasha-reign-california-condom-law-proposition-60.

could be effectively enforced in the pornography industry, amateurs could still film and distribute pornography without using condoms, so condom requirements would not effectively prevent people from making porn without condoms. Instead, such regulations would only prevent them from doing so as part of larger production and distribution firm where their work is more likely to be profitable. Actors and studios already have strong incentives to avoid the sexual transmission of infections at work and take other steps to self-regulate their industry and ensure workers' safety.

I am not suggesting that the industry's ability to self-regulate is always effective. Employers' failure to comply with industry standards can put workers at risk. But like other industries, the judicial system can address these harms better than preemptive legislative interference and law enforcement.[38] For example, courts could hold employers liable for injuries sustained at work as a result of negligence and require that they pay compensation to injured workers. Workers could also purchase insurance to compensate them for workplace injuries.

Burdensome regulation may also undermine the benefits that proponents of decriminalization sought to achieve. Health screenings and condom requirements onerous to comply with and the monitoring and enforcement of these requirements takes time and money and workers risk financial penalties.[39] Heavy-handed health and safety

38. On the other hand, for a compelling counter-argument to this claim see Andrei Shleifer, *The Failure of Judges and the Rise of Regulators* (Cambridge, MA: MIT Press Books, 2012).

39. Editorial Board, "Heavy-Handed Proposition 60 Would Deputize Every Californian as a Condom Cop," *The Los Angeles Times*, September 28, 2016, sec. Opinion, https://www.latimes.com/opinion/editorials/la-ed-vote-no-proposition-60-20160922-snap-story.html.

regulations for sex workers could then cause a two-tiered system of legal sex work alongside black markets.[40] In general, licensing requirements and other barriers to employment deter economic mobility and disproportionately harm the economically worst off.[41] Requirements that prohibit persons under age 21 from selling sex could backfire by causing 19- and 20-year-old sex workers to work in black markets instead. These considerations weigh against even a broadly permissive approach that includes some licensing, such as proposals to enforce criminal penalties only against the clients of unlicensed sex workers.[42]

Policies that prohibit third parties from facilitating sex work, such as laws against brothel-keeping and pimping, also compromise sex workers' safety. Workers report increased control over client interactions, greater capacity to refuse sex and a heightened ability to avoid violence from clients in indoor workplaces with access to other sex workers.[43]

---

40. Emily Bazelon, "Should Prostitution Be a Crime?," *The New York Times*, May 5, 2016, sec. Magazine, https://www.nytimes.com/2016/05/08/magazine/should-prostitution-be-a-crime.html.

41. "Trends in Occupational Licensing and Best Practices for Smart Labor Market Regulation," whitehouse.gov, July 28, 2015, https://obamawhitehouse.archives.gov/blog/2015/07/28/trends-occupational-licensing-and-best-practices-smart-labor-market-regulation. Edward Rodrigue and Richard V. Reeves, "Four Ways Occupational Licensing Damages Social Mobility" (Brookings, February 24, 2016), https://www.brookings.edu/blog/social-mobility-memos/2016/02/24/four-ways-occupational-licensing-damages-social-mobility/.

42. For an explanation and theoretical defense of this proposal see Samuel Lee and Petra Persson, "Human Trafficking and Regulating Prostitution" (NYU Law and Economics Research Paper No. 12-08, 2015).

43. Andrea Krüsi et al., "Negotiating Safety and Sexual Risk Reduction With Clients in Unsanctioned Safer Indoor Sex Work Environments: A Qualitative Study," *American Journal of Public Health* 102, no. 6 (May 9, 2012): 1154–59.

Yet regulations prohibit sex workers form sharing premises in the United Kingdom, so workers who do work together in order to protect themselves from the violence are then deterred from reporting violence when it does occur because of regulations that prohibit brothel-keeping.[44] Similarly, in India sex workers are prohibited from living with adult family members out of concerns about pimping and exploitation. But rather than making sex work safer, these policies either make criminals of sex workers' parents and adult children or force workers to leave their families and work alone in more costly and dangerous environments.[45]

In response to these concerns, one may instead favor regulations that *require* sex workers to work in licensed brothels and prohibit street-based sex work or working independently. Though these regulations are safer for sex workers than outright bans, licensing brothels also has drawbacks.[46] The main problem with brothel requirements is that they isolate unlicensed workers.[47] In the Netherlands,

44. Jane Pitcher and Marjan Wijers, "The Impact of Different Regulatory Models on the Labour Conditions, Safety and Welfare of Indoor-Based Sex Workers," *Criminology & Criminal Justice* 14, no. 5 (November 1, 2014): 549–64.

45. Harsh Mander, "Emerging from the Shadows," *The Hindu*, May 18, 2016, https://www.thehindu.com/opinion/columns/Harsh_Mander/emerging-from-the-shadows/article5664286.ece.

46. Barbara G. Brents and Kathryn Hausbeck, "Violence and Legalized Brothel Prostitution in Nevada: Examining Safety, Risk, and Prostitution Policy," *Journal of Interpersonal Violence* 20, no. 3 (March 1, 2005): 270–95.Teela Sanders and Rosie Campbell, "Designing out Vulnerability, Building in Respect: Violence, Safety and Sex Work Policy," *British Journal of Sociology* 58, no. 1 (March 1, 2007): 1–19.

47. Christine Harcourt et al., "The Decriminalization of Prostitution Is Associated with Better Coverage of Health Promotion Programs for Sex Workers," *Australian and New Zealand Journal of Public Health* 34, no. 5 (October 2010): 482–86.

a system of licensed brothels has effectively created a dual system where illegal sex workers have few legal protections and sex workers in licensed brothels lack independence from their employers and are therefore more vulnerable to be victims of workplace violence from their bosses.[48] In Queensland, Australia, police require sex workers to either act as independent service providers or to become licensed as brothels, which means that sex workers who work together without licensing as a brothel are deterred from seeking police protection or legal remedies if they are harmed because they can face legal penalties as well.[49] Bans on street-based sex work can also force outdoor sex workers to work in more dangerous settings in order to avoid detection by police.[50] And as a group, street-based sex workers are also more vulnerable than indoor sex workers because they are more likely to be homeless.

On the other hand, if the call for regulation means that sex work is treated like other industries and subjected to industry-specific regulations, then regulation is not meaningfully different from decriminalization. In New Zealand, officials still require that employers such as brothel owners comply with industry-specific health and safety regulations,

48. Pitcher and Wijers, "The Impact of Different Regulatory Models on the Labour Conditions, Safety and Welfare of Indoor-Based Sex Workers."

49. Alison Brown, "Sex Workers 'Have to Choose between Working Legally, or Working Safely,'" *Brisbane Times*, November 23, 2018, https://www.brisbanetimes.com.au/politics/queensland/sex-workers-have-to-choose-between-working-legally-or-working-safely-20181120-p50h42.html.

50. Hendrik Wagenaar and Helga Amesberger, *Designing Prostitution Policy: Intention and Reality in Regulating the Sex Trade* (Bristol, UK: Policy Press, 2017).

and offer the same labor protections as employers in other industries such as holiday pay and sick pay.[51] To the extent that regulation is not so burdensome that it amounts to backdoor criminalization, proponents of decriminalization and regulation may be entrenched in a verbal dispute while they broadly agree about which policy is best for workers.[52] Decriminalization does not mean that sex work would not be subject to any laws. It means that sex workers would not be subject to industry-specific regulations that burdened workers and effectively criminalized parts of the industry.

4.2.3 Law and Stigma

For these reasons, the decriminalization of sex work is better for sex workers' health and safety than alternative policy approaches. When public officials treat buying or selling sex as an illicit act they also perpetuate the stigma that surrounds the industry. Stigma contributes to higher rates of violence against sex workers.[53] And all policies that

51. Occupational Safety and Health Service, "A Guide to Occupational Health and Safety in the New Zealand Sex Industry" (Department of Labour, New Zealand, June 2004), http://espu-usa.com/espu-ca/wp-content/uploads/2008/02/nz-health-and-safety-handbook.pdf.

52. A verbal dispute occurs when two people appear to disagree about a substantive issue but they really disagree about which words to use. In this case, proponents of regulation and proponents of decriminalization may disagree more about what to call a particular set of policies than they disagree about the policies themselves. David J. Chalmers, "Verbal Disputes," *Philosophical Review* 120, no. 4 (2011): 515–66.

53. Clarissa Penfold et al., "Tackling Client Violence in Female Street Prostitution: Inter-Agency Working between Outreach Agencies and the Police," *Policing and Society* 14, no. 4 (December 1, 2004): 365–79, 377; John Lowman, "Violence and the Outlaw Status of (Street) Prostitution in Canada," *Violence Against Women* 6, no. 9 (September 1,

subject sex workers and their clients to the discretionary power of the police put sex workers at risk because in these contexts people work to evade detection and avoid reporting. Criminal penalties also expose sex workers and their clients to violence simply because criminal law enforcement necessarily involves threats of violence, and encounters with law enforcement always carry the possibility of escalation to violence.

In contrast, decriminalization would not only enable sex workers to report violence and work in safer conditions, it would also improve workplace health and safety for sex workers. To those who argue that participating in the sex industry is inherently dangerous, due to the risk of sexual transmission of disease, it is worth noting that the material deprivation and impoverishment that cause many workers to sell sexual services is also bad for people's health. And if sex work were decriminalized, sex workers would have more access to larger labor unions, group health insurance plans, worker's compensation insurance and legal remedies for workplace injuries.

In addition, laws that prohibit sex work reduce workers' ability to negotiate the terms and conditions of their labor and report violations, meaning that prohibitive policies undermine sex workers' capacity to ensure condom use. Critics who are concerned with the health and safety risks that workers are exposed to in the sex industry should instead support the public provision of free medical services and mental health support, instead of using tax dollars to

2000): 987–1011; Jody Miller and Martin D. Schwartz, "Rape Myths and Violence against Street Prostitutes," *Deviant Behavior* 16, no. 1 (January 1, 1995): 1–23.

finance policing and incarceration for workers and their clients.[54]

4.2.4 Clients' Well-Being

So far I have focused on the effects of sex work and sex work policy for workers, but clients' well-being is also relevant to assessments of the overall consequences of various policy proposals. Clients' well-being is often overlooked in conversations about the decriminalization of the sex industry, but it shouldn't be. Overlooking the well-being of clients trivializes the morally significant benefits sex workers provide including companionship, access to intimacy and room to explore one's sexual identity without fear or judgment.[55] These benefits are especially significant in social contexts that are more generally sexually repressive or for clients who would otherwise have difficulty accessing intimate relationships. Some clients can only receive the psychiatric and health benefits associated with sex or developing an intimate partnership by paying for sex.[56]

54. Steven P. Kurtz et al., "Barriers to Health and Social Services for Street-Based Sex Workers," *Journal of Health Care for the Poor and Underserved* 16, no. 2 (2005): 345–61.

55. Philip Birch, *Why Men Buy Sex: Examining Clients of Sex Workers* (New York, NY: Routledge, 2015); Christine Milrod and Ronald Weitzer, "The Intimacy Prism: Emotion Management among the Clients of Escorts," *Men and Masculinities* 15, no. 5 (2012): 447–67; Christian Grov et al., "Male Clients of Male Escorts: Satisfaction, Sexual Behavior, and Demographic Characteristics," *Journal of Sex Research* 51, no. 7 (October 1, 2014): 827–37.

56. Robert T. Muller, "Sexual Surrogates Help Many Who Suffer Alone," *Psychology Today*, May 27, 2013, http://www. psychologytoday.com/blog/talking-about-trauma/201305/ sexual-surrogates-help-many-who-suffer-alone.

The moral significance of clients' well-being in these cases weighs in favor of decriminalization. One may object that instead of decriminalization, people who lack access to intimate partnerships due to sexual dysfunction or disability should be permitted to pay licensed sex therapists or sexual surrogates. But even clients who are not substantially disadvantaged or otherwise unable to have sex or explore their sexuality benefit from decriminalization. Like any other form of entertainment, sex workers provide people with pleasure. On most accounts, pleasure is an important component of well-being, and all people's well-being is morally significant, especially if promoting it does not undermine anyone else's rights.

Many sex workers see themselves as providing morally significant benefits, just as other entertainers and performers do. Some conceive of their jobs as continuous with other caregiving professionals, similar to therapy or massage, and participate in other caregiving professions either before or after working in the sex industry.[57] Perhaps one explanation for people's reluctance to recognize the benefits that sex workers provide is that a culture of masculinity often downplays men's emotional well-being or the value of caregiving services for adult men while simultaneously discounting the value of the caregiving services that women typically provide. But sex workers provide the same social benefits associated with some other caregiving industries, and the moral significance of these benefits weighs in favor of decriminalizing the sex industry.

57. Diane Taylor, "Most Sex Workers Have Had Jobs in Health, Education or Charities—Survey," *The Guardian*, February 27, 2015, sec. Society, http://www.theguardian.com/society/2015/feb/27/most-sex-workers-jobs-health-education-charities-survey.

4.2.5 Public Well-Being

In addition to the benefits of decriminalization for workers and their clients, decriminalization may also benefit the general public. This claim may seem surprising at first because many people disapprove of the sex industry. But even though decriminalization would plausibly increase the prevalence of sex markets, which people disapprove of, the public may nevertheless benefit on balance from decriminalization because it reduces the risks and harms associated with a more prohibitive approach.

Consider an analogy to other prohibitive policies. Early in the 20th century, the United States prohibited the production and sale of alcohol. This policy was clearly bad for the well-being of people who wanted to buy or sell alcohol, but many people disapproved of the alcohol industry. In light of this widespread disapproval, alcohol prohibition was justified on the grounds that it would promote the general welfare by reducing rates of domestic violence and corruption associated with saloons.[58] Yet prohibition backfired—it is likely that crime increased in major cities, including higher rates of theft, assault, and homicide.[59] Prohibition probably

58. Catherine Gilbert Murdock, *Domesticating Drink: Women, Men, and Alcohol in America, 1870–1940* (Baltimore, MD: Johns Hopkins University Press, 2002).

59. Though there were higher rates of convictions for these crimes in some major cities, it is difficult to definitively claim that prohibition increased crime because prohibition may have been correlated with higher rates of enforcement and also there were not uniform national crime statistics before 1930. Wayne Hall, "What Are the Policy Lessons of National Alcohol Prohibition in the United States, 1920–1933?," *Addiction* 105, no. 7 (2010): 1164–73. Mark Asbridge and Swarna Weerasinghe, "Homicide in Chicago from 1890 to 1930: Prohibition and Its Impact on Alcohol- and Non-Alcohol-Related Homicides," *Addiction* 104, no. 3 (2009): 355–64.

did not effectively stem rates of excessive consumption of alcohol either, though it did lead to the consumption of riskier forms of black-market alcohol.[60]

In general, black markets are associated with higher rates of violence because participants cannot use the police and courts to protect themselves and settle disputes. Black markets are also more dangerous because they are less transparent, so it is more difficult for consumers or provider to implement screening, certification, and truthful labeling standards. In the case of sex work, it is difficult to decisively establish that eliminating black markets in sex work through decriminalization would reduce rates of violence on balance but there is a fair amount of theoretical and observational evidence that it would. One methodological challenge for establishing a clear causal link between decriminalization and lower rates of violence is that rates of violence fall for a variety of reasons, and the same considerations that cause some places to see a decline in violent crime may also be associated with deregulating or decriminalizing sex work.

60. Here again, the policy lessons of prohibition are unclear. On some estimates, millions of Americans stopped drinking during Prohibition. But those who continued drinking faced greater dangers from drinking. Also, because prohibition coincided with the Great Depression, it is difficult to isolate the independent effects of the policy. For two contrasting perspectives on this controversy see Jeffrey A. Miron, "The Effect of Alcohol Prohibition on Alcohol Consumption No. w7130" (National Bureau of Economic Research, 1999). And Mark Thornton, "Cato Institute Policy Analysis No. 157: Alcohol Prohibition Was a Failure" (Washington DC: Cato Institute, 1991), in comparison to Hall, "What Are the Policy Lessons of National Alcohol Prohibition in the United States, 1920–1933?"

Large-scale meta-analyses can overcome some of the methodological challenges associated with studying sex work. And a recent meta-analysis suggests that decriminalizing the sex industry would reduce rates of sexual violence. The authors write that on average, the repressive policing practices associated with criminalization were associated with an increased risk of sexual or physical violence.[61] This claim is supported by 9 studies and 5,204 participants. Smaller studies provide further evidence of a causal link between decriminalization and lower rates of violence. For example, Rhode Island briefly decriminalized prostitution in 2003, rates of sexual violence did not increase—rather rates of rape significantly decreased compared to similar states that did not decriminalize sex work.[62] On the other hand, the recriminalization of sex work in 2009 did not cause a statistically significant increase in rates of sexual assault, so this evidence is not decisive. It could be that decriminalization was only correlated with lower rates of rape or it could be that the effects of decriminalization persisted after recriminalization for a time.[63]

Other evidence that compares rates of violence before and after decriminalization of access to sexual services is similarly favorable to decriminalization. [64] When Dutch

61. Platt et al., "Associations between Sex Work Laws and Sex Workers' Health."

62. Scott Cunningham and Manisha Shah, "Decriminalizing Indoor Prostitution: Implications for Sexual Violence and Public Health," *Review of Economic Studies* 85, no. 3 (2017): 1683–1715.

63. Ibid.

64. The evidence is not indisputable on this point. For a subset of men who are already violent and who seek out violent pornography, pornography does seemingly legitimate sexual violence. See Gert Martin Hald, Neil M. Malamuth, and Carlin Yuen, "Pornography and Attitudes

cities designated legal street prostitution zones, known as tippelzones, rates of sexual assault decreased by 30 to 40%.[65] In Queensland, rates of sexual violence increased by 149% after legal brothels were closed in 1959.[66] Further evidence comes from New Zealand, where rates of sexual violence did not increase after decriminalization but sex workers' reporting of sexual violence did increase.[67] In the Czech Republic, rates of sexual violence decreased when people gained legal access to pornography.[68] Similar effects were found in Japan, as people gained access to the internet.[69] When Denmark deregulated pornography in the 1970s allegations of sexual violence decreased as well.[70] Other studies confirm that access to pornography correlates with lower rates of sexual violence in a range of international contexts.[71]

Supporting Violence against Women: Revisiting the Relationship in Nonexperimental Studies," *Aggressive Behavior* 36, no. 1 (2009): 14–20.

65. Paul Bisschop, Stephen Kastoryano, and Bas van der Klaauw, "Street Prostitution Zones and Crime," *American Economic Journal: Economic Policy* 9, no. 4 (2017): 28–63.

66. Linda M. Rio, "Psychological and Sociological Research and the Decriminalization or Legalization of Prostitution," *Archives of Sexual Behavior* 20, no. 2 (1991): 205–18.

67. Though sex workers remained reluctant to carry out the process of investigating reports. "Report of the Prostitution Law Review Committee on the Operation of the Prostitution Reform Act 2003" (Wellington New Zealand: Ministry of Justice, New Zealand Government, May 2008).

68. M. Diamond et al., "Pornography and Sex Crimes in the Czech Republic," *Archives of Sexual Behavior* 40 (2011):1037.

69. M. Diamond and A. Uchiyama. "Pornography, Rape, and Sex Crimes in Japan," *International Journal of Law and Psychiatry* 22 (1999): 1.

70. B. Kutchinsky, "The Effect of Easy Availability of Pornography on the Incidence of Sex Crimes: The Danish Experience," *Journal of Social Issues* 29 (1973): 163.

71. M. Diamond, "The Effects of Pornography: An International Perspective," in *Pornography 101: Eroticism, Sexuality, and the First*

Another relevant social consequence of the sex industry relates to the public health effects of the sex industry. Critics allege that the sex industry ought to be prohibited because it puts people at risk of sexual transmission of contagious infections. Yet these claims are also not supported by the evidence. [72] Decriminalization enables public health officials to investigate and address the sexual transmission of infections and effectively promote safe sex better than prohibitive models. [73] Black markets may also further deter condom use in the general population because condoms can be seen evidence of a criminal encounter where sex work is prohibited. [74] It is primarily for these reasons that organizations such as UNAIDS and the World Health Organization support the decriminalization of prostitution as a component of preventing transmission and treating people affected by sexually transmitted infections. [75]

Amendment, ed. J. Elias et al. (Amherst, NY: Prometheus Press, 1999); and B. Kutchinsky, "Pornography and Rape: Theory and Practice? Evidence from Crime Data in Four Countries Where Pornography Is Easily Available," *International Journal of Law and Psychiatry* 14 (1991): 47.

72. Chris Beyrer et al., "An Action Agenda for HIV and Sex Workers," *Lancet* 385, no. 9964 (January 2015): 287–301; Stefania Boccia, Paolo Villari, and Walter Ricciardi, *A Systematic Review of Key Issues in Public Health* (New York: Springer, 2015), 10; Pippa Grenfell et al., "Decriminalising Sex Work in the UK," *BMJ* 354 (August 16, 2016): i4459, "Decriminalisation of Sex Work: The Evidence Is In," *Australian Federation of AIDS Organisations*, accessed September 25, 2017, https://www.afao.org.au/article/decriminalisation-sex-work-evidence/.

73. Harcourt et al., "The Decriminalization of Prostitution Is Associated with Better Coverage of Health Promotion Programs for Sex Workers."

74. Ine Vanwesenbeeck, "Sex Work Criminalization Is Barking Up the Wrong Tree," *Archives of Sexual Behavior* 46, no. 6 (2017): 1631–40.

75. "UNAIDS Guidance on HIV and Sex Work"; World Health Organization, "Policy Brief: Consolidated Guidelines on HIV Prevention, Diagnosis, Treatment and Care for Key Populations, 2016 Update"

A meta-analysis that included 12,506 participants from 11 studies found that repressive policing of sex workers was associated with an increased risk of HIV STI infection compared to decriminalization. [76] The same analysis found that decriminalization was also associated with a decreased risk of condomless sex. Specific studies echo this finding. In Rhode Island, decriminalization also reduced female cases of gonorrhea statewide.[77] And a 2012 report on sex markets in Asia found,

> Evidence from the jurisdictions in the region that have decriminalized sex work (New Zealand and New South Wales) indicates that the approach of defining sex work as legitimate labor empowers sex workers, increases their access to HIV and sexual health services and is associated with very high condom use rates. Very low STI prevalence has been maintained among sex workers in New Zealand and New South Wales, and HIV transmission within the context of sex work is understood to be extremely low or nonexistent.[78]

Instead of criminalizing the sex industry, public health experts who focus on STI prevention advocate an approach that focuses on education and prevention. Decriminalization may even improve public health on balance if it enables more workers to provide services

(World Health Organization, 2017), http://apps.who.int/iris/bitstream/10665/258967/1/WHO-HIV-2017.05-eng.pdf?ua=1.

76. Platt et al., "Associations between Sex Work Laws and Sex Workers' Health."

77. Cunningham and Shah, "Decriminalizing Indoor Prostitution."

78. John Godwin, *Sex Work and the Law in Asia and the Pacific: Laws, HIV and Human Rights in the Context of Sex Work* (UNDP, 2012): 29..

in legal brothels.[79] A study conducted in Ecuador found that sexual transmission of infections was more likely in street-based sex work and that enforcement against workers in brothels exacerbated public health problems by causing sex workers to resort to less visible, street-based work.[80]

Looking beyond the health and safety effects of decriminalization, it is worth considering the other benefits that decriminalization can bring to members of a political community. First, even if a person never uses the option to become a sex worker or to pay for sex, merely having the option could be valuable, because people benefit from having additional options. Second, to the extent that the decriminalization of sex work eliminates the expressive harms of prohibition that sex workers and their clients suffer from, everyone benefits from a safer and more inclusive community that respects all its members.

4.2.6 Summary

The consequentialist case in favor of decriminalization is supported by a pluralistic conception of well-being. Whether one's conception of well-being refers to the health, safety, preference-satisfaction, or overall welfare of sex workers, clients, or the public more generally, decriminalization likely promotes well-being better than

79. Platt et al., "Associations between Sex Work Laws and Sex Workers' Health."

80. Paul J. Gertler and Manisha Shah, "Sex Work and Infection: What's Law Enforcement Got to Do with It?," *Journal of Law and Economics* 54, no. 4 (November 1, 2011): 811–40.

alternatives. This argument relies on empirical claims which I acknowledge are contestable. Partly due to the fact that sex markets are typically regulated or prohibited, it is difficult to establish a clear causal connection between decriminalization and improved health, safety, or general welfare. But recent empirical evidence, including a mixed-methods review and meta-analysis that includes 134 studies from 1990 to 2018, suggests that the benefits of decriminalization has better consequences than policies that criminalize the sex trade.[81]

4.3 SEX WORK AND EQUALITY

Readers who are unpersuaded by rights-based arguments for decriminalization and skeptical about the empirical claims offered in support of arguments for decriminalization may maintain their support for some legal interference with the sex industry on egalitarian grounds. Egalitarians maintain that many social and economic inequalities are unjust, and that public officials should enforce policies that mitigate these inequalities. In this section, I make the case that egalitarians should support decriminalization because decriminalization will mitigate unjust social and economic inequality better than alternative policies. Here again, I first address the effects of decriminalization for sex workers, then clients, and to close I argue more generally treating sex work as work would have egalitarian externalities as well.

81. Platt et al., "Associations between Sex Work Laws and Sex Workers' Health."

4.3.1 Sex Workers and Equal Status

Watson develops an egalitarian argument in favor of the Nordic Model. Her argument begins with the empirical premise that in general, sex work involves men paying for sex with women. She then suggests that part of the reason that sex work exists is because of social and economic inequalities between the sexes, which are a result of systematic discrimination against women and sexist social norms. These social and economic inequalities, along with laws that would permit and normalize sex work, keep women in a position of powerlessness with respect to male employers and clients who threaten them with violence or who manipulate them into selling sex. In a just society, the law would not reinforce or exacerbate women's social and economic subordination to men. So, in a just society, the law would not permit men to pay for sex.

As a first pass, it is worth clarifying that proponents of decriminalization, like me, also do not condone relationships where people are threatened with violence to sell sex. But Watson's argument poses a challenge to decriminalization even if it excludes cases where sex workers are threatened with violence, so I will consider the parts of the argument that oppose decriminalization, not those parts of the argument that oppose threats of violence.

Watson's conception of equality is sometimes called *social egalitarianism*. This view identifies equality with an absence of hierarchy or unequal status, in contrast to egalitarian views that identify equality with an equal distribution of resources. Watson writes, "dismantling power structures that serve to subordinate some relative to others is essential to securing conditions of equality." On her view, public officials should enforce laws that actively aim to reduce or prevent the emergence of socio-economic hierarchies and the subordination of women by men.

I grant that sex workers are generally women who sell sex to men. And for the sake of argument, I will also grant that a just society would be one which diminished socioeconomic hierarchies and unequal status relations between citizens and public officials. But social egalitarian arguments against decriminalization overlook the fact that political hierarchy is also a form of hierarchy. Though citizens do form subordinate relations between each other, these relations are often a result of political choices, such as tax policies that determine the distribution of wealth, income, and social services, and penalize or incentivize marriage and parenting among different social groups. In addition, citizens are also directly subordinate to public officials in that people who hold legal authority have the power to dictate others' behavior by issuing threats of penalties like fines and incarceration. The egalitarian case against sex work overlooks these power dynamics, especially to the extent that it amounts to a defense of paternalistic limits on women's occupational freedom and bodily rights that are enforced by public officials using threats of fines and incarceration.

Additionally, there are non-ideal considerations related to the enforcement of prohibitive policies that should make all social egalitarians very wary of any policies which give public officials greater discretion to interfere with citizens' choices and to impose punishment. Even if the social egalitarian case for the Nordic Model succeeded in principle, which I don't think it does, it does not succeed in practice given existing conditions of socio-economic inequality. Egalitarian considerations also do not clearly justify criminalization, prohibition, and regulation, especially if we grant that subordination to public officials is as much of an affront to egalitarian ideals as social and economic subordination.

Social egalitarians generally emphasize the injustice of subordinating and dominating relations between citizens or groups of citizens. If, for example, people treated members of an ethnic minority as second-class citizens, excluded them from positions of power and prestige and discriminated against them, then such a society would be unjust in this way. In response to patterns of social hierarchy, many social egalitarians favor governmental solutions, such as the enforcement of non-discrimination law and reforms to housing and education policy. Yet social egalitarians often overlook that some governmental solutions introduce a different form of hierarchy—hierarchy between citizens and public officials. For example, the practices of unaccountable police violence and civil asset forfeiture illustrate that the same harms associated with domination from a powerful social majority are also associated with domination by a politically empowered group. Oftentimes socially dominant groups are politically dominant as well. There is little reason in principle that social egalitarians should overlook domination by officials when it takes the same form as domination between citizens but is more likely to be violent and inescapable.

In response to this line of argument, social egalitarians may reply that domination by public officials is different because citizens are not subordinate to particular persons or a socially dominant group when they are subordinate to officials, but rather they are all equally subordinate to particular offices which are collectively authorized by citizens who participate in fair democratic procedures. [82]

But this response is unpersuasive for two reasons. First, the fact that a person occupies an official role does not sanitize their oppressive behavior. If it were the case that merely occupying an official role could license interference with citizens' choices for the sake of social equality between people, then officials would be authorized to interfere a great deal more than they do in most liberal democracies. Second, we cannot assume that the assignment of official roles and the priorities of government officials will align with social egalitarian aims rather than working against them. For example, social egalitarians should be troubled by immigrants' lack of freedom relative to citizens, but should not assume that furthering empowering law enforcement would mitigate the oppression of immigrants.

Proponents of the Nordic Model seem to implicitly acknowledge that citizens' subjugation to public officials is a threat to social equality. This is why the Nordic Model does not criminalize the sale of sex, because to do so would be to further subject female sex workers to threats of violence and subordination. In light of this observation, social egalitarians discussing sex work should acknowledge tradeoffs between subordination at the social level and subordination between citizens and officials. Even if the Nordic Model did effectively advance the position of women relative to men, this alone would not settle the social egalitarian position on sex work. And social egalitarians should also be

82. For elaboration on this point, see Elizabeth Anderson, "Expanding the Egalitarian Toolbox: Equality and Bureaucracy," *Proceedings of the Aristotelian Society, Supplementary Volumes* 82 (2008): 139–60.

skeptical that the Nordic Model would effectively advance the relative status of women because policies that criminalize the purchase of sex still reduce female sex workers bargaining position and make it more difficult for them to safely screen clients. So even if the Nordic Model reduced the number of female sex workers by shrinking the market for sex work, it could at the same time make conditions even more oppressive for female sex workers who remain in the industry, compared to decriminalization.

Instead, social egalitarians should acknowledge the close connection between the conditions of social inequality that emerge between citizens and the political choices that facilitated those conditions. Unequal social and economic conditions between citizens emerge partly because of citizens' own patriarchal traditions, racist and sexist beliefs, and otherwise inegalitarian preferences. But these traditions, beliefs, and preferences are shaped and reinforced by public policy. Officials craft tax policies and property systems that fail to provide citizens with a basic income. Local governments implement educational policies that produce unequal opportunities. Law enforcement administer immigration restrictions and zoning regulations that create and sustain social divisions between social and economic groups.

Rather than treating the symptoms of social inequality by criminalizing exchanges which may reflect particularly stark conditions of social and economic hierarchy, social egalitarians should favor solutions to inequality that treat the underlying causes. So for example, rather than responding to the observation that men are socially and economically empowered relative to women by prohibiting men from using that position of power to pay women for sex, social egalitarians should instead advocate for a basic income, which would diminish the conditions of economic vulnerably that women face.

Of all the policies that could directly mitigate social and economic inequality, proponents of the Nordic Model favor a solution that treats the symptoms of inequality but not the cause. One may respond that I am posing a false dichotomy here because the Nordic Model does not rule out addressing the factors that cause some women to choose sex work alongside the criminalization of payment for sex. But even in the absence of a basic income, the Nordic Model is not even a second-best solution to structural injustices which socially and economically marginalize sex workers. For the aforementioned reasons associated with the harms of stigmatization and potential police abuse associated with working in a criminal industry, the Nordic Model could worsen the social and economic position of sex workers instead of improving it. Criminalizing the purchase of sex not only subjects workers to governmental interference (even under the Nordic Model), it also makes it more difficult for workers to find clients, requiring them to work longer hours with less negotiating power. And because sex workers have less political power within a social hierarchy they are still likely to be harmed in interactions with law enforcement even if selling sex is not itself criminalized.

These pragmatic concerns about the Nordic Model should be especially worrying to egalitarians, who may either advance the Nordic Model as a principled ideal of equal gender relations or as a pragmatic solution to gendered inequities. It is unclear why anyone would endorse the Nordic Model as an ideal policy though. Presumably if it were possible to effectively enforce any egalitarian policy solution, then officials would enforce policies that directly minimized structural social and economic disadvantages, such as a basic income, rather than the Nordic Model which legally entrenches gender dichotomies and subordinates citizens to the government. So the best case for the Nordic Model is that it is a pragmatic solution to inequality in non-ideal circumstances.[83] But in practice, the Nordic Model compounds violence against sex workers and contributes to their marginalization, so it is not a pragmatic solution to non-ideal conditions inequality either.

4.3.2 Clients and Equal Status

There are also egalitarian reasons in favor of decriminalizing the sex industry for the sake of clients. Social egalitarians who are concerned about hierarchy should also reject the Nordic Model because the Nordic Model disproportionately subjects socioeconomically vulnerable and otherwise marginalized men to criminal penalties. The Nordic Model also harms these men because, if enforcement is an effective deterrent, the policy would prevent at least some men from having any intimate experiences.

Egalitarians should also favor decriminalization insofar as enforcement of criminal penalties disproportionately harms socially marginalized men who are either more likely to encounter law enforcement due to "hot spot" policing or who have fewer financial resources to effectively avoid

---

83. One may press this position in light of concerns about the feasibility or desirability of a Universal Basic Income. For a challenge to Basic Income proposals see Hilary W. Hoynes and Jesse Rothstein, "Universal Basic Income in the US and Advanced Countries. No. w25538" (National Bureau of Economic Research, 2019).

criminal sanctions. Proponents of the Nordic Model may reply that they oppose the sale of women's sexual service on the grounds that women are systematically oppressed by men, so even if particular men are more disadvantaged than particular women in general the policy is justified on the grounds that all else equal, men are a dominant social group. But such a response would fail to account for the full range of social disadvantages that people can experience with respect to each other. This concern is especially pressing for people with disabilities, but extends to other multiply-disadvantaged men as well.

Some egalitarians cite the harms associated with lack of intimacy and social isolation as targets of egalitarian concern.[84] Many people who see sex workers do so because they otherwise would lack intimate partnerships or even companionship in their lives. Even if the relationships between sex workers and their clients may fall short of some people's idea of a loving relationship, these relationships could still be preferable to circumstances where people entirely lack social connection and intimacy in their lives. The Nordic Model therefore effectively criminalizes the only means that some people have to experience intimate relationships.

Egalitarian concerns about a lack of access to intimacy are especially pressing given that people who are overweight, socially awkward, poor, or members of marginalized or stigmatized groups are likely to have fewer options for intimate partners than multiply advantaged groups. This

---

84. See e.g. Chiara Cordelli, "Distributive Justice and the Problem of Friendship," *Political Studies* 63, no. 3 (August 1, 2015): 679–95. Aaron James, "Power in Social Organization as the Subject of Justice," *Pacific Philosophical Quarterly* 86, no. 1 (2005): 25–49.

does not characterize all sex buyers. Some people simply prefer to pay for sex or prefer sex workers to other potential intimate partners. But clients' social disadvantages can partly explain their decision to pay for sex. For example, a survey of sex buyers in Australia found that

> Clients were significantly older, less likely to have been educated beyond high school, less likely to report having a regular partner in the past 6 months, and more likely to report that their most recent sexual encounter was with a casual partner.[85]

A less systematic report of sex buyers describes the following motivations for seeing a sex worker. One client writes,

> I am single and have been so for all my life. I am somewhat overweight, even though I would not consider myself to be ugly. Before visiting a sex worker for the first time I was a kissless virgin . . . I think I visit sex workers for two reasons. First of all to satisfy my sexual needs. I decided to lose my virginity to a sex worker, essentially "just to get it over with." But I've also noticed that visiting a sex worker satisfies my need for physical intimacy. Additionally, I think that trying out new or niche kinks is easier with somebody who already has experience but does not expect you yourself to be experienced.[86]

85. Marian K. Pitts et al., "Who Pays for Sex and Why? An Analysis of Social and Motivational Factors Associated with Male Clients of Sex Workers," *Archives of Sexual Behavior* 33, no. 4 (August 1, 2004): 353–58.

86. Miranda Kane, "Why Do Men in Their 20s Pay for Sex? We Asked Them," *Metro* (blog), January 22, 2018, https://metro.co.uk/2018/01/22/why-do-men-in-their-20s-pay-for-sex-we-asked-them-7237965/

Another writes,

> I'm just really lonely. I do a couple of online dating apps but
> I don't get many matches and then trying to get dates from
> those matches is even less likely. Trying to actually date
> someone a few times is nearly impossible for me. I've been
> using these apps for almost a year and I'm not sure why it's
> so hard for me. I have good photos and a good profile and am
> polite and respectful but even the matches I do get are with
> women I'm not really that interested in. Outside of the apps,
> I literally have no friends so there's not much opportunity for
> me to meet women. [87]

Teela Sanders' interviews with clients broadly affirms this
picture, though clients are also varied in their characteristics
and motivations for paying for sex.[88]

Some people have sexual dysfunctions or injuries that
make it difficult for them to form intimate partnerships.
In some cases, their condition can be successfully treated
by paying for the services of a sexual surrogate.[89] Yet the
same reasons in favor of allowing sexual surrogacy are also
reasons to permit payment for sex more generally. In cases
where sexual surrogacy is not therapeutic, intimacy is still
important to people with disabilities who lack access to intimate partners because of challenges associated with being

---

87. Ibid.

88. Teela Sanders, *Paying for Pleasure: Men Who Buy Sex* (Milton,
Oxfordshire, England: Willan Publishing, 2013).

89. Bruce Rybarczyk, "Sexual Surrogate Therapy," *Encyclopedia of
Clinical Neuropsychology* (2011): 2281; Muller, "Sexual Surrogates Help
Many Who Suffer Alone"; Joshua A. Bodie, William W. Beeman, and
Manoj Monga, "Psychogenic Erectile Dysfunction," *International Journal
of Psychiatry in Medicine* 33, no. 3 (2003): 273–93.

disabled. For these populations, Ezio De Nucci argues that the sex should be donated to disabled or elderly people as charity.[90] But this proposal is unlikely to effectively meet the demand for intimacy among these populations. For this reason, medical ethicists who claim that disabled people have a moral right to access the goods of sexual intimacy support a legal right to pay for sex in these cases.[91] But as Brian Earp argues, the case in favor of sex rights for the disabled effectively demonstrates why all people should have a legal right to pay for sex, because nondisabled people face other disadvantages which may make it difficult for them to form intimate partnerships without paying.[92]

In addition to the egalitarian case for allowing heterosexual male clients to pay for sex, social egalitarians should also favor decriminalization on the grounds that some clients are not enacting any form of patriarchal subjugation because they are men who pay male sex workers. In defense of the decriminalization of the male escort service rentboy. com, Scott Schackford writes,

> While the increased acceptance of homosexuality has made
> it easier for gay men and women to come out earlier in their
> lives, we still have untold numbers of older gay men who
> came out late (or still aren't comfortable coming out at all)

90. Ezio Di Nucci, "Sexual Rights and Disability," *Journal of Medical Ethics* 37, no. 3 (2011): 158–61.

91. Jacob M. Appel, "Sex Rights for the Disabled?," *Journal of Medical Ethics* 36, no. 3 (2010): 152–54. Frej Klem Thomsen, "Prostitution, Disability and Prohibition," *Journal of Medical Ethics* 41, no. 6 (2015): 451–59.

92. Brian D. Earp and Ole Martin Moen, "Paying for Sex—Only for People with Disabilities?," *Journal of Medical Ethics* 42, no. 1 (November 2015): 54–55. medethics—2015.

and didn't move to big gay metropolises like New York City
or San Francisco to find love. Gay men (and women!) are
still a small part of the population. It is inaccurate—even
heartless—to assume that all gay men are able to find a
sexual companion through conventional means.

Schakford's argument appeals to a relational egalitarian
ideal. In many places, homosexuality is still stigmatized.
In these contexts, it is difficult for gay men to find love in
virtue of unfair social conditions that prevent them from
coming out.

But the same relational egalitarian case that Shackford
presents for allowing gay men to find sexual companions
through online escort services are also reasons for allowing
other men who are the victims of unfair social conditions
to pay for sexual companionship as well. Just as it is unfair
that gay men are unable to find partners "through conventional means" in places where being gay is stigmatized, it is
also unfair that overweight, unattractive, socially awkward
men, poor men, or men of color are unable to find partners through conventional means. And so just as it is heartless to then exclude gay men in these circumstances from
having rewarding sexual experiences, it is also heartless
to exclude other unfairly disadvantaged men from finding
sexual companions.

Proponents of the Nordic Model may reply that it is
less problematic if gay men pay for companionship because
participants in the market for gay male escorts are not in
relations of social subordination (they're both gay men),
unlike participants in the market for female escorts. If so,
then proponent of the Nordic Model could endorse policies
that only criminalize men paying for sex with women, not
men paying for sex with men. But this policy would amount

to an overly narrow focus on relations of hierarchy between the sexes, whereas I have argued that relational egalitarians should widen their view and consider a wider scope of social and economic disadvantages which may partly explain why some people pay for sex.

4.3.3 Sex Work and an Egalitarian Society

There are also several reasons to think that decriminalization would advance the more general cause of equality between the sexes better than the Nordic Model, both in practice and in principle. In practice, decriminalization could have egalitarian externalities by destigmatizing female sexuality rather than casting sex either as sacred gift or as a tool of patriarchal oppression. In principle, decriminalization is more compatible with the ideal of an egalitarian society than the Nordic Model because a true society of equals would not entrench gender dichotomies in the justification for the law nor would it prohibit mutually beneficial exchanges.

For example, one threat to equality between the sexes today is purity culture. Though egalitarian proponents of the Nordic Model do not generally support purity cultures, they find common ground with those who advocate for norms of chastity and modesty when they treat markets that are characterized by sexual promiscuity as a distinctive social problem relative to other occupational choices. Even if proponents of the Nordic Model do not intend to stigmatize or degrade female sex workers, by focusing their attention on the dangers of sexual markets specifically, they affirm traditionalists' conviction that unrestricted female sexuality is dangerous to women and society. In contrast, the case for decriminalization is a case for legitimizing a wider range of expressions of female sexualities in people's personal and professional lives.

Furthermore, contrary to the claim that the sex industry fuels a culture of male dominance, there is also evidence that suggests that it can have the opposite effect. For example, one study suggests that people who watch porn hold more gender-egalitarian views than those who do not.[93] Others have argued that purity cultures and the policies that stigmatize female sexuality contributes to rape cultures, in contrast to social practices that normalize female sexual promiscuity.[94] Even if decriminalization did not counteract a culture of male dominance though, proponents of the Nordic Model have not established that decriminalization promotes a culture of male dominance to a greater extent than more prohibitive systems, especially given that prohibitive systems including the Nordic Model do not eliminate the practice of men paying for sex with women, they merely drive the practice underground and relegate female sex workers and their clients to a black market industry.

Proponents of the Nordic Model may reply that the egalitarian and consequentialist objections I raise against it are pragmatic concerns, but that in ideal theory the best

93. Taylor Kohut, Jodie L. Baer, and Brendan Watts, "Is Pornography Really about 'Making Hate to Women'? Pornography Users Hold More Gender Egalitarian Attitudes Than Nonusers in a Representative American Sample," *Journal of Sex Research* 53, no. 1 (January 2, 2016): 1–11.

94. Jennifer Mathieu, "The Troubling Connection Between Modesty Culture and Rape Culture," *Time*, July 8, 2015, http://time.com/3918215/modesty-culture-rape-culture/.

egalitarian sex work policy would be the Nordic Model. Yet as socialist thinker G. A. Cohen argues, a truly egalitarian society would be a stateless society, one where all people related as equals not because they were forced to do so by a powerful public official but because they had an egalitarian ethos.[95] In this way, the Nordic Model also fails to live up to its egalitarian ideals in principle. The ideal egalitarian society would not be one where people were prohibited from exchanging sex for money. Rather, the ideal egalitarian society would be one where no one needed to exchange any form of labor for money in order to meet their basic needs, a society where people of different sexes and races related to each other as equals, and where people had an egalitarian ethos of mutual respect and solidarity.

Even in an ideal egalitarian society though, we might imagine that some people would still choose to make exchanges, including exchanges that involved sex. If such cases emerged in such a society it would be worse by the lights of egalitarian ideals for a public official to interfere and coercively prevent people from trading their resources and talents for mutual advantage. Such interference would make both parties to the exchange worse off than they would have been. Officials' interference with sex markets would also establish a subordinating relationship between citizens and officials, which I argued earlier, egalitarians should oppose just as they oppose other forms of structural hierarchy. For this reason, even the ideal egalitarian society would be one where sex work was decriminalized.

95. G. A. Cohen, *Rescuing Justice and Equality* (Cambridge, MA: Harvard University Press, 2009), 119. See also Jonathan Wolff, "Fairness, Respect, and the Egalitarian Ethos," *Philosophy & Public Affairs* 27, no. 2 (1998): 97–122.

4.3.4 Summary

Egalitarian proponents of the Nordic Model have a blind spot when it comes to the subordination that law enforcement necessarily involves. Paying attention to the inegalitarian effects of law enforcement strengthens the case for decriminalization. In a true egalitarian society, women would not only be free of male-domination, all citizens would be free of governmental subordination as well.

4.4 CONCLUSION

Whatever one thinks about the potential for exploitation or injury associated with sex work, prohibiting people from selling and paying for sex will only make things worse. The case for decriminalization does not appeal to a particularly optimistic view of sex work. I recognize that sex work is a dangerous profession and that even decriminalization cannot protect workers from all the risks associated with it. Rather, the case for decriminalization appeals to a pessimistic view of alternative policy proposals. The Nordic Model doesn't stop sex work; it only stops sex workers from working with law-abiding citizens in the safety of a legal marketplace. Though proponents of the Nordic Model claim they are motivated by a concern for women's' rights, health and safety, and equality, they favor a policy that empowers public officials to interfere with women's most intimate choices, endangers their health and safety, and subordinates them to paternalistic public officials and moralistic majorities.

Moreover, critics of sex work overlook the benefits of the industry for workers and clients. Sex workers may quite reasonably prefer their industry to alternative occupations because it offers flexible hours, a comparatively high hourly rate, the opportunity to meet new people and to provide care-giving services, and an outlet for creative expression. Clients also benefit from the intimate services that sex workers provide. When workers judge that their best occupational option is sex work and clients judge that their preferred (or only) opportunity for sexual intimacy is to pay a sex worker, public officials should believe that they are making decisions that are in their interests. And while sex work is work, sex work is also sex. So even if some sex workers' occupational choices aren't in their interests, selling sex is still an intimate choice that workers are entitled to make. For these reasons, the best thing that public officials can do for sex workers is to get out of the way and let them decide for themselves.

Defending
Decriminalization

IN THE PREVIOUS CHAPTER I MADE the case for decriminalization. There I argued that sex work should be decriminalized because criminal penalties violate the rights of sex workers and their clients, compromise health and safety, and are especially burdensome to people who are already socially or economically disadvantaged. In response to arguments like these, proponents of regulation, prohibition, and the Nordic Model question whether people have rights to sell or pay for sex, whether criminal penalties really do have bad consequences on balance, and whether an egalitarian society would allow people to sell or pay for sex. In this chapter, I will describe and respond to some of the strongest objections to the foregoing case for decriminalization.

5.1 RIGHTS-BASED OBJECTIONS

The first group of objections to decriminalization question my argument that criminal penalties violate the rights of sex workers and their clients. Some critics of this argument argue that while people may have rights to consensually

Debating Sex Work. Lori Watson, Jessica Flanigan, Oxford University Press (2020). © Oxford University Press.
DOI: 10.1093/oso/9780190659882.001.0001

choose their sexual partners and their occupations, sex workers cannot consent to sex or work when they are acting as sex workers. Relatedly, one may grant that sex work is consensual, but question whether consent is enough to establish that a choice is within someone's rights when some workers only choose to sell sex because their other options are much worse. In response, I argue that these objections to decriminalization typically prove too much because they cannot establish why sex work in particular is non-consensual or non-voluntary, in contrast to other occupational choices. I also argue that even if these objections succeeded, they would not decisively undermine the case for decriminalization.

Another line of objections denies my claim that economic liberties are basic liberties, and then argues that since economic liberties are nonbasic, the regulation or prohibition of the sex industry is permissible as long as public officials have good reason. I think that economic liberties are basic, but even if this line of objection succeeded, critics of the industry must also establish that officials have good reason to prohibit or regulate sex work. I then consider two other rights-based arguments against decriminalization. First, some claim that a system of legal sex work would undermine the sexual autonomy of workers in other industries. Second, critics of decriminalization sometimes appeal to members of a political community's rights to define and enforce standards of decency. These arguments appeal to the idea that decriminalization could be justified for the sake of bystanders' rights. In response, I argue that bystanders do not have rights to have their sexual choices institutionally protected from pecuniary considerations nor do they have rights to impose controversial conceptions of decency on other people.

5.1.1 Sex Work Is Not Consensual

Consent is a normative power that changes the moral landscape of permissions and obligations between people.[1] By consenting, people authorize actions that would otherwise be wrong. For example, people are not permitted to injure each other or remove people's organs. But if a patient consents to surgery then that patient's physician is authorized to do these things. The conception of consent that is used in medical contexts can helpfully illustrate what meaningful consent requires more generally. In order to consent, a person ought to be informed, uncoerced, unforced, and mentally capable of giving consent. Adult sex workers can meet these conditions. The defense of decriminalization does not amount to a defense of nonconsensual sex, such as sex that results from fraud, coercion, or force or sex with people who are incapable of consenting.

Yet some critics of decriminalization argue that sex work is not consensual because sex workers are implicitly threatened with violence if they refuse sex with a client. There are two versions of this objection. The first is that many sex workers are implicitly threatened with violence from clients or employers if they refuse to sell sex, and that their decision to sell is therefore non-consensual. The second is that if sex work was decriminalized, sex workers

1. David Owens, "The Possibility of Consent," *Ratio* 24, no. 4 (December 1, 2011): 402–21.

could be threatened with legal penalties for refusing sex in some cases. And since legal penalties are coercively enforced with threats of force, decriminalized sex work that enabled clients to legally threaten workers for refusing sex would make it so that some people were only having sex in order to avoid being subjected to force.

The first version of this objection characterizes sex work as forced labor. In some cases, this is an apt characterization of sex work. If a client or employer violently threatens a sex worker for refusing to provide sexual services or assaults her, then she does not consent to sell sex. But there are cases like this in all other industries as well, where it is apt to characterize some labor in an industry as forced labor. If an employer violently forces his workers to stay at the factory or farm for long hours, then his workers do not consent to work. If a customer threatens his taxi driver to take him across town, the driver does not consent to provide taxi services. These cases illustrate that the morally objectionable aspect of forced sex work is not that it involves sex but that it is forced work, and that it would be a mistake to dismiss an entire industry as nonconsensual on the grounds that in some cases people in the industry are forced to work.

Some people point out that sexual encounters between women and men very often carry an implicit threat of male force against a woman.[2] As an empirical matter, it is plausible that many sex workers do feel pressured to have sex and do fear physical retaliation if they refuse. Many women

---

2. Dorothy E. Roberts, "Rape, Violence, and Women's Autonomy," *Chicago Kent Law Review* 69 (1993): 359; Susan Estrich, "Rape," *Yale Law Journal* 95, no. 6 (1986): 1087–1184.

246 | DEBATING SEX WORK

who are not sex workers feel similar pressure in their sexual encounters. Many women who are not sex workers also reasonably fear physical retaliation. Pressure and physical intimidation are legitimate concerns regarding sexual encounters, but they are not concerns that are specific to sex work. Prohibiting the sale or purchase of sexual services does not address these concerns though, it only makes workers more fearful of reporting violence or threats of violence. And if sex work were decriminalized then sex workers could be less likely than non-sex workers to experience these threats because sex workers are more likely to clarify the terms of a sexual encounter beforehand and to hire security services.

Other critics of the sex industry argue that the implicit threat of legal penalties can in some circumstances invalidate sex workers' ability to consent. For example, Watson writes that "if specific performance were granted as a relief [for the violation of sex contracts] requiring specific performance with a john would be to Court order rape and would run afoul of 13th Amendment and other legal prohibitions of involuntary servitude."

But existing standards within contract law make room for circumstances like these. In general, courts require that workers or contractors who break contracts provide refunds and compensation or pay a penalty instead of requiring specific performance of a service.[3] A house cleaner cannot be legally forced to uphold a cleaning contract by cleaning her client's home, even if she can be required to provide a

---

3. Paul H. Rubin, "Unenforceable Contracts: Penalty Clauses and Specific Performance," *Journal of Legal Studies* 10, no. 2 (June 1, 1981): 237–47.

refund. [4] So, too, even if sex workers make contracts with their clients they may avoid being compelled to have sex.

One may reply that laws that require sex workers to pay damages for breaches of contract are also wrong, even if they do not require specific performance, because no one should face financial penalties for refusing sex. This reply would either amount to a critique of the more general practice of contracting for labor, or it would require further justification to explain why no one should face financial penalties for refusing sex when refusing to do other forms of contractually mandated labor can permissibly result in financial penalties. This reply also has unappealing policy implications. Rejecting the enforceability of some contracts would entail either the prohibition of contractually mandated sex work or officials' refusal to enforce contracts for sex work. The first policy would be paternalistic toward sex workers; in that it would prohibit them from making binding contracts that they judge to be in their interest on the grounds that being bound by the contract could be bad for them. Prohibiting contractually mandated sex work would also amount to empowering public officials and law enforcement (usually men) to use violence

---

4. This analogy also challenges Pateman's claim that "The client makes direct use of the prostitute's body, and there are no 'objective' criteria through which to judge whether the service has been satisfactorily performed. Trades unions bargain over pay and conditions for workers, and the products of their labors are 'quality controlled.' Prostitutes, in contrast, can always be refused payment by men who claim (and who can gainsay their subjective assessment?) that their demands have not been met." Yet other service providers face the same risk, and if sex work were decriminalized then they could develop industry standards, norms, and protections from these risks, just as home cleaners or massage therapists do. Carole Pateman, *The Sexual Contract* (Hoboken, NJ: John Wiley & Sons, 2014), 61.

to control women's sexual choices. The second policy of officials' refusing to enforce sex workers labor agreements would only make the sex industry worse for sex workers by locking them into a grey market economy that lacks access to formal legal protections.[5]

5.1.2 Sex Work Is Not Voluntary

A more frequent rights-based objection to decriminalization is that even if sex workers consent, in that they are not forced, tricked, or coerced into having sex, their consent is insufficiently voluntary because they only choose to sell sex because they lack better options. For example, though Melissa Farley writes that "what's wrong with prostitution, and what's wrong with buying sex, are the same things that are wrong with other forms of violence against women, incest, rape, and battery," she then goes on to describe a series of cases where women chose to sell sex so in light of poor alternatives. On this view, a consensual sexual encounter is relevantly similar to rape if the worker only consents because of unacceptable or unjust circumstances.

Watson makes a similar point when she writes, "'choices' made from circumstances of inequality that additionally harm persons are 'choices' that the state should prevent for the sake of equality." Watson then cites the choice to sell an organ or to work in a sweatshop as the sorts of choices that, while consensual, amount to modern day slavery. Watson thinks that sex work is analogous to these choices because like organ sellers and sweatshop workers,

5. Jessica Flanigan, "Rethinking Freedom of Contract," *Philosophical Studies* 174, no. 2 (2017): 443–63.

sex workers only choose to sell sex because they lack acceptable alternatives. Other critics of decriminalization echo this worry. Similarly, Catharine MacKinnon writes,

> When material conditions preclude 99 percent of your options, it is not meaningful to call the remaining 1 percent— what you are doing—your choice . . . when force is a normalized part of sex, when no is taken to mean yes, when fear and despair produce acquiescence and acquiescence is taken to mean consent, consent is not a meaningful concept.[6]

These arguments are similar to Serena Olsaretti's more general argument that that a worker's consent is normatively deficient whenever she lacks acceptable alternatives to work. Olsaretti writes,

> A choice is voluntary if and only if it is not forced, and it is forced if and only if it is made only or primarily because the alternative to it is unacceptable, where the standard for the acceptability of options is an objective standard of wellbeing and unacceptable options are those which by that standard fall below a certain threshold. A paradigmatic example of an unacceptable option is a hazardous job that threatens frustration of people's basic needs.[7]

Critics of decriminalization appeal to this notion of voluntariness when they argue that even if a woman consents to sell sex, if she only does so because otherwise she will be

6. Catharine A. MacKinnon, "Liberalism and the Death of Feminism," in *The Sexual Liberals and the Attack on Feminism*, ed. Dorchen Leidholdt and Janice G. Raymond (Oxford, UK: Pergamon Press, 1990), 3–13.

7. Serena Olsaretti, "Self-Ownership and Coercion," in *Oxford Handbook of Freedom*, ed. David Schmidtz (Oxford, England: Oxford University Press, 2018), 444.

unable to meet her basic needs, then the decision to sell sex is not voluntary.

There are two ways of responding to this objection. First, we should question whether a lack of voluntariness on its own renders an otherwise consensual choice normatively deficient. If a cancer patient consents to chemotherapy because she lacks acceptable alternatives, her physicians would not commit medical battery by administering it. The same insight applies to the labor market. People may only choose to work in difficult industries such as sex work, factory work, or cleaning commercial buildings because they cannot meet their needs if they are unemployed or because they consider their other employment options to be unacceptable.

Second, we should question whether a lack of acceptable alternatives is relevant to the case against decriminalization. Even if sex workers do lack acceptable alternatives and resort to "survival sex" to meet their basic needs, this consideration does not clearly weigh against decriminalization. As Peter de Marneffe's argues in response to this argument, prohibiting survival sex without providing acceptable alternatives to sex work only makes it more difficult for people to meet their basic needs.[8] In addition, de Marneffe points out that some sex workers are citizens of Scandinavian countries that provide unemployment benefits and nationalized healthcare services.[9] Though de Marneffe does not support decriminalization, this

8. Peter de Marneffe, *Liberalism and Prostitution* (New York: Oxford University Press, 2010), 70.
9. Though on de Marneffe's view, the fact that sex workers have alternatives weighs in support of prohibition or regulation because limiting the industry in these contexts is less likely to harm workers.

argument effectively undermines a central justification for the Nordic Model. And even outside of Scandinavia, many sex workers are educated and capable of finding work in other industries.[10] In these cases, the decision to sell sex would be voluntary and consensual.

If sex work is not a voluntary choice because workers lack acceptable alternatives then prohibiting it would only worsen the position of workers by depriving them of one of their only legal means of surviving. If workers have acceptable alternatives to selling sex then critics of decriminalization cannot cite workers' lack of voluntariness as a grounds for prohibiting the sale or purchase of sexual services.

5.1.3 Sex Workers Do Not Give Enthusiastic Consent

In arguing that officials should not prohibit sex work on the grounds that sex workers' lack acceptable alternatives, I compared sex work to work in other industries. But one might reply that the sex industry is different from other industries because it involves sex, and the standards

10. For example, A recent survey of internet-based sex workers in the United Kingdom found that 38% had college degrees and 17% had postgraduate degrees. And a survey of sex workers in eight cities in the United States found that more than 75% of sex workers had graduated high school or received a GED and 33% had some college. Teela Sanders, Laura Jarvis King, and Laura Connelly, "Internet-Based Sex Workers: Working Conditions and Job Satisfaction," Wellcome Trust, 2015. "Estimating the Size and Structure of the Underground Commercial Sex Economy in Eight Major US Cities," Urban Institute, accessed March 8, 2017, http://www.urban.org/research/publication/estimating-size-and-structure-underground-commercial-sex-economy-eight-major-us-cities/view/full_report.

for consent to sex should be higher than the standards of consent to other kinds of work. Namely, some argue that people are morally required to obtain enthusiastic mutual consent to sex.[11] There are several reasons one might think that the standards for consent to sex should be higher. Some people argue that there should be higher standards of consent for sex given its importance to people's humanity. Others think that consent to sex should be held to higher standards because of the potential for abuse. On any version of this view, a sex worker's lack of acceptable alternatives to sex work or the threat of legal penalties associated with contractual violations could undermine her ability to meet this higher standard for consent to sex if sex workers do not give enthusiastic consent.

I agree that, all else being equal, it is better if people give enthusiastic consent to sex. Yet a narrow focus on enthusiastic consent is an inadequate benchmark for distinguishing morally good sex from morally problematic sex that should be legislated against. A person may give consent to sex that is unwanted and unwelcome. In these cases, Robin West writes,

> If unwelcome sex is a constant in a woman's life—for weeks, months, years, and decades—it is likely to be alienating and oppressive—in a word, injurious. We might decide for all sorts of reasons that we cannot imagine a legal response to such a private injury. It doesn't follow though that we should deny or ignore it.

11. Jaclyn Friedman and Jessica Valenti, *Yes Means Yes!: Visions of Female Sexual Power and A World Without Rape* (Boston: Da Capo Press, 2008), 21.

Like West, I am skeptical that an enthusiastic consent or welcome sex standard is a sound basis for public policy. For one thing, many sexual encounters outside of the marketplace fall short of this standard. People have non-commercial sex for all sorts of reasons. People may even have non-commercial sex in order to meet their basic needs, such as sugaring or cases where a person remains in a relationship that she would otherwise leave because she cannot find acceptable housing elsewhere. If public officials could prohibit people from having unenthusiastic sex for economic reasons, then they could in principle prohibit these sorts of arrangements. But interfering with people's relationships in these ways would an obvious overreach. This is not to say that unwelcome sex is morally unproblematic, only to say that moral objections to unwelcome sex are not sufficient grounds for interventionist public policy.

One may reply that prohibition of unwanted or unenthusiastic sex would only be an overreach in private contexts because such relationships happen outside of the marketplace. But officials rightly prohibit sexual assault in private contexts, so if unenthusiastic consent was insufficiently consensual than in principle officials would have the authority to interfere with a private sex-for-housing arrangement. Yet it would be wrong to require enthusiastic consent not just pragmatically but also in principle because while some women (or anyone) may not want to have sex in particular cases, women may also have a desire to have the freedom to have sex even in those particular cases where they do not desire sex.

There is also reason to doubt whether enthusiastic consent should be considered an ideal for sexual encounters. An enthusiastic consent standard may backfire if it effectively means that women are expected or required to perform the emotional labor of mustering a sufficient degree of enthusiasm when having sex.[12] Women are already required to calibrate their emotions to perform sympathy, enthusiasm, or affection in other domains of their lives, and these expectations can be disproportionately burdensome to women who are more likely than men to be sanctioned for failing to emotionally engage with people. Taken too far, an ideal of consent may amount to yet another expectation for women to conform to gendered expectations. Expectations of emotional performance can be especially burdensome in workplaces, and sex work is no different. Like any worker, the way that sex workers feel about their jobs isn't central to questions of whether they consent to work. To say otherwise is to suggest that sex workers, who are most often women, should not only work but enjoy their work, while fewer people object to workers' lack of fulfillment or enthusiasm in traditionally male industries.

5.1.4 Economic Rights Are Nonbasic

Another set of rights-based objections to decriminalization reject my claim that respect for workers' autonomy requires protections for their economic freedom and argue further that protections for workers' autonomy may actually require limits on their economic freedom. The first of these objections is that economic liberty is generally nonbasic, unlike other liberties which merit strong institutional

---

12. De Marneffe cites the emotional labor required by sex workers as a harm associated with the industry. But if the expectation that women perform sexual desire is a harm, it is also a harmful expectation that may be entrenched by prohibiting or regulating the industry.

protections, so it is permissible for officials to limit worker's economic freedom through regulations and prohibitions. The second objection is that the exercise of economic liberty threatens other liberties and reduces workers' overall freedom. The third objection is that some sexual choices, in the context of the marketplace, undermine workers' sexual autonomy. All three of these objections grant that sex work may be a consensual and voluntary choice but nevertheless denies that it is the sort of choice that merits protection for rights-based reasons.

The first objection is that all economic liberty is nonbasic and can therefore be limited for the sake of other social goals. In the previous chapter I argued that sex workers' rights are entailed by other basic liberties including sexual rights and economic rights. Sex work is an economic right because it is an occupational choice and a choice to employ someone as a worker. One may object to the claim that economic rights are basic though, and if so then they may claim that officials can limit and regulate sex work as they regulate other choices within the economic realm.

Say we grant that economic freedom is nonbasic and therefore that sex work is nonbasic. Even still, this argument cannot on its own establish that the Nordic Model or prohibitive approaches are preferable to decriminalization. Even those philosophers who accept these distinctions agree that public officials should adopt a "presumption of liberty" and protect economic and other, nonbasic freedoms unless there is not another acceptably costly other way to advance a compelling interest of the political community. So even if my claims in the previous chapter about the basic status of the rights to sell and pay for sex are false, public officials still should not limit people's freedom to buy and sell sex unless there is no other available alternative way to promote their goals of women's' rights, public health and safety, and equality. But there certainly are other available alternative ways of advancing these goals, such as by improving access to law enforcement and judicial services for women, investing in public health, and by promoting economic policies that give economically and socially disadvantaged workers more and better options rather than taking their options away. Since limiting the freedom of sex workers and their clients isn't necessary to achieve the goals that people cite in favor of prohibitive policies, even those who are skeptical that the rights to sell and pay for sex are basic liberties should still be skeptical of prohibitive policies.

The second objection is that market choices limit autonomy on balance. Here the idea is that some jobs involve working for an oppressive employer or signing non-compete agreements that limit worker's autonomy in the long run. Watson presses this objection specifically against the sex industry when she argues against the claim that decriminalization would be good for workers' autonomy by giving sex workers the protections that other employees have. Watson is skeptical that employees autonomy is protected or promoted under most existing labor agreements. Watson writes, "(sex workers) maintaining status as an independent contractor may appear to give the veneer of autonomy, but it fails insofar as economic burdens associated with this status place 'workers' in a position of vulnerability not simply with respect to buyers/clients/johns but also the persons in charge of the club or brothel."

Elizabeth Anderson develops a similar argument against modern corporatized workplaces in general. On her view the modern corporation is like a mini-dictatorship with total control over workers' lives.[13] Since workplaces have so much power over their workers today, their policies should be subject to principles of justice. And these principles of justice would prohibit labor agreements that were subordinating, demeaning, disrespectful, or oppressive to workers. Instead, a just workplace would give people greater autonomy in the workplace and more of a voice in the terms and conditions of their labor.

Let's grant for the sake of argument that Watson and Anderson are correct about the conditions of independent contractors and workers in a modern workplace. Anderson's arguments show that sex workers are not the only employees who work from a position of vulnerability and who lack autonomy in their workplaces. And many sex workers may judge that despite the hardships Watson cites, the hardships associated with other workplaces would be a greater burden. Public officials should believe these workers. Even if these arguments entailed that officials should intervene in some way to make both kinds of workplaces better, such arguments cannot justify a policy that diminished the autonomy of workers on balance by restricting workers' occupational choices even further without replacing their poor options with better ones.

The third objection of this sort is that economic choices that involve alienating sexual autonomy in the marketplace, should not be legally protected because they can undermine workers' sexual autonomy. For example, Hallie

13. Elizabeth Anderson, *Private Government: How Employers Rule Our Lives* (Princeton, NJ: Princeton University Press, 2017).

Liberto contrasts cases where a sex worker trades sex for money with cases where a sex worker can be legally bound to a contract that gives a client rights to have sex with her for a specified time without an "opt out" option. Liberto writes that "legalizing prostitution does not entail the market alienability of sexual rights." Yet she is reluctant to endorse a policy that allowed for the market alienability of sexual rights on the grounds that contractually mandated sex work would threaten workers' sexual autonomy. In support of this claim, Liberto points out that if there were market alienability for sexual rights then sex workers could be required to pay damages for refusing sex, but these legal penalties can "render contract breaking an unavailable option for contractors" in some cases, thereby undermining their sexual autonomy.[14]

Previously, I made the case that this concern is not unique to sex work, it relates more generally to any contracts that would seemingly require specific performance or damages for non-performance. But Liberto and others seem to worry that contracts for sex work would be morally distinctive, because sexual autonomy is distinct from the autonomy that workers have over their bodies in other contexts. For example, Margaret Radin, writes,

> Having to pay damages for deciding not to engage in sex with someone seems very harmful to the ideal of sexuality as integral to personhood. Moreover, it seems that determining the amount of damages due is tantamount to complete commodification. Granting a damage remedy requires an official

14. Hallie Rose Liberto, "Normalizing Prostitution versus Normalizing the Alienability of Sexual Rights: A Response to Scott A. Anderson," *Ethics* 120, no. 1 (October 1, 2009): 138–45.

entity to place a dollar value on the "goods"; commodification is thus officially imposed.[15]

Like Liberto, Radin does not favor prohibition. But Radin does favor regulations that limit the threat of legal penalties that sex workers would face for breaking contractual agreements.

Radin therefore concludes that "we should continue to make prostitution contracts unenforceable" and that officials should instead either enforce only restitution or refuse to involve themselves in settling contract disputes for sex workers altogether. I suggested earlier that refusing to accommodate contracts for sex work is an unappealing solution because it relegates sex workers to a gray-market economy where they lack the ability to make legally binding and enforceable contracts. In this way, Radin's solution would limit sex workers' autonomy. But proponents of this solution may reply that it would promote workers' autonomy on balance.

At this point the dialectic stalls. In part, it is an empirical question whether the market alienability of sexual rights would promote or undermine sex workers' sexual autonomy on balance. But even if we grant that it would undermine their autonomy on balance, as the critics allege, this would raise a further question of whether public officials ought to promote autonomy or respect autonomy. If officials ought to respect autonomy and if the market alienability of sexual rights undermined autonomy, then this would be a reason

15. Margaret Radin, "Contested Commodities," in *Rethinking Commodification: Cases and Readings in Law and Culture*, ed. Martha Ertman and Joan C. Williams (New York: New York University Press, 2005).

in favor of some limits on sex workers' economic freedom. I deny that officials ought to promote autonomy though. On my view, officials should respect autonomy. But one may argue that refusing to uphold contracts that involved the market alienability of sexual rights is not disrespectful to sex workers autonomy because it does not involve interfering with their choices. I think such refusal would be disrespectful all the same because it expresses paternalistic judgments about sex workers' ability to form contracts that are in their interest. Even if the foregoing anti-paternalistic argument fails, these concerns about sexual autonomy would only successfully undermine the case for decriminalizing a narrow subset of sex work. Liberto writes, "permitting the alienation of one's sexual rights arguably limits rather than promotes sexual liberty. Permitting the exchange of money for sex does not."[16] In this way, even if one could defend an autonomy-based argument against the decriminalization of some sex work, this argument would not justify legal limits on most existing forms of sex work.

5.1.5 Sex Work Undermines Bystanders' Sexual Autonomy

In addition to arguments against decriminalization that appeal to sex workers' sexual autonomy, Scott Anderson and Margaret Radin also argue that decriminalization would threaten the sexual autonomy of other workers too. On this view, treating sex work as work could create social and economic pressure for people to become sex workers or

16. Liberto, "Normalizing Prostitution versus Normalizing the Alienability of Sexual Rights."

to provide sexual services as part of other jobs when they would not have sold sex were it illegal to buy or sell sexual services.[17] Some pornography may also change norms surrounding sex acts which cause people to feel pressure to participate in sex acts that they would not otherwise consider.[18] Radin worries that a legal sex industry would have a "domino effect" which causes other industries to trade in sexual services as well.[19] The general concern is that once sex work is normalized as part of the broader economy; the provision of sexual services would be expected in other domains and people would feel more pressure to have sex in the context of their social and economic relationships.

Though women have historically been expected to provide sexual labor as part of their professional duties, there are several reasons to doubt that decriminalization would normalize the sale of sexual services across industries today. First, as Ann Lucas argues, decriminalization is just as likely to contain the commodification of sexual services to a designated legal sector thereby preventing the normalization of sexual services in other industries.[20] So in theory, decriminalization is as likely to reduce the expectation of sexual services in other industries as to have a domino effect on other industries. Yet there is further reason to suspect that decriminalization

17. Scott A. Anderson, "Prostitution and Sexual Autonomy: Making Sense of the Prohibition of Prostitution," *Ethics* 112, no. 4 (2002): 748–80.

18. Nick Cowen, "Millian Liberalism and Extreme Pornography," *American Journal of Political Science* 60, no. 2 (April 1, 2016): 509–20.

19. Radin, "Contested Commodities."

20. Ann Lucas, "The Currency of Sex: Prostitution, Law and Commodification," in *Rethinking Commodification: Cases and Readings in Law and Culture*, ed. Martha Ertman and Joan C. Williams (New York: New York University Press, 2005), 248–64.

would not have a domino effect because the commodification of other services has not caused similar domino effects. For example, when women entered the labor force childcare became a pervasive industry when childcare had previously been provided for free by mothers who worked in the home. Yet the normalization of paid childcare did not cause employers to systematically demand that their employees in other industries babysit their children, nor did it cause women to feel more social pressure to provide childcare for money. If anything, making childcare a paid profession may liberate women from the expectation that they will watch other people's children since the industry is now professionalized and associated with a specialized skill set.

Anderson and Radin object that the presence of a legal social practice could change norms in ways that make people who don't engage in that practice worse-off. But one might have offered a similar objection against revising norms that valued female virginity. When unmarried women were expected to remain celibate, women likely felt less pressure to have sex outside of the context of marriage because premarital sex was not expected. Today, as people become more accepting of polyamory, spouses may feel more pressure to have sex outside the context of their marriage to the extent that it is seen as an acceptable option. But even if normalizing premarital sex or polyamory does make some people feel pressured to have sex when otherwise they wouldn't, this threat to their sexual autonomy is not a decisive reason against normalization. So too, even if decriminalization did make some people consider sex work when they would have preferred not to have the option to sell sex, this would not establish that people were impermissibly pressured to sell sex or that sex work should not be treated like other forms of labor.

5.1.6 Sex Work Normalizes Sexual Harassment

A related concern about normalizing sex work, which Watson raises, is that it would also entail the broader tolerance for workplace sexual harassment.[21] Here the argument is that officials' enforcement of sexual contracts or labor agreements would enable any employer to add the provision of sexual services as a condition for continued employment, which is incompatible with our existing understanding of sexual harassment.

Yet fully decriminalized sex work needn't be incompatible with a general presumption against sexual harassment. Sexual harassment is wrong because employers and coworkers are not entitled to require people to perform sexual tasks or labor when they did not previously disclose that a job required it. As Japa Pallikkathayil argues, sexual harassment typically involves a radical change in a person's job description when "instead of being, say, a secretary, the employee must also act as a prostitute."[22] However, if the requirement to perform sexual tasks and labor were previously disclosed, and a worker consented to it, then

21. See also Anderson, "Prostitution and Sexual Autonomy."

22. Robert Epstein, "Why Shrinks Have Problems," *Psychology Today*, July 1997, http://www.psychologytoday.com/articles/199707/why-shrinks-have-problems; Annalee Yassi et al., "Protecting Health Workers from Infectious Disease Transmission: An Exploration of a Canadian-South African Partnership of Partnerships," *Globalization and Health* 12 (March 31, 2016); Andrea C. Tricco et al., "Work-Related Deaths and Traumatic Brain Injury," *Brain Injury* 20, no. 7 (January 1, 2006): 719–24.

assuming that sex work is permissible an employer would not be violating the workers' rights by including sex work within a labor agreement.

A proponent of this argument against decriminalization may reply however that sexual harassment law doesn't just protect the right to know whether a job will potentially or surely require the provision of sexual services, it also protects people's right to be insulated from the choice to provide sex as a condition of employment. Any theory of the scope of sexual harassment law must make reference to a theory about the scope of people's rights. On my view, people have rights against deception, but assuming that consensual sex work is not a rights violation, they do not have rights to be insulated from labor agreements that include sex work. In order to establish that fully transparent labor agreements that include the provisions of sexual services violates rights, one must assume that workers have additional rights that rule out even transparent labor agreements that include sex.

It's worth walking through this argument for the claim that sex work should not be decriminalized because it would legitimize sexual harassment. It goes like this. First, the objection assumes that sexual harassment is wrong. Second, it defines sexual harassment in a way that not only includes labor agreements where the requirement to provide sexual services was not fully disclosed, but also labor agreements where the expectation of sexual services was disclosed. Third, the objection then states that if sex work were legal, then labor agreements where the requirement to provide sexual services was fully disclosed would be legal. Therefore, the objection concludes, if sex work were legal, then sexual harassment would be legal. When we spell it out in this way it is clear that this seeming reductio of decriminalization is actually a question-begging argument. Because the objection relies on a definition of sexual harassment that characterizes all sex work as instances of sexual harassment, the objection implicitly assumes the conclusions it is meant to establish.

If we do not define sexual harassment in a way that characterizes all labor agreements that involve sexual services as sexual harassment, then sex workers could also be legally protected from sexual harassment. In New Zealand an unnamed sex worker successfully sued a brothel owner for sexual harassment when her employer made demeaning and derogatory comments and she felt debased by the management.[23] In this case, sex workers were capable of consenting to perform sexual labor in some previously disclosed and defined contexts at work but not others, and courts were able to uphold these protections. This example shows that a decriminalized sex industry is not incompatible with legal protections against sexual harassment, even for sex workers.

5.1.7 Sex Work Violates Citizens' Rights to Uphold Community Standards

A final rights-based objection to the decriminalization of sex work is that members of a political community have rights to enforce laws that uphold their communities' values or community standards. There are two versions of this objection. The first version of the objection is that

---

23. Lizzie Crocker, "Sex Worker Sues Brothel—And Wins," *The Daily Beast*, March 5, 2014, sec. World, http://www.thedailybeast.com/articles/2014/03/05/sex-worker-sues-brothel-and-wins.

people may not want sex workers in their community because exchanging sex for money is seen as a vice or because people worry that it will change the nature of their community or hurt their property values. Few academic critics of sex work press this objection, but in actual political communities it is often raised as a consideration against more liberal laws.[24] The second version of the objection, which Watson does advance, is that communities are entitled to limit the sex industry in order to uphold, express, or affirm their liberal commitment to equality between the sexes.

Consider first the view that citizens are entitled to prohibit certain industries in order to preserve some other value they hold in their community. Officials in many communities enforce zoning restrictions which restrict which kinds of businesses can operate within their jurisdiction. Officials may claim that they are entitled to ban brothels and strip clubs for the same reasons that they ban or regulate liquor stores, bars, tattoo parlors, and other industries that they would prefer remained outside their borders.

Three responses to this objection. First, there are limits to what officials may prohibit in the name of community standards. In the early 20th century majorities in some communities within the United States judged that interracial relationships were morally wrong, but they nevertheless were not morally entitled to prohibit it and anti-miscegenation laws were unjust policies that violated couples' freedom of association and rights to make intimate and personal, self-regarding choices. Earlier, I argued that

24. See e.g. Gere Clark, "Brothel Ban Would Be a Fiscal Win for Lyon County: Clark," *Reno Gazette Journal*, July 18, 2018, https://www.rgj. com/story/opinion/voices/2018/07/18/brothel-ban-would-fiscal-win-lyon-county-clark/798482002/.

sex workers and their clients are exercising similar rights to make intimate choices and freedom of association. So even if officials had the authority to enforce zoning restrictions and licensing requirements, to the extent that some indoor sex work is functionally identical to consensual sex outside of the market context, officials would not be entitled to prohibit all forms of sex work on these grounds.

Second, communities can permit markets in sexual services while still respecting community members' interest in limiting the visible effects of the sex industry on their community. For example, in Zurich, Switzerland some neighborhoods now provide "sex boxes"—garages for sex workers to meet their clients.[25] These boxes were constructed by public officials in response to community opposition to outdoor prostitution. Decriminalization may make it more feasible to find these sorts of compromises as well because decriminalization eliminates the negative externalities of the industry that are attributable to black markets.

Third, I am skeptical that public officials have the authority to enforce zoning regulations and licensing requirements for business owners within their borders anyhow. It is at least controversial whether these policies are socially beneficial because licensing restrictions and zoning restrictions can entrench existing patterns of social and economic privilege and limit people's economic freedom and freedom of association.[26] If zoning restrictions and

25. Agence France-Presse, "'Sex Drive-in' Hailed as Success after Year-Long Experiment in Zürich," *The Guardian*, August 26, 2014, sec. Society, http://www.theguardian.com/society/2014/aug/26/sex-drive-in-hailed-success-switzerland-zurich-experiment.

26. Jessica Trounstine, *Segregation by Design: Local Politics and Inequality in American Cities* (Cambridge, England: Cambridge University Press, 2018).

licensing requirements are generally unjustified, they are unjustified when used to restrict markets in sexual services as well. A further reason to be skeptical of the enforcement of zoning restrictions to discourage sex work is that it may effectively criminalize sex workers who work in suburban areas, thereby reintroducing the harms associated with black markets that decriminalization aims to mitigate.[27]

Few academic critics of decriminalization object to it on the grounds that political communities are entitled to keep certain industries and businesses out of their borders. But they do advance a version of this "community standards" argument when they argue that public officials are entitled to limit the sex industry in order to publically express disapproval of the sexist and inegalitarian nature of sex work. For example, Watson writes that decriminalized sex work would consist in public affirmation and endorsement of patriarchy, since sex work is intrinsically a patriarchal industry yet decriminalizing it would require public officials to then provide supportive law enforcement and supportive services for participants in the sex industry. Carol Pateman writes that a legal sex industry would perpetuate the political fiction that women consent to their subordinate status and would invite people to extend property norms to women's bodies and labor and to view men as women's sexual masters.[28]

27. Gillian M. Abel, "A Decade of Decriminalization: Sex Work 'down under' but Not Underground," *Criminology & Criminal Justice* 14, no. 5 (November 1, 2014): 580–92.

28. Pateman writes, "In contract theory universal freedom is always a hypothesis, a story, a political fiction. Contract always generates political right in the forms of domination and subordination." And elsewhere, "There need be no such ambiguities in relations between men and women, least of all when a man has bought a woman's body for his

I also accept that political communities should maintain their commitments to moral values like sex-equality. But in the previous chapter I argued that the goal of sex-equality is not best advanced through the Nordic Model because it effectively subordinates women to the will of public officials by violating their rights to choose their intimate partners. Also, the Nordic Model is ineffective at its stated aim of abolishing sex work, it only makes sex work more dangerous for workers. In addition to these worries, this argument also implicitly appeals to the premise that citizens and officials are entitled to prohibit otherwise permissible conduct on the grounds that publically supporting or acknowledging that conduct would be wrong. This premise would have unacceptable implications beyond debates about sex work though. For example, many people morally oppose alcohol use and there are good health and safety reasons for this opposition. Yet they must nevertheless pay public officials to enforce laws that uphold the property and occupational rights of bartenders. Pacifists must pay for defense. Even if citizens were correct in their judgment that their political community should not publically express support for sex work, alcohol use, or militarism, it would not follow from this judgment that public officials should therefore prohibit people from selling sex, alcohol, or weapons.

use as if it were like any other commodity. In such a context, 'the sex act' itself provides acknowledgment of patriarchal right. When women's bodies are on sale as commodities in the capitalist market, the terms of the original contract cannot be forgotten; the law of male sex right is publicly affirmed, and men gain public acknowledgment as women's sexual masters—that is what is wrong with prostitution." Pateman, *The Sexual Contract.*

5.1.8 Summary

The foregoing objections to decriminalization focused on the rights-based arguments that I developed in the previous chapter. One theme that emerged from this analysis is that it is difficult to distinguish sex work from other kinds of labor and rights to sell sex from other kinds of rights. The justification for the Nordic Model relies on the claim that sex is different from other kinds of labor, and in some ways it obviously is. But when it comes to the decision to work in an industry or choose a sexual partner, sex workers decide under similar conditions as other workers and have many of the same interests as other workers. For this reason, rights-based objections to decriminalization potentially undermine rights-based justifications for occupational freedom and the freedom to form intimate partnerships as well.

5.2 CONSEQUENTIALIST OBJECTIONS

The second group of objections to decriminalization question the empirical claim that decriminalization has better consequences than prohibition, Nordic Model or extensive regulation of the sex industry. The first set of consequentialist objections deny the antipaternalist arguments for decriminalization, which state that even if sex work did make sex workers worse off in some senses, officials should still permit sex work. Rather, they begin with an assumption that paternalism is justified and then go on to say that prohibiting people from buying or selling sex would be in their interests. Many of these consequentialist arguments against decriminalization focus on the fact that sex work is difficult and dangerous work that often affects workers even after they leave the profession. The second set of consequentialist objections focuses on the effects of sex work for people who are not sex workers. I argued that a decriminalization is not as harmful to political communities as black markets. But if decriminalized sex work did lead to higher rates of rape, sex trafficking, disease transmission, or other forms of crime then one may oppose decriminalization on public health and safety grounds. However, proponents of criminalization and the Nordic Model have not met the burden of proof to establish a consequentialist case for decriminalization. Often consequentialist arguments for these policies either fail to establish a causal link between interventionist polices and better health and safety outcomes, or they implicitly conflate decriminalization with a lack of any law enforcement to prevent sexual assault and trafficking.

5.2.1 The Case for Paternalism

Peter de Marneffe argues in favor of some forms of prohibition and regulation of the sex industry on the grounds that sex work is psychologically destructive and limits sex workers' opportunities. He favors legal limits on the industry on the grounds that laws against paying for sex would reduce the number of people who sell sexual services and reduce the amount of services provided.[29] De Marneffe's argument rests on an empirical claim that sex workers commonly experience their work as "humiliating

---

29. de Marneffe, *Liberalism and Prostitution*, p. 4.

and abusive, and [it] results in lasting feelings of worth-lessness, shame, and self-hatred," and symptoms of post-traumatic stress disorder in some cases.[30] Part of this harm is attributable to the "emotional pretense" sex work requires, which causes sex workers to lose their ability to form healthy and respectful intimate relationships even after they leave the industry. As evidence for this claim, de Marneffe cites many empirical studies, which are gener-ally case studies or observational analyses, that document the emotional consequences of participating in the sex in-dustry. In particular, de Marneffe focuses on the harm to sex workers' relationships, since by its very nature the job is incompatible with sexual monogamy.

De Marneffe's paternalistic argument does not sup-port prohibitive policies that subject sex workers them-selves to criminal penalties. Instead, he favors either the Nordic Model or what he calls "impermissive regulation" which would include age requirements and other strict restrictions that aim to reduce the demand for sex work by discouraging opportunistic purchasing of sexual services. De Marneffe's argument for restricting the sex industry walks a middle pathway between anti-paternalism and paternalism. He accepts that if a person has the capacity to reason and a policy restricts an important liberty in a way she opposes, then the policy cannot be justified on the grounds that it benefits her.[31] But de Marneffe's disputes the claim that regulation or the Nordic Model would de-prive sex workers of important liberties. So on his view, sex workers needn't have a valid complaint against laws that

30. Ibid., p. 13.
31. Ibid., p. 67.

restrict the industry as long as the laws are passed and enforced fairly.

Other critics of the sex industry also endorse paternalism as a basis for restricting the sex industry. These paternalists oppose legal sex markets on the grounds that working in the industry is bad for the people who do it. For example, some religious scholars suggest that buying or selling sex is bad for people's character.[32] Melissa Farley cites the physical and psychological risks associated with being a sex worker, even in a decriminalized context, as a sufficient reason to prohibit people from paying for sex.[33]

But even if we were to grant that the right to sell sex is not especially important and instead focused only on the other effects of selling sex, paternalistic arguments that appeal to the harms of sex work would nevertheless struggle to explain why the harm of sex work *in particular* is morally wrong and merits legal intervention. Paternalistic arguments against sex work appeal to the harms associated with the industry, but when we look closer at plausible conceptions of harm, the sex industry is not distinctively harmful relative to other industries.[34] And even if we accept that there are some harms associated with the industry, many of the harms that paternalists attribute to sex work are also experienced by people in other professions. Also, even if there were a harm associated

32. Robert P. George, *Making Men Moral: Civil Liberties and Public Morality* (Oxford: Clarendon Press, 1995).

33. Melissa Farley, "'Bad for the Body, Bad for the Heart': Prostitution Harms Women Even If Legalized or Decriminalized," *Violence Against Women* 10, no. 10 (October 1, 2004): 1087–1125.

34. This discussion of harm is informed by Ben Bradley's work on defining harm. Ben Bradley, "Doing Away with Harm," *Philosophy and Phenomenological Research* 85, no. 2 (2012): 390–412.

with the industry, decriminalization could still reduce harm to sex workers on balance.

Say an act is harmful if it makes the person who acts worse than she would have been otherwise. This conception of harm cannot justify paternalism because, as I discussed in the previous chapter, many sex workers choose to sell sex only because it is their best economic option. This is an observation that many critics of the industry acknowledge. Yet this observation suggests that at least in the short-term, sex workers may be better off because they choose to sell sex in which case it is not harmful on this characterization. So while it may be true that selling sex damages some people's relationships, character, or emotional wellbeing, it could also be true that these costs are worth it to them on balance. Paternalists may deny this assertion, but I argued in the previous section they would then face substantial epistemic challenges in arguing that selling sex is on balance harmful to sex workers, given that sex workers' seemingly judge that it is in their overall interest.

Alternatively, one could characterize the harm of sex work as the mere presence of emotional suffering or physical pain. On this view, a person has been harmed by her profession if she has a particular negative experience, even if she also would have been badly off or worse off in a different profession. This conception of harm may hold that sex workers are harmed by selling sex whenever they experience accidental injury or unanticipated emotional distress as part of their job. But this conception of harm is not well-suited to justify paternalism in public policy. Many other personal and professional choices also expose people to accidental injury or potential emotional pain in this way, but are beneficial on balance and should not be prohibited on these grounds. Factory workers and farmers often risk physical injury, health workers expose themselves to a higher risk of illness, and psychiatrists are vulnerable to unanticipated emotional distress, yet these occupations can nevertheless be rewarding and beneficial on balance.[35]

Another account of harm may hold that the harms associated with the sex industry are wrongful harms because they violate people's rights. On this view, to establish the paternalistic case against sex work one would need to establish that sex workers' rights are violated. Yet paternalistic arguments are generally developed on the assumption that sex workers consent to sell. Typically, consent is not present if a person has been subjected to force or coercion. No one who defends decriminalization of sex work defends the decriminalization of assault or coercion, but it would be inaccurate to characterize all sex work as rights-violating in these ways. This is why critics of decriminalization appeal to paternalistic arguments.

This overview of various conceptions of harm shows that once we look closer at plausible conceptions of harm, paternalists' claim that sex work is harmful looks less plausible. In any case, whatever the harms are associated with sex work those very same harms are also associated with other industries. For example, physicians also experience a high rate of burnout related to their professions.[36] Casino

35. Andrea C. Tricco et al., "Work-Related Deaths and Traumatic Brain Injury," *Brain Injury* 20, no. 7 (January 1, 2006): 719–24; Robert Epstein, "Why Shrinks Have Problems," *Psychology Today*, July 1997, http://www.psychologytoday.com/articles/199707/why-shrinks-have-problems; Annalee Yassi et al., "Protecting Health Workers from Infectious Disease Transmission: An Exploration of a Canadian-South African Partnership of Partnerships," *Globalization and Health* 12 (March 31, 2016).

36. Tait D. Shanafelt et al., "Changes in Burnout and Satisfaction With Work-Life Balance in Physicians and the General US Working Population

managers,' bartenders,' and flight attendants' marriages are especially unlikely to succeed.[37] Pilots, roofers, and trash collectors face a comparatively high risk of death.[38] Plumbers, cleaners, and sanitation workers may experience disgust related to encountering other people's bodily fluids. Police officers and people in the military are at a high risk of violence associated with their occupation. And many occupations are harmful in virtue of the boring, repetitive, de-skilling, or tedious nature of the work.[39]

The difference, de Marneffe claims, is that these harms are more extreme for sex workers. Even if the kinds of harms involved are similar, other professions are not similarly harmful on balance, though de Marneffe acknowledges that sex work also can be a beneficial occupation on balance for some people.[40] To support the claim that sex work is generally harmful on balance, de Marneffe also disputes my claim that workers are generally the best judges of whether sex work will be harmful to their overall wellbeing, on the grounds that potential workers are not adequately informed about the risks and long-term consequences of sex work. De Marneffe argues that unlike other professionals,

Between 2011 and 2014," *Mayo Clinic Proceedings* 90, no. 12 (December 1, 2015): 1600–1613.

37. Nathan Yau, "Divorce and Occupation," *Flowing Data* (blog), July 26, 2017, https://flowingdata.com/2017/07/25/divorce-and-occupation/.

38. Bureau of Labor Statistics, "Census of Fatal Occupational Injuries—Hours-Based Rates" (US Bureau of Labor Statistics, March 5, 2010), https://www.bls.gov/iif/oshnotice10.htm.

39. For a discussion of this aspect of the workplace see Samuel Arnold, "The Difference Principle at Work," *Journal of Political Philosophy* 20, no. 1 (2012): 94–118.

40. de Marneffe, *Liberalism and Prostitution*, p. 16.

would-be sex workers typically have little interaction with the industry beforehand and they may have unrealistic expectations about what it will be like to sell sex for a living.[41]

This argument for some paternalistic regulation of the sex industry can be characterized as an argument for soft paternalism, which refers a class of cases where paternalistic interference with a seemingly voluntary and consensual choice is nevertheless justified on the grounds that the subject on interference is uninformed or misinformed.[42] Just as it would be permissible to stop a person from walking across a faulty bridge, the argument goes, it is permissible to prevent workers from exposing themselves to the harms and risks associated with the sex industry. Soft paternalism cannot justify legal penalties for selling or paying for sex though, for three reasons. First, as in the bridge crossing case, if it possible to inform someone of the risks then informing her is morally preferable to interfering with her. It is possible to inform sex workers of the risks associated with the profession, so this argument cannot justify paternalistic interference. Second, one of the reasons that sex workers may not have an entirely accurate understanding of the industry is because it is prohibited and stigmatized, so sex workers and their clients may be reluctant to publically discuss their experiences and a more representative range of voices and experiences may not be included in public conversations about the sex industry. And third, there are many other experiences, which people

41. Ibid.
42. Gerald Dworkin, "Paternalism," in *The Stanford Encyclopedia of Philosophy*, ed. Edward N. Zalta (Palo Alto, CA: Metaphysics Research Lab, Stanford University, Winter 2017), https://plato.stanford.edu/archives/win2017/entries/paternalism/.

cannot anticipate the effects of beforehand. Some of these experiences can also be emotionally damaging or harmful or can be beneficial and meaningful. These experiences include people's first sexual experiences, breaking up with a first love, using psychedelic drugs, childbirth, skydiving, chemotherapy, or performing in public. Yet the fact that people are unable to know what these experiences are like, and that they may be harmful and emotionally damaging, would not be sufficient grounds for legally limiting people's access to these experiences, nor is it sufficient grounds for legal limits on the sex industry.

5.2.2 Sex Workers Don't Like Their Jobs

Following de Marneffe, a critic of decriminalization may accept my claim that people are generally the best judges of their own wellbeing but then reject decriminalization by pointing out that empirically, sex workers don't seem to like their jobs as much as workers in other industries.[43] These accounts would seem to indicate that workers themselves judge that sex work is bad for them. And if so, a proponent of paternalism may justify a more interventionist policy on the very grounds that I cited in arguing for decriminalization—by arguing for deference to sex workers' own testimony about their experiences.

Here again, there are few empirical studies of sex workers' job satisfaction in context where sex work is not prohibited. But what studies there are find that despite anecdotal accounts of the difficulty of sex work, sex workers generally prefer their jobs to their other economic options

---

43. de Marneffe, *Liberalism and Prostitution*, p. 25.

and enjoy sex works' flexible hours and relatively high pay.[44] In addition, to the extent that workers do report low satisfaction with the sex industry (or any industry) it is difficult to establish that a profession itself causes lower subjective wellbeing for workers in contrast to the possibility that it is merely correlated with low job satisfaction. For example, one study of job satisfaction finds that workers are generally more satisfied if one of their central life interests relates to their profession, but people with non-work central life interests, who are more likely to be dissatisfied with their jobs, may systematically select into industries that give them the flexibility or means to pursue other projects.[45] Moreover, one impediment to job satisfaction may be the stigma associated with sex work, even if it were legal.

On the other hand, sex work is relatively dangerous and can it involves a level of entrepreneurship, financial unpredictability, and emotional labor that may be burdensome to some workers. I do not mean to deny that some sex workers may not like their jobs. But even if sex workers generally did not enjoy their jobs and even if we grant that paternalism could sometimes justify prohibiting a profession, such an argument still would not justify limits on the sex industry without undermining a broad range of other professions. Many workers do not enjoy their jobs as much as workers in

44. Teela Sanders, Laura Connelly, and Laura Jarvis King, "On Our Own Terms: The Working Conditions of Internet-Based Sex Workers in the UK," *Sociological Research Online* 21, no. 4 (November 1, 2016): 1–14; Jade E. Bilardi et al., "The Job Satisfaction of Female Sex Workers Working in Licensed Brothels in Victoria, Australia," *Journal of Sexual Medicine* 8, no. 1 (January 1, 2011): 116–22,.

45. Robert Dubin and Joseph E. Champoux, "Central Life Interests and Job Satisfaction," *Organizational Behavior and Human Performance* 18, no. 2 (April 1, 1977): 366–77.

other industries, but they choose their profession for other reasons. Some of the most widely enjoyable jobs, such as professions that involve the arts or athletics, are most competitive or lowest paying. A narrow focus on workplace satisfaction fails to reflect the many ways in which a person's life can go well. Work is not central to everyone's identity or wellbeing. For these reasons, paternalists cannot cite workers' feelings about their jobs in order to justify limiting a profession—instead paternalists should be concerned with workers' overall wellbeing, and accounts of low job satisfaction, even if they were representative, would not establish that the sex industry is bad for workers relative to other professions.

5.2.3 Sex Workers Have Adaptive Preferences

Some critics of the sex industry reject the argument that sex workers can generally predict or know what's best for them on the grounds that sex workers have maladaptive preferences—preferences that are formed only in response to injustice or oppression. The charge of maladaptive preferences assumes that a person's objective interests can differ from their subjective or stated preferences in circumstances of injustice. Martha Nussbaum, who is generally supportive of sex worker's rights, elsewhere describes the problem of maladaptive preferences through the example of uneducated Bangladeshi women who had no desire for education, due to the fact that they were not educated enough to see the value of education.[46] Feminist theorists

46. Martha Nussbaum, "Women's Education: A Global Challenge," *Signs: Journal of Women in Culture and Society* 29, no.2 (2004): 325–355.

have long appealed to the idea of maladaptive preferences to explain why women seem to make sexual choices that entrench their own oppression or otherwise appear contrary to their interests. This objection casts doubt on the claim that officials should defer to women's testimony that they prefer sex work to alternatives.

The allegation of maladaptive preferences may apply either to women who have sex with men in general or to women who have sex with men for money specifically.[47] Catharine Mackinnon questions whether women eroticize male dominance only because their cultural environment assigns greater power to men.[48] Ariel Levy suggests that some women see pornography and public nudity as empowering because of maladaptive preferences.[49] Carol Pateman argues that markets in sex reflect a more general dynamic that ties masculine identity to a patriarchal and capitalist dominant culture and socializes women to think of themselves as commodities that can meet this demand. [50]

47. Adrienne Rich argues that many women may only seem to prefer heterosexuality because the dominant culture has conditioned them to idealize sexually gratifying and marrying men. Adrienne Rich, "Compulsory Heterosexuality and Lesbian Existence," in her *Blood, Bread and Poetry: Selected Prose, 1979–1985* (New York: WW Norton & Company, 1994), 39.

48. Catharine MacKinnon, *Toward a Feminist Theory of the State* (Cambridge, MA: Harvard University Press, 1989), 177–78.

49. Ariel Levy, *Female Chauvinist Pigs: Women and the Rise of Raunch Culture*, 1st ed. (New York: Free Press, 2006).

50. Carole Pateman, "Defending Prostitution: Charges Against Ericsson," in Cass R. Sunstein, ed., *Feminism and Political Theory* (Chicago: University of Chicago Press, 1990), 204. See also her "Women and Consent," in *Political Theory* 8 (May 1980): 162.

Arguments that focus on maladaptive preferences challenge the view that women's choices generally reflect their judgments about their best interests when those choices are shaped by patriarchal institutions. Even if women do meaningfully consent to sex or sex work in these cases, critics claim that a narrow focus on consent may also be ill-advised if focusing on consent alone causes officials to overlook problems with the way that the preferences that led her to consent were formed.[51] So the fact that sex workers around the world overwhelmingly support decriminalization, on this view, may only reflect the fact that sex workers around the world are forming their preferences in response to unjust circumstances.

To the extent that arguments about maladaptive preferences are true, they still would not justify criminalization or regulation of the sex industry for four reasons. First, in some cases, the best way of responding to a person's maladaptive preferences may consist in nevertheless respecting her preference. A person's interest in being seen and treated as the best judge of her own wellbeing may outweigh her interest in developing preferences in the absence of oppression or other preference-constraining conditions. Treating a person as if they are a competent judge of their own interests may even improve her ability to form preferences that promote her interests in the long run. For example, maladaptive preferences may develop because people never deliberated about their values but instead developed preferences unreflectively. This lack of deliberation may be a result of learned helplessness or the

51. Lisa H. Schwartzman, "Can Liberalism Account for Women's 'Adaptive Preferences'?," *Social Philosophy Today* 23 (2007): 175–86.

fact that sometimes, if a person has few options, it is not worthwhile to deliberate about preferences over outcomes that seem impossible. In these circumstances, discounting a persons' authority as a competent judge of her own interests could be counterproductive and could confirm a person's suspicion that she is an unreliable deliberator and that further investment in deliberating about her options is not worthwhile. In this way even if a person is not in fact as competent a judge of her own interests due to maladaptive preferences, overriding a choice that reflects a maladaptive preference could still be harmful on balance and could make a person's already challenging epistemic circumstances even worse by further undermining her ability to deliberate about what's best for her.

Second, in some cases a person may have an adaptive preference due to injustice, but even if her preference were not formed in response to oppression or marginalization she could have developed that preference anyhow. For example, a woman's desire to have children may be a result of unfair social expectations that women will perform unpaid reproductive labor, but it could also be the case that she would also desire children in the absence of those expectations. So even if in principle maladaptive preferences merited less deference than preferences that were formed under better conditions, in practice it can be difficult to know how to respond to a maladaptive preference if it is robust enough that a person could have formed it anyhow. Policymakers who are concerned about occupational choices that they attribute to maladaptive preferences therefore face substantial epistemic hurdles to establish the case for interfering with those who act on their preferences.

Third, a person's decision to be a sex worker could be a maladaptive preference in some sense but she may nevertheless have a genuine, non-maladaptive preference to not be subjected to criminal penalties.[52] So even if the preference to be a sex worker merited less deference in virtue of the fact that it is a response to oppressive conditions, the preference to not work in a black market would nevertheless warrant respect. When considering whether sex work should be decriminalized the question should not be "do workers genuinely prefer to sell sex?" but "do workers genuinely prefer decriminalization?"

Fourth, to the extent that people *do* support criminalization of the sex industry, one might press the same charge of maladaptive preferences against them, on the grounds that citizens' support for government intervention is shaped by their own history of oppression by public officials.[53] For example, maybe people only support criminal penalties because they have been conditioned to support existing governmental interventions and to obey authority or because they were raised in religious traditions that value virginity and monogamy or oppose sex outside of marriage.

For these reasons, paternalistic arguments for prohibitive approaches are unlikely to succeed by appealing to the

52. Relatedly, as Rosa Terlazzo argues, an adaptive preference can itself both be prudentially bad and prudentially good for its holder, depending on one's temporal perspective. Rosa Terlazzo, "Must Adaptive Preferences Be Prudentially Bad for Us?," *Journal of the American Philosophical Association* 3, no. 4 (ed 2017): 412–29, https://doi.org/10.1017/apa.2018.1.

53. Huemer, *The Problem of Political Authority*.

claim that people's preferences are unreliable when they are the victims of injustice or oppression.

5.2.4 Sex Work Causes Trafficking

It is worth repeating that no one who favors decriminalization of sex work supports the decriminalization of sexual assault or forced labor. Yet a broadly consequentialist set of arguments against sex work disputes my claim that permitting the sale of sexual services is good for the general welfare on the grounds that decriminalized sex work causes higher rates of rape and human trafficking, that decriminalized sex work is a threat to public health, and that decriminalized sex work is a threat to public safety.

I will first address the claim that decriminalized sex work causes higher rates of rape and human trafficking. Watson argues that the Nordic Model is preferable to decriminalization partly on the grounds that it "curbs the demand for commercial sex that fuels trafficking." Watson connects decriminalization to sex trafficking at several points. First, Watson cites a claim from the European Parliament's 2014 report on "Sexual exploitation and prostitution and its impact on gender equality" which references "conservative estimates" that 1 in 7 sex workers in Europe are victims of trafficking, and some member states reporting 60–90% of sex workers as trafficked."[54] Watson links the prevalence of trafficking in Europe to the presence of regulated sex

54. E. Schulze, "Sexual Exploitation and Prostitution and Its Impact on Gender Equality," Directorate General for Internal Policies, Policy Department C: Citizens' Rights And Constitutional Affairs, Gender Equality, 2014, p. 6, http://www.europarl.europa.eu/RegData/etudes/etudes/join/2014/493040/IPOL-FEMM_ET(2014)493040_EN.pdf

markets because "legalization and decriminalization in particular locales impacts neighboring locales, increasing sex trafficking over all."

Yet the trafficking statistics that are the basis of Watson's causal between legal sex markets and trafficking are unreliable for two reasons. First, the evidence that Watson cites relies on the Palermo Protocol, a set of standards that define trafficking as:

> The recruitment, transportation, transfer, harboring or receipt of persons, by means of the threat or use of force or other forms of coercion, of abduction, of fraud, of deception, of the abuse of power or of a position of vulnerability or of the giving or receiving of payments or benefits to achieve the consent of a person having control over another person, for the purpose of exploitation.[55]

This definition of trafficking is overly-broad and it seemingly cannot distinguish trafficking from ordinary exchanges with people where there is asymmetric power or when one person is in a position of vulnerability. As I previously argued, an exchange can be voluntary and even mutually beneficial even in the presence of asymmetries of power. Building on the Palermo Protocol, the report Watson cites is a bit more specific about the definition of trafficking. There, the authors write,

> The following six elements characterize a forced labor situation; usually two or more are imposed on a worker in a

---

55. Christina A. Seideman, "The Palermo Protocol: Why It Has Been Ineffective in Reducing Human Sex Trafficking," *Global Tides* 9, no. 1 (2015): 5.

combined fashion: a) physical or sexual violence; b) restriction of movement of the worker; c) debt bondage/bonded labour; d) withholding wages or refusing to pay the worker at all; e) retention of passports and identity documents; f) threat of denunciation to the authorities.

In addition, trafficking can include other forms of sexual exploitation such as "abuse of a position of vulnerability" which refers to

abuse of any situation in which the person involved has no real and acceptable alternative to submitting to the abuse. The vulnerability may be of any kind, whether physical, psychological, emotional, family- related, social or economic. The situation might, for example, involve insecurity or illegality of the victim's administrative status, economic dependence or fragile health. In short, the situation can be any state of hardship in which a human being is impelled to accept being exploited. Persons abusing such a situation flagrantly infringe human rights and violate human dignity and integrity, which no one can validly renounce.

So by this definition, "abusing the economic insecurity or poverty of an adult hoping to better their own and their family's lot" is a form of abuse just as threatening a worker with violence is a form of trafficking. By this definition, sex workers who support their families are trafficked, sex workers who are in debt are trafficked, and sex workers who have chronic health conditions are trafficked. Imagine if this standard were applied to other forms of labor—if baristas who support their families, have credit card debt, and suffer from chronic health conditions where characterized as victims of abuse. More generally, there are many challenges associated with studying sex trafficking due to misleading data (because people define sex trafficking differently) that depends on the nature of each country's enforcement policies.[56]

The second reason to doubt a link between permissive policies and sex trafficking is that the evidence for a market-trafficking link is decidedly mixed. On one hand, there is some evidence that permitting the sale or purchase of sexual services in some contexts is correlated with higher rates of trafficking. Specifically, European countries that regulate and allow some prostitution have higher human trafficking inflows on average.[57] But this evidence does not establish a causal connection, it only establishes a correlation which could be explained by a third factor, such as the populations' attitudes toward sex or broader economic conditions which influence both inflows of trafficked persons and people's willingness to buy and sell sex. And on the other hand, decriminalization in New Zealand did not increase sex trafficking.[58]

56. Maggie McNeill, "Lies Damned Lies and Sex Work Statistics," *The Washington Post*, March 27, 2014, https://www.washingtonpost.com/news/the-watch/wp/2014/03/27/lies-damned-lies-and-sex-work-statistics/?utm_term=.7879d2fb535d.Noah Berlatsky, "'Human Trafficking' Has Become a Meaningless Term," *The New Republic*, October 30, 2015, https://newrepublic.com/article/123302/human-trafficking-has-become-meaningless-term.

57. Seo-Young Cho, Axel Dreher, and Eric Neumayer, "Does Legalized Prostitution Increase Human Trafficking?," *World Development* 41 (2013): 67–82; Niklas Jakobsson and Andreas Kotsadam, "The Law and Economics of International Sex Slavery: Prostitution Laws and Trafficking for Sexual Exploitation," *European Journal of Law and Economics* 35, no. 1 (February 1, 2013): 87–107.

58. Tracey Tyler, "Legalized Brothels 'fantastic' for New Zealand, Prostitutes Say," *The Toronto Star*, September 29, 2010, sec. GTA, https://www.thestar.com/news/gta/2010/09/29/legalized_brothels_fantastic_for_new_zealand_prostitutes_say.html.

Elsewhere, Watson argues that the German experience illustrates that legal sex work could result in some women immigrating to a country specifically for the purposes of sex work, and that allowing legal sex work and legal immigration would effectively serve to make a country even more unequal by adding inequalities between citizens and noncitizens to the long list of inequalities that predict women's participation in sex markets.

She argues that where sex work is legal, states would be encouraged to impose citizenship restrictions on who can legally perform sex work in order to prevent sex trafficking, but these citizenship requirements would be unlikely to effectively prevent sex trafficking because it would result in "thriving illegal markets alongside the legal markets."

On my view, states should not impose citizenship restrictions on who can legally perform any work, including sex work. Human trafficking occurs in part because employers are able to threaten people with deportation if they do not work for low wages or in unsafe conditions. But workers are victims of trafficking in these cases because they are threatened with the enforcement of unjust immigration restrictions, not because they are required to work. In this way, citizenship requirements cause human trafficking, not labor markets. So to the extent that human trafficking motivates one's opposition to markets in sex work for citizen workers, they ought to oppose the restriction of the markets to citizens, not the expansion of labor markets to include sex work.

I grant that many migrants chose to work in the sex industry because they cannot find work in other industries or in their countries of origin.[59] But anti-trafficking advocacy

59. Chang-Ryung Han, "Is the Immigration of Korean Sex Workers to the United States Sex Trafficking or Migrant Smuggling?," *Brookings*

does more harm than good, to sex workers in general and to migrant sex workers in particular. Legal penalties for migrant sex workers' clients are harsher than the penalties that public officials impose on people who pay for sex with citizens which further disadvantages migrant workers.[60] And even in places that follow the Nordic Model and only prohibit people from paying for sex, migrant sex workers remain vulnerable to deportation in virtue of their citizenship status, so criminalizing the purchase of sex still harms them by exposing them to interference from the police and the threat of deportation.[61]

But even if we grant that permitting sex work would increase trafficking by increasing the scale of the sex industry more generally, it would not follow from this claim that public officials should prohibit people from selling or paying for sex. As the authors of one of the studies that found higher rates of sex trafficking in European countries that permit some prostitution also caution that using this research to support prohibitive policies "overlooks potential benefits that the legalization of prostitution might have on those employed in the industry . . . [and] raises tricky

(blog), November 30, 2001, https://www.brookings.edu/research/is-the-immigration-of-korean-sex-workers-to-the-united-states-sex-trafficking-or-migrant-smuggling/.

60. See for example, Brigette Noel, "How Canada's Immigration Laws Make Migrant Sex Workers' Jobs More Dangerous—VICE," *Vice*, October 13, 2016, https://www.vice.com/en_us/article/kwkz4z/how-canadas-immigration-laws-are-making-migrant-sex-workers-jobs-more-dangerous.

61. As previously noted, this concern extends to the Nordic Model as well. Kulick, "Sex in the New Europe"; Holmström and Skilbrei, "The 'Nordic Model' of Prostitution Law Is a Myth."

'freedom of choice' issues concerning both the potential suppliers and clients of prostitution services."[62] Watson is implicitly committed to the claim that officials cannot always limit markets in sexual services for the purpose of reducing trafficking. After all, trafficking is even lower in countries that fully prohibit sex work, but Watson opposes full prohibition in light of the liberty interests at stake and the harmful effects of prohibition for sex workers.[63] Given that public policy should not be exclusively informed by the goal of reducing rates of trafficking, it is an open question whether, if there is a marginal increase in trafficking, that increase justifies the Nordic Model, especially considering all of the other aforementioned costs of criminalizing the sale.

Finally, the recent effects of the "Stop Enabling Sex Trafficking Act" (SESTA) and "Fight Online Sex Trafficking Act" (FOSTA) legislation in the United States further supports the view that conflating sex work with sex trafficking undermines officials' ability to effectively prevent sex trafficking, in addition to harming sex workers and the general public. The acts enable public officials to prosecute internet service providers and online platforms that are used by sex traffickers. As a consequence, the legislation resulted in the abolition of sex-worker platforms and websites that enabled sex workers to find and safely screen clients. It also makes it more difficult for law enforcement to find nonconsensual trafficking victims and to identify criminals involved in nonconsensual trafficking. In

---

62. Cho, Dreher, and Neumayer, "Does Legalized Prostitution Increase Human Trafficking?"

63. Jakobsson and Kotsadam, "The Law and Economics of International Sex Slavery."

addition, the legislation undermined all citizen's freedom of online expression by encouraging websites and platforms to engage in preemptive censorship and policing of users' online speech. The consequences of SESTA/FOSTA are representative of a broader phenomenon. Criminalization or Nordic Model polices that aim to end or limit the demand for sex work that are justified on the grounds that they will reduce trafficking but often these policies are so wide in scope that they substantially harm a large number of people (e.g. sex workers and internet users more generally) in order to achieve (at best) limited benefits to a small group of victims of nonconsensual trafficking. Potentially, these policies can also make it more difficult to investigate and prosecute nonconsensual trafficking in other ways, thereby creating more victims in the long run.

5.2.5 Sex Work Would Introduce New Public Health Risks

Against the claim that decriminalized sex work would have better public health outcomes than the Nordic Model, Watson raises the following dilemma. If sex work were treated like other forms of work, then either it would or would not be wrong to discriminate against sex workers on the basis of their medical status, including whether they have an illness that could be sexually transmitted. If it would not be wrong to discriminate against sex workers, for example if officials prohibited people with HIV to sell sex, then Watson argues that this policy is incompatible with a broader commitment to nondiscrimination. On the other hand, if it were legally permissible for people with HIV to sell sex, then such a policy would introduce unnecessary new public health risks. Proponents of decriminalization encounter a similar dilemma regarding whether it would be wrong for sex workers to discriminate against clients on this basis.

In response to this objection, I maintain that neither horn of the dilemma undermines the case for decriminalization. Say officials enforce policies that prohibit workers with sexually transmittable infections from selling sex. This policy would only constitute an unjust form of discrimination if having a sexually transmittable infection were normatively extraneous to the act of selling sex.[64] If a person's STI status is relevant to the sale of sex in the way that health or ability status can be relevant to other professions then excluding people with STI's from the sex industry would be no more of an injustice than excluding people with significant vision impairments from working as bus drivers.

Say officials do not enforce policies that prohibit workers with HIV and other STI's from selling sex. This is the approach I favor because I think that sex workers and their clients should have the benefits of participating in a legal marketplace whatever their health status. Such a policy would not discriminate against workers or clients on the basis of their medical status. But one may worry that permitting people with HIV to sell and pay for sex would introduce unnecessary health risks. This is an empirical worry though, and there are several reasons to be skeptical that decriminalizing sex work for people who have STI's would reduce rates of STI transmission. Decriminalizing sex work would enable public officials to enforce protections against

---

64. Sophia Moreau, "What Is Discrimination?," *Philosophy & Public Affairs* 38, no. 2 (2010): 143–79.

fraudulent and misleading marketing. In this way, by bringing sex work into the formal economy officials could offer legal protection against the risk of sex workers and clients being misled about their partners health status. In principle, officials could even enforce legal penalties for contagious transmission if either a worker or client failed to disclose their health status.

Also, if sex work were a legal industry where workers and clients were required to disclose their health status, then people would have a strong incentive to take due care to minimize and avoid the risk of culpable contagious transmission. For this reason, legal sex work would provide incentives for workers and clients to get tested that are absent in the current system of black markets. Decriminalization could also enable coordination and standardization of practices by sex workers and their clients, and if sex workers had more bargaining power in a legal marketplace they could more effectively enforce policies that require condom use. Finally, sex workers and clients can partly protect themselves from contagious transmission of HIV by taking a pre-exposure prophylaxis that further reduce the risk of HIV infection beyond the protection provided by condoms. Just as sex workers may use hormonal birth control to provide protection against the risk of pregnancy, these drugs can reduce the occupational risks of sex work. Since there are means available to prevent the risks of contagious transmission besides prohibition and there is insufficient evidence to support the claim that prohibition would recue contagious transmission anyhow, concerns about contagious transmission cannot justify support for a prohibitive approach, including the Nordic Model.

5.2.6 Sex Work Makes Communities Less Safe

The final group of broadly consequentialist objections relates to public safety. Critics of the sex industry argue that communities are entitled to prohibit sex work on the grounds that the sex work has negative consequences for the broader community.[65] These negative effects may either be merely associated with the industry or intrinsic to it. [66] Negative effects that are merely associated with the sex industry include crime, noise complaints, and potential threats to the public health, though it is plausible that people merely perceive higher rates of crime and that in the long run decriminalization reduces these outcomes on balance.[67] And as I argued in the previous chapter, these negative effects can be mitigated or eliminated through decriminalization or by addressing the negative effects of sex work directly rather than preventing people from paying for or selling sex. For example, sex work is associated with

65. This is the argument in favor of prohibiting sex work on the grounds that it is a "quality of life" crime that harms communities. Public officials in New York City engaged in this approach to law enforcement in the 1990's and it was enforced in London in the early 2000s as well. These law enforcement efforts, which identified sex work as a public nuisance, further marginalized sex workers and were ultimately unsustainable. For more on this approach to policing sex work see, Rosie Campbell and Maggie O'Neill, *Sex Work Now* (Milton Park, England: Routledge, 2013), 12–20.

66. R. J. McDougall, "Intrinsic Versus Contingent Claims About the Harmfulness of Prostitution," *Journal of Medical Ethics* 40, no. 2 (2014): 83.

67. Paul Bisschop, Stephen Kastoryano, and Bas van der Klaauw, "Street Prostitution Zones and Crime," *American Economic Journal: Economic Policy* 9, no. 4 (2017): 28–63.

crime partly because laws against sex work makes sex worker's clients' criminals, and makes it more likely that sex workers will encounter people who are comfortable breaking the law and working in an underground industry. Decriminalization would go some way to address criminal behavior associated with sex work and to the extent that it persists officials ought to police crime directly.

But following Watson, one may reply that decriminalization makes sex crimes more likely. Watson cites research that finds that "the experience of buying sex has substantial explanatory power over the probability of one committing a sex crime." Watson's interpretation of this research is that sex buyers are more likely to accept rape myths, and hence more likely to commit sex crimes. But it is unclear what follows from this analysis even if it is true. After all, the probability of one committing a sex crime is also correlated with experience of drinking alcohol, but this correlation would not establish any all-things-considered conclusions about alcohol prohibition.[68] It wouldn't even show that alcohol consumption caused people to commit sex crimes because the correlation could instead be explained by behavioral traits or contexts that caused both alcohol consumption and sexual assault.[69] Another plausible interpretation of this research is that people who are willing to disregard a legal prohibition on paying for sex, who have hostile attitudes toward women,

68. Antonia Abbey, "Alcohol-Related Sexual Assault: A Common Problem among College Students," *Journal of Studies on Alcohol, Supplement*, no. 14 (2002): 118–28.

69. Maria Testa and Michael J. Cleveland, "Does Alcohol Contribute to College Men's Sexual Assault Perpetration? Between- and Within-Person Effects Over Five Semesters," *Journal of Studies on Alcohol and Drugs* 78, no. 1 (December 12, 2016): 5–13.

and who seek out casual sex, are also the sort of people who will disregard other legal prohibitions related to sexual conduct and commit sex crimes. So even if these findings are valid, they do not establish the case for the Nordic Model. Further, the evidence for Watson's claims about sex buyers draws on an analysis of sex buyers in Korea, where paying for sex is illegal. This research could just as easily support decriminalization on the grounds that shows that there are sex offenders in Korea who see sex workers, and decriminalizing the sex industry would make it easier for workers to report crimes and for law enforcement to investigate sex crimes more generally.

5.2.7 Summary

The consequentialist case against decriminalization takes two forms. First, some argue in favor of decriminalization on paternalistic grounds. This argument appeals to the idea that sex work is bad for sex workers and should therefore be prohibited. In addition to the controversial claim that public officials may permissibly prohibit consensual self-regarding conduct on the grounds that it is bad for those who do it, this argument also assumes an implausible theory of wellbeing. Others argue that decriminalization is bad for other people, and should therefore be prohibited. But for both arguments, even if the sex industry has some bad effects for workers or communities, it doesn't follow that officials should prohibit it even on consequentialist grounds because the bad effects of the sex industry often persist whether it is decriminalized or not and prohibition has bad effects as well.

5.3 EGALITARIAN OBJECTIONS

The third group of objections to decriminalization question egalitarian arguments against criminal penalties for sex workers or their clients. Recall that I argued that criminal penalties were inegalitarian because they were enforced in discriminatory ways and because they subjected workers and their clients to subordination by public officials and political communities. But critics of decriminalization may grant that while there is some degree of subordination involved in the enforcement of criminal penalties, prohibiting sex work along the lines of the Nordic Model or regulatory systems would result in less subordination of women on balance than decriminalization.

The first set of egalitarian objections focuses on equality in the workplace. One may argue that sex work is a form of wrongful exploitation, that the regulation or prohibition of sex work provides the public good of better working conditions, enables the enforcement of workplace protections, or prevents discrimination on the basis of race. In response, I make the case that many of these concerns about sex work apply to all jobs, but that egalitarians may be right to advocate for some workplace regulations that are specific to the sex industry. Even if the sex industry did merit a distinctive set of regulations, these regulations would not be as extensive as those which proponents of the Nordic Model or a legalization advocate for.

A second set of egalitarian objections is that decriminalization has inegalitarian externalities because the presence of legal markets in sex is degrading to women, perpetuates racist and sexist stereotypes, and can effectively objectify all women. These objections rest on empirical assertions about the broader effects of the sex industry which we may have reason to doubt. Even if these assertions were warranted though, they still would not justify interference with the industry.

5.3.1 Sex Work Exploits Unjust Circumstances

Watson argues that sex work is exploitative and that this is a reason to favor the Nordic Model. As Watson writes, exploitation occurs when people make an exchange which is mutually beneficial, but which only exists because one party to the exchange is especially vulnerable. Part of the objection to exploitative exchanges, which I address in a previous section, is that people do not voluntarily work when they only work because they lack acceptable alternatives. But Watson also argues that exploitation is also objectionable because it is a symptom of state policies that structure people's lives in ways that make them vulnerable to unequal labor conditions. Watson writes,

> To argue that the state should legalize prostitution on the grounds that prostitution is the best option, the best deal, that some people can get, ignores that the state itself is a primary source of structuring the options available to its citizens.

On her view, the government permitting sex work on the grounds that it is a mutually beneficial between a vulnerable worker and a more powerful client is analogous to a person abandoning someone on an island and then permitting the sale of extravagantly expensive rescue services. She writes "they justify their actions by saying "well, this is the best deal you can get," all the while never acknowledging that their actions partly explain why they are on the island in the first place."

For the sake of argument, let's grant Watson's claim that the government places some workers in a position of vulnerability by enforcing a property system and social welfare policies (or lack thereof). If so, then they should acknowledge that they are partly responsible for the disadvantaged circumstances of some would-be sex workers. As Watson notes, many people who argue that public officials should permit mutually beneficial exchanges argue that the government should pay people a basic income. This is my view as well. I think that the basic income can compensate citizens for the coercive imposition of unjust property rules. A basic income could serve as an acknowledgement of the government's culpability for people's vulnerability and also as a partial remedy for that vulnerability by making work more voluntary.

In response to the basic income proposal, Watson replies that nothing like a universal basic income is available in most countries, suggesting that the Nordic Model is at least justified in circumstances where a basic income is unavailable. And Watson argues further that a basic income would only address economic inequality, "other layers of inequality similarly structure the lives and choices of people who enter into prostitution."

This response reveals a puzzling asymmetry in the case for the Nordic Model though. Say the government is responsible for placing women in a position of social and economic disadvantage and vulnerability, yet at the same time public officials are incapable of passing and enforcing a simple tax and transfer policy that would mitigate that disadvantage and vulnerability. Yet the same reasons in favor of these assumptions in Watson's argument for the Nordic Model are reasons to doubt the prospects of the Nordic Model. If public officials cannot pass or effectively enforce other policies that mitigate women's disadvantage and vulnerability, the same barriers to effective enforcement would presumably remain for any attempts to criminalize the purchase of sex for the sake of vulnerable groups.

To the extent that public officials are the architects of the unjust circumstances that sex workers face, proponents of the Nordic Model misplace their faith in officials to protect vulnerable sex workers just in this case. If we grant the premise that sex workers are disadvantaged largely as a result of public officials, then we should reject the conclusion that public officials could solve the problem.

5.3.2 Sex Workers Face Collective Action Problems

Another egalitarian objection favors legalization or substantial regulation of the industry rather than full decriminalization. This objection begins with a characterization of sex workers as the victims of the more general failure to coordinate for better working conditions that many workers face. On this view, sex workers only accept the unfavorable conditions that characterize their industry because low wage workers are unable to coordinate and unionize for better working conditions.[70] This characterization is

70. Teela Sanders and Kate Hardy, "Devalued, Deskilled and Diversified: Explaining the Proliferation of the Strip Industry in the UK," *British Journal of Sociology* 63, no. 3 (2012): 513–32.

particularly common among sex workers who work as independent contractors and support more extensive workplace protections than decriminalization would offer.[71] The idea is that since workers would demand better conditions if they were capable of coordinating and unionizing, those conditions should be required by law.

I am not opposed to voluntary unionization, but I am opposed to workplace regulations that constrain individual workers' labor-market options for the sake of similarly situated workers as a group. This same argument extends to any low wage workers who fail to coordinate for better wages and working conditions. Elsewhere, I address this argument in its more general form, as a justification for extensive labor protections for low-wage workers, such as sweatshop workers. [72] There, I argue that even if individual workers do struggle to coordinate in ways that would ensure better conditions for all workers as a group, this failure to coordinate does not on its own establish that public officials ought to intervene and enforce legal regulations on workers' behalf.

There are also other reasons to reject policies that aim to secure better conditions for workers who would otherwise fail to coordinate and unionize. First, it could be that workers fail to unionize because there is not a united interest for them to organize around. Workers are not homogenous in their preferences over the tradeoffs between

71. Melissa Gira Grant, "Organized Labor's Newest Heroes: Strippers," *The Atlantic*, November 19, 2012, https://www.theatlantic.com/sexes/archive/2012/11/organized-labors-newest-heroes-strippers/265376/.sone

72. Jessica Flanigan, "Sweatshop Regulation and Workers' Choices," *Journal of Business Ethics* 153, no. 1 (2018): 79–94.

wages and working conditions. Though many sex workers may have valid complaints about the sex industry, their complaints may not all align. Workers may fail to coordinate because they have different preferences about how to trade off wages, conditions, and hours. And if sex workers as a group do not have clear, unified, collective preferences about how to make tradeoffs between wages, conditions, and hours, it is not clear that sex workers as a group would coordinate for better conditions if only they were able to coordinate for better working conditions. Furthermore, sex workers may favor voluntary unionization or sex workers' cooperatives while also opposing the enforcement of workplace regulations. Sex workers may value better working conditions but also value the freedom to negotiate for working conditions that work best for them. Sex workers may worry that the regulation of working conditions in the industry could heighten stigma as well. They may also (reasonably) be skeptical that public officials can enforce policies that promote their interests better than they can, especially in contexts where public officials were not historically friendly to sex work.

Lastly, the case for legal interference with the sex industry in order to solve coordination problems for laborers relies on the questionable premise that sex workers are unable to advocate for themselves. Yet even in existing contexts where sex work is criminally prohibited, sex workers have proven remarkably adept at forming collectives and cooperatives and advocating for better working conditions.[73] Given the success of sex workers'

73. Gregor Gall, *Sex Worker Union Organising: An International Study* (New York: Springer, 2006).

advocacy organizations to date, it would at least be premature to assume that sex workers would be unable to successfully coordinate and voluntarily adopt standards and policies that advanced the interests of their members without state intervention.

5.3.3 Sex Work Is Incompatible with Workplace Protections

The question of unionization and enforceable workplace protections prompts a related egalitarian objection—that sex work is incompatible with existing workplace protections that are currently enforced in other industries. Watson develops an argument along these lines. She argues that if decriminalization were justified, then the justification for decriminalization would invalidate the justification for a range of occupational health and safety regulations that are currently enforced. But these occupational health and safety regulations are justified. Therefore, justifications for decriminalization fail.[74]

Watson's argument takes the form of a reductio. In response, one can either deny that the justification for decriminalization avoids the reductio, deny that occupational health and safety regulations are justified, or agree with Watson's argument while denying that it tells in favor of decriminalization. I am sympathetic to all three responses. Watson frames the argument as a challenge to the "sex work is work" slogan. To defend the industry against regulation one would need to show that there is something distinctive

74. Lori Watson, "Why Sex Work Isn't Work," *Logos Journal* (blog), 2014, http://logosjournal.com/2014/watson/.

about sex work that means that sex workers should be allowed to work under heightened risks that other workers are protected from or make the case against existing health and safety regulations in other industries.

The first response denies that the justification for decriminalization undermines the justification for existing workplace protections. The sex industry may merit industry-specific exemptions from some labor laws. There are several reasons to favor exemptions over a policy that required sex workers to comply with occupational health and safety regulations. As I argued previously, industry-specific regulations may amount to a form of backdoor criminalization. And other industries are granted exemptions to occupational health and safety regulations, including caregiving and entertainment industries that are similar to sex work. For example, in-home childcare providers in the United States are exempt from many workplace regulations, including the Occupational Health and Safety Act (OSHA).[75] Independent contractors are also held to different standards of workplace protection than the employees of large companies. These examples show that even if occupational health and safety legislation were justified, it would not follow that the justification is incompatible with justified exemptions. To the extent that the justifications for exemptions for similar industries apply to sex work, occupational health and safety standards are compatible with a decriminalized sex industry.

75. Siobhán McGrath and James DeFilippis, "Social Reproduction as Unregulated Work," *Work, Employment and Society* 23, no. 1 (March 1, 2009): 66–83.

Second, even granting that the justification for de-criminalization undermines the justification for existing labor standards and policies, perhaps that's not such a bad thing. As I previously argued, occupational licensing and health and safety requirements often backfire and either create black markets or only serve the interests of politically and economically empowered stakeholders. We can imagine a different approach to labor that did not subject workers to burdensome and paternalistic regulations but instead enforced policies that protected workers from fraud and ensured that people knew the risks of their chosen occupation.

Watson responds to this general skepticism of workplace regulation by arguing that economic choices should be regulated differently than private choices because "employment brings with it additional vulnerabilities to workers (not the least of which is economic dependence)" which merit additional regulation. As an aside, I'm not sure that this is necessarily the case. People can make private choices such as the choice to marry or to leave the workplace and raise children for reasons of economic dependence. And this would not justify the enforcement of safety regulations for marriages and motherhood.

But even if people do have specific rights to workplace protections in economic contexts, they should be permitted to waive those rights as well. To deny that people have the right to waive their rights against risk would rule out not only sex work, but other risky professions in the health and security industries. Watson then claims that these industries are different because police and medical professionals take on heightened risks at work to provide a beneficial public good, unlike sex workers.

Setting aside whether health workers provide public goods (their labor is excludable), this argument would at least struggle to explain why health workers who perform elective surgery should be permitted to take on the occupational risks associated with their jobs. Yet if people were permitted to waive their rights against occupational risks, then health and safety regulations would be ineffective.

Third, even if it were true that sex work violated justified occupational health and safety standards and other workplace regulations in ways that undermined the justifiability of sex work, this insight would favor legalization or a great deal of regulation, but not the Nordic Model or criminalization. It would be excessively burdensome to criminalize an entire industry on the grounds that many workers in the industry would be exposed to some risks of injury or disease, when public officials could instead enforce industry-specific safety standards and prohibit the violation of those standards.

I don't like this response any more than I suspect Watson does. Watson and I agree that sex workers should have extensive protections against violence and fraud. But Watson thinks that these protections should in part include Nordic policies that reduce the prevalence of sex work. Watson likely rejects this response then, because she is skeptical that effective enforcement of adequate safety standards is possible for an industry like sex work. But many of the risks she cites, including the risk of crime and violence and the health risks of sex work, can be effectively prohibited without prohibiting the entire industry. It is unclear why Watson would presume that public health officials and police are capable of effectively preventing contagious transmission of illness and crime in other contexts but not for sex workers.

In contrast, I think this is an effective response to Watson's objection that sex work is unacceptably dangerous because workers are exposed to the risk of violence. I favor decriminalization as a means of preventing black markets that operate beyond the reach of the judicial system, and think that the best response to a risk of violence is to enforce laws against violence, not to preemptively limit people's freedom on the grounds that exercising their freedom could put them at risk to have other rights violated. But I am less satisfied by this response as a means to protect workers from the health risks of their occupation because, as I mentioned, I worry that regulations of the sex industry that aim to promote public health are paternalistic to workers who are willing to take on heightened risks to their health. Also, such regulations could be excessively burdensome to workers and may backfire to create a black market industry that evades effective regulation.

5.3.4 Discrimination Law

One of Watson's arguments against decriminalization is that legal sex work is either incompatible with anti-discrimination law or it would require sex workers to provide sexual services against their will to avoid discriminating against clients. Watson describes accounts from sex workers in New Zealand and Nevada who did not feel that their right to refuse clients was respected, especially when brothel owners disagreed that the woman had a good reason to refuse.

On the other hand, if sex workers are permitted to refuse sex on the basis of their clients' race, one may also object that the resultant patterns racial discrimination is an injustice toward clients.[76]

It is generally unethical to discriminate against people on the basis of their race, meaning that there are strong moral reasons against doing so and that a person who discriminates on the basis of racial animus against a disadvantaged group is making a moral mistake. But it does not follow from this that public officials are entitled to censor speech or prohibit people's intimate choices on the grounds that they are racist.[77] In these cases, discrimination within the sex industry is an example of a right to do wrong, meaning that though objectionable, it doesn't warrant a legal response that limits people's rights.

Sex workers' discrimination in choosing clients is insufficient grounds for legal intervention because it is not clear that prohibiting discrimination could or should be effective. If a sex worker can refuse sex with a client for any reason, as long as it is not on the basis of race, then it would be extremely difficult for any particular client to establish that he was the victim of racial discrimination. But even if enforcing anti-discrimination statutes could be effective, it's not clear that officials should do it. Watson frames the question of discrimination as one where sex

76. Price discrimination on the basis of race seems to persist even in competitive sex markets. See e.g. Huailu Li, Kevin Lang, and Kaiwen Leong, "Does Competition Eliminate Discrimination? Evidence from the Commercial Sex Market in Singapore," *The Economic Journal*, 2017.

77. Matt Zwolinski, "Why Not Regulate Private Discrimination?," SSRN Scholarly Paper (Rochester, NY: Social Science Research Network, April 11, 2007), https://papers.ssrn.com/abstract=978937.

310 DEBATING SEX WORK

workers are effectively employees for brothel owners, and
as employees they could be legally required to provide services to customers without discriminating. But another
way of viewing the issue is that sex workers are temporary
workers who are entitled to choose their employers. Anti-
discrimination laws do not prohibit workers from taking
race into account when choosing their employers. In this
way, decriminalized sex work is not necessarily incompatible with anti-discrimination law.

And even if enforcing anti-discrimination law against
sex workers could be effective and even if sex workers' relations with clients are best understood as service-providers
and customers rather than service-providers and temporary
employers, all antiracists should be skeptical of any policies that empower the police to interfere with the people's
self-regarding and morally permissible choices. People of
color are disproportionately harmed by excessive law enforcement. Sex workers of color are especially vulnerable to
the harms associated with racialized policing, even if the
law only officially authorizes the prohibition of paying for
sex and not selling it.[78] So if the motivation behind one's
support for anti-discrimination law is a broader commitment to antiracism and racial justice, if one must choose
between granting an exemption from anti-discrimination

78. For example, the Chicago Reporter finds that 97% of prostitution-
related felonies are enforced against sex workers in Cook County despite
local law enforcement's vocal commitment to focusing on clients and
the "End Demand" model. Christie Thomson, "Escorted to Jail," *Chicago
Reporter*, November 1, 2012, http://chicagoreporter.com/escorted-jail/.
At the same time, the Cook County justice system has also faced forceful
criticism for racialized patterns of enforcement and punishment. See e.g.
Nicole Gonzalez Van Cleve, *Crook County: Racism and Injustice in America's
Largest Criminal Court* (Palo Alto, CA: Stanford University Press, 2016).

law or criminalizing the sex industry, antiracists should favor exemptions from anti-discrimination law.

In non-market contexts, people's sexual choices privilege certain racial groups and discriminates against others outside of the marketplace as well. For example, Sonu Bedi describes the pervasive sexual racism of online dating sites.[79] Bedi argues that just institutions should attend to discrimination, stereotyping, and racial hierarchy within patterns of romantic and intimate partnership. If people's romantic choices entrench racial hierarchy by expressing racial favoritism, then "these are not benign sexual preferences but problematic conditions that structure the very formation of romantic relationships."[80] But Bedi stops short of prohibiting people from choosing intimate partners based on racial favoritism or disgust because people have rights to select intimate partners even if they do so on the basis of racist reasons. Instead, Bedi favors policies that prohibit online dating sites from allowing users to search for partners on the basis of race. Bedi's proposal could extend to the sex industry too. Online platforms could prohibit workers from screening clients on the basis of their race but acknowledge workers right to choose their intimate partnerships. But in both cases, even though people should not discriminate against potential partners on the basis of their race, it would be more wrong for public officials to interfere with people's intimate choices in order to promote racial justice.

79. Sonu Bedi, "Sexual Racism: Intimacy as a Matter of Justice," *Journal of Politics* 77, no. 4 (October 1, 2015): 998–1011.
80. Ibid.

5.3.5 The Sex Industry Is Racist and Sexist

A related argument against decriminalization is that the sex industry is irremediably racist in ways that perpetuate racism within the broader culture and subject sex workers to bigotry.[81] Sex workers are potentially subject to racial discrimination in brothels, online forums, and high-wage work.[82] Aspects of the sex industry can reinforce harmful racist stereotypes in the way that it also reinforces sexist stereotypes.[83] For example, black women are more frequently the targets of aggression in pornography than white women and black men are less frequently depicted as intimate partners than white men.[84]

One may object to the foregoing argument by asking, if public officials should exempt sex workers from anti-discrimination law, could similar considerations justify a right for clients and brothel owners to discriminate when employing sex workers? Two responses are available to a proponent of decriminalization on this point. First, the aforementioned concerns about effective enforcement apply to the enforcement of anti-discrimination policies

81. Cheryl Nelson Butler, "A Critical Race Feminist Perspective on Prostitution & Sex Trafficking in America," *Yale JL & Feminism* 27 (2015): 95.

82. English Collective of Prostitutes, "The Work Black Prostitute Women Face of Dealing with Racism," *English Collective of Prostitutes* (blog), June 29, 1995, http://prostitutescollective.net/1995/06/the-work-black-prostitute-women-face-of-dealing-with-racism-including-from-clients/.

83. Kamala Kempadoo and Jo Doezema, *Global Sex Workers: Rights, Resistance, and Redefinition* (New York: Psychology Press, 1998), 9.

84. Gloria Cowan and Robin R. Campbell, "Racism and Sexism in Interracial Pornography: A Content Analysis," *Psychology of Women Quarterly* 18, no. 3 (September 1, 1994): 323–38.

for the benefit of sex workers with equal force as they applied to the enforcement of anti-discrimination policies for the benefit of clients. Second, as Sophia Moreau argues, discrimination ought to be illegal when traits like race or gender are normatively extraneous to the job description. Physical appearance, sex, and gender, are not normatively extraneous to professions such as performance art (e.g. casting someone to play the role of Hamlet) but they are normatively extraneous to other professions (e.g. medicine). For this reason, public officials may legitimately prohibit discrimination against employees unless a person's traits are relevant to job performance in some way. In some cases, a sex workers' race or sex is relevant to the job description, so to the extent that performance industries are exempt from anti-discrimination law it would be consistent with this precedent to exempt the sex industry as well.

One may object that this response is unpersuasive because a person's race should not be normatively relevant to the provision of sexual services, and that it is only considered relevant because clients and employers have racist attitudes. Julie Bindel emphasizes the racist dynamics in sex work in arguing for an abolitionist approach.[85] Bindel writes,

In the Netherlands, racist attitudes of sex-buyers towards prostituted women are commonplace. For these men, selecting a woman of color is all about fulfilling a fantasy that is grounded in racist and colonialist stereotypes. This is also reflected in advertising: African-Caribbean women are billed

85. Julie Bindel, "What the Sex Trade Has in Common with the Slave Trade—Julie Bindel | Aeon Essays," *Aeon*, June 26, 2018, https://aeon.co/essays/what-the-sex-trade-has-in-common-with-the-slave-trade.

as more sexually adventurous, Chinese and eastern European women are presented as more submissive, and Latina women are deemed more sensuous.

On Bindel's account, the sex industry is part of a long-standing legacy of racial oppression, and Bindel equates the persistence of the sex industry with the persistence of racial hierarchy. Bindel advocates for the abolition of the sex industry partly on these grounds.

It is difficult to know, however, whether the persistence of the sex industry contributes to the persistence of racial hierarchy or if it merely reflects broader social trends. The suggestion that the sex industry perpetuates racism is at odds with the observation that the creation of the internet, which expanded access to sexual services and pornography, coincided with continued advances in civil rights, so the empirical link between the sex industry and racial injustice is at least uncertain.

A critic of the sex industry may respond that it does promote racism by teaching people racist stereotypes and glorifying racist behavior. But even if this were true, it would not justify a prohibitive approach. Consider two analogies to illustrate this point. Plausibly, the religious and cultural traditions of heterosexual marriage perpetuate sexist stereotypes about women and sets back the equal status of all women, even those who are unmarried. But even if this were true, it would nevertheless be wrong to prohibit traditional heterosexual marriages in ways that violate people's religious freedom, freedom of association, or rights to form intimate partnerships. Similarly, social media sites like Twitter permit people to form communities of racists who disseminate racist ideas and imagery. Plausibly, these users undermine the equal status of racial minorities, including people who do not use Twitter at all. But even if this were true, it would still be wrong for officials to regulate or prohibit people from using Twitter on the grounds that some people exercise their freedom of expression and association in racist ways. Such censorship would not only violate the rights of all users, it also would not solve the problem of racism online. Rather, it would merely send those users to different sites which were less surveilled and where they were more likely to be radicalized or encouraged to use violence.

So too, participation in the sex industry is a form of expression and association that sometimes perpetuates offensive stereotypes and reflects and reinforces patterns of historical injustice, but it doesn't follow from this observation that the industry should be abolished. If anything, as Martha Nussbaum argues, the stigmatization of sex work may itself be based on racial stereotypes which denounce industries that people of color are likely to participate in.[86] Instead of perpetuating stigma and stereotypes through calls to treat the sex industry differently, sex work should be treated like other forms of work and those who are concerned with sex workers' wellbeing should focus on improving their conditions and providing alternatives to sex work for those who want them.

Moreover, policies that empower public officials to police sex work for the sake of racial equality are unlikely to

86. Martha C. Nussbaum, "Ignore the Stigma of Prostitution and Focus on the Need," *New York Times*, April 19, 2012, sec. Room for Debate, https://www.nytimes.com/roomfordebate/2012/04/19/is-legalized-prostitution-safer/ignore-the-stigma-of-prostitution-and-focus-on-the-need.

be effective given the prevalence of black markets and the difficulty of regulating speech online. Such polices would also be over inclusive to the extent that they censored all speech or associations that perpetuated racist imagery or preferences. And it would be moralistic and arbitrary if officials only limited pornography and sex work on these grounds. Even if decriminalization effectively permits people to engage in racist speech and behavior, alternatives are worse for the cause of racial justice on balance.

5.3.6 Sex Work Is Degrading to Women

So far I have addressed objections related to potential economic and racial inequalities associated with the sex industry. But perhaps the most prominent set of egalitarian objections to the sex industry focus on equality between the sexes. For example, Christine Overall develops a view like this when she argues it is immoral in part because it is necessarily unequal between the sexes. On her view, "the fact that it is men and not women who buy prostitutes services is not, surely, just for women's lack of equal opportunity to do so." [87] Rather, Overall argues that the industry depends on constructed gender roles where women are taught to provide sexual services and men are taught to seek them out. The thing that is wrong with prostitution therefore is that it "epitomizes men's dominance" and reinforces patriarchal attitudes that cause men to perceive themselves as "needing" sexual services and it causes

87. Christine Overall, "What's Wrong with Prostitution? Evaluating Sex Work," *Signs: Journal of Women in Culture and Society* 17, no. 4 (July 1, 1992): 705–24.

women to internalize their own oppression by buying into these patriarchal attitudes through their occupational choices.[88]

This argument is similar to the previous concern that the sex industry reinforces racist stereotypes and perpetuated racism, thereby undermining racial justice. Here the worry is that the industry reinforces sexist stereotypes and perpetuates sexism, to the detriment of the cause of feminist justice. In the same vein, Carol Pateman argues that prostitution as a social and economic institution reflects an implicit agreement among men in society that they are entitled to sexual access to women.[89] This objection to the industry is that it consists in the public recognition that a woman's sexual submission is a legitimate object of sale within the marketplace, which it shouldn't be. Though Overall and Pateman identify the wrongfulness of the sex industry as a species of the more general injustices of capitalism and patriarchy, they also support sex industry-specific laws, such as Nordic Model, that would prohibit or limit individual men's participation in the sex industry without punishing the women who participate in it. For example, Overall writes that "men must take individual responsibility for hiring prostitutes" but does not support prohibiting sex workers from selling to them.[90]

Here the analogy between racism and sexism is instructive in illustrating where this argument misfires. Even if it were wrong to endorse the gendered dynamics of the sex industry, permitting the sale of something needn't amount

88. Ibid.
89. Pateman, *The Sexual Contract*, p. 2.
90. Overall, "What's Wrong with Prostitution?"

to public endorsement of the sale of it. Public officials could support decriminalization and also publically recognize that a woman's sexual submission or services is not a legitimate object of sale within the marketplace, just as they allow other markets such as markets in offensive or racist speech to persist while also publically condemning them. In addition, to the extent that one's concern about sex work is it's broader social significance within a patriarchal society, the meaning of the practice of sex work within society can change as can broader dynamics of male domination or female subordination. In response to this argument, Debra Satz suggests that this reply is unrealistic under current conditions.[91] Referring to feminist proponents of decriminalization Satz writes,

> I agree that in a different culture, with different assumptions about men's and women's gender identities, prostitution might not have harmful effects on women in prostitution and as a group. But I think these feminists have minimized the cultural stereotypes that surround contemporary prostitution and exaggerated their own power to shape the practice. . . . I doubt that ethnographic studies of prostitution would support the claim that prostitution contributes to images of women's dignity or empowerment. [92]

Yet to justify regulation, criminalization, or a policy like the Nordic Model, critics of decriminalization must show that regulating the industry or prohibiting men from paying for sex would effectively address or mitigate male domination

91. Debra Satz, *Why Some Things Should Not Be for Sale: The Moral Limits of Markets*, Reprint ed. (New York: Oxford University Press, 2012), 149.
92. Ibid., p. 149.

or economic subordination relative to decriminalization. They do not show that this is the case, and as I previously argued, I am skeptical that they can. If public officials could legitimately prohibit male participation in the sex industry on the grounds that the industry depends on sexist and harmful socially constructed gender roles, then such an argument would also justify prohibition in other industries, such as cosmetics or fashion. After all, these industries also can teach women to see themselves as the providers of sexual gratification and cause men to see themselves as consumers of female sexuality.

Satz replies to this argument that the "negative image effect" of the sex industry exceeds the negative image effect of other industries because it is a largely gender-segregated profession that is stigmatized which thereby stigmatizes all women, and because it involves men viewing women as objects for their use. For this reason, Satz is open to regulating sex work. Though Satz is also aware of the dangers of a prohibitive approach. She emphasizes that "if we are troubled by prostitution. . . then we should direct much of our energy to putting forward alternative models of egalitarian relations between men and women," rather than a prohibitive approach.[93]

Elsewhere, Pateman develops a different feminist argument against the sex industry when she argues that the sex industry requires women to sell their womanhood, and therefore to sell themselves, since a person's body and sexual capacities are so integrally connected to her sense of self.[94] Other feminist scholars have similarly objected that

93. Ibid., p. 153.
94. Carole Pateman, "Defending Prostitution: Charges against Ericsson," *Ethics* 93 (April 1983).

the problem with prostitution is that it values people on the basis of their bodies as objects or their sexual capacities.[95] They view the purchasing of sexual services as a form of impermissible objectification because buyers value sex workers not as people but as body parts that can provide sexual gratification.[96]

I grant that a female's biological sex can often be one of the primary bases of value in the sexual marketplace, just as it is a primary basis of value in markets for commercial surrogacy. Biological traits that are more commonly found in males, such as physical strength or athletic ability are a primary basis of value in other markets. It is not intrinsically wrong if a market primarily values a bodily service that is closely associated with one's womanhood (or manhood). Womanhood, sexuality, or bodily services needn't be closely connected to all people's senses of themselves, and so participation in these markets needn't be alienating for all workers.

Moreover, as Patricia Marino argues, concerns about sexual objectification are justified because it is reasonable to be concerned about autonomy, but as long as the social and political conditions are present for a person to autonomously choose sexual objectification, "there is nothing wrong with anonymous, one-sided, or just-for-pleasure kinds of sexual

95. Laurie Shrage, "Feminist Perspectives on Sex Markets," in *The Stanford Encyclopedia of Philosophy*, ed. Edward N. Zalta (Palo Alto, CA: Metaphysics Research Lab, Stanford University, Fall 2016), https://plato.stanford.edu/archives/fall2016/entries/feminist-sex-markets/; Anne Phillips, "It's My Body and I'll Do What I Like with It: Bodies as Objects and Property," *Political Theory* 39, no. 6 (2011): 724–48.

96. Melinda Vadas, "The Manufacture-for-Use of Pornography and Women's Inequality," *Journal of Political Philosophy* 13, no. 2 (2005): 174–93.

objectification."[97] Or, on a broadly Kantian view, treating a person as a mere means consists in using them in a way that does not engage with their own will, whereas if a person consents then she is a participant in the interaction and she is not being used as a mere means.[98] So since sex workers consent, paying for sex is not objectionable in this sense. Some people may have a legitimate interest in being degraded, disrespected, or used during sex. So even if expressing these attitudes is generally impermissible it is only because it is contrary to people's interests or it violates their rights but it would not be impermissible in the context of a consensual sexual encounter.[99] I'm not even sure that it is possible to degrade, disrespect, or treat someone as a mere means if he or she consents to be treated in that way.

Even if we grant that objectification is wrong even when the objectified party consents, such an argument still would not warrant a specific legal response to sex work. Even if clients do see sex workers as objects or body parts rather than people, consumers in other industries and people who have non-commercial sex can make the same mistake. And if it is wrong to treat a person as an object or a mere means, not all sex buyers do, and consumers in other industries objectify and disrespect service providers as well.[100]

97. Patricia Marino, "The Ethics of Sexual Objectification: Autonomy and Consent," *Inquiry* 51, no. 4 (2008): 345–64.

98. For more on this point see Christine M. Korsgaard, *Creating the Kingdom of Ends* (Cambridge, England: Cambridge University Press, 1996), esp. p. 141.

99. By analogy, it does not violate a moral requirement for an actor to take a role where his character is treated disrespectfully because the role serves the actor's broader aims.

100. Laurie Shrage, "Exposing the Fallacies of Anti-Porn Feminism," *Feminist Theory* 6, no. 1 (2005): 45–65.

5.3.7 Summary

Egalitarians may object to decriminalization on the grounds that it maintains economic inequality by undermining support for workplace protections or on the grounds that it contributes to social inequality by undermining anti-discrimination law and perpetuating sexism. In response to these objections, I have argued that decriminalization does not necessarily exacerbate inequality, rather, these problems are more often the symptoms of the broader social conditions that also explain in part the persistence of the sex industry. Moreover, as I argued in the previous chapter, even if decriminalization does not advance socio-economic equality, and even if in some cases it enables racism and sexism to persist, egalitarian values still weigh in support of decriminalization more than alternatives that subject marginalized workers to subordination by public officials.

5.4 CONCLUSION

The slogan "Sex Work is Work" aims to normalize and destigmatize sex work by challenging the double standards that are implicit in laws that penalize sex workers and their clients. The claim that sex work is work suggests that sex work is on a continuum with other kinds of labor, and that there is no non-arbitrary way to distinguish it from other labor that involves performance, emotional support, providing physical pleasure, caregiving, or entertainment.

I have argued in favor of this slogan. Public officials should treat sex work like other kinds of work. Prohibiting the sale or purchase of sex not only violates the rights of sex workers and their clients, it has bad consequences on balance and it is inegalitarian. Treating sex work like other kinds of work may prompt people to re-evaluate certain workplace regulations, such as laws that prohibit unsafe conditions, discrimination, sexual harassment, or sex work may be the kind of industry that merits exemption from these laws when others do not.

Critics of the sex industry often mischaracterize sex work either as sexual assault or forced labor. But as long as sex work is consensual then it is neither forced sex nor forced labor. These mischaracterizations are not only used to justify the unjust criminalization of sex work but also divert resources from the prevention and punishment of actual instances of sexual assault and forced labor. And the criminalization of all sex work may also cause higher rates of sexual assault and sex trafficking by relegating all paid sexual labor to black markets and deterring sex workers from reporting crimes in their industry.

Readers who remain reluctant to support decriminalization despite the foregoing arguments and evidence in favor of it should consider the relative risks of prohibition versus decriminalization. If proponents of prohibition are wrong, then public officials are enforcing an unjust policy that coerces some of societies' most vulnerable populations, forces people to comply with moralistic sexual norms, puts people's health at risk, and unjustly fines and imprisons people who are not liable to be punished. If I am wrong about the injustice of prohibition, then decriminalization would consist of officials' failure to enforce a policy that would have public health benefits and which would improve would-be sex workers' lives.[101]

So the risk of prohibition is that public officials are currently violating sex workers' and their clients' rights by unjustly coercing and punishing them. The risk of decriminalization is that public officials may fail to deliver morally significant benefits to their constituents. Since it is morally worse to unjustly threaten or punish a person than to fail to deliver morally significant benefits, the moral risks associated with prohibition exceed the moral risks associated with decriminalization. For this reason, even readers who remain uncertain about the case for and against sex work ought to support decriminalization in light of their uncertainty.

101. On the other hand, concerns about moral risk could weigh in the other direction when it comes to whether a person should personally choose to pay for sex. Then again, as Ann Ferguson argues, other sexual practices such as BDSM and sex in the context of marriage are also morally risky in some of the same ways, but nevertheless should not be prohibited. Ann Ferguson, "Prostitution as a Morally Risky Practice," in *Daring to Be Good*, ed. Bat-Ami Bar On and Ann Ferguson (New York: Routledge, 1998).

INDEX

For the benefit of digital users, indexed terms that span two pages (e.g., 52–53) may, on occasion, appear on only one of those pages.